Tradition
and
Liberation

Tradition and Liberation

The Hindu Tradition in the
Indian Women's Movement

Catherine A. Robinson

Bath Spa University College

St. Martin's Press
New York

St. Martin's Press, Scholarly and Reference Division,
175 Fifth Avenue, New York, N.Y. 10010

First published in the United States of America in 1999
Printed in Great Britain

ISBN: 0–312–22718–3

Library of Congress Cataloging-in-Publication Data

Robinson, Catherine A.
Tradition and liberation : the Hindu tradition in the Indian
women's movement / Catherine A. Robinson.
p. cm.
Includes bibliographical references and index.
ISBN 0–312–22718–3 (cloth)
1. Feminism–South Asia–History–20th century. 2. Women and
religion–South Asia–History. 3. Women in Hinduism–India-
-History. 4. Hinduism and politics–India–History. 5. Women in
politics–South Asia–History–20th century.
HQ1735.3.R63 1999
305.42'0954–dc21 99-31639
CIP

For Ellen Rose Ryan

who first introduced me to feminism,
and who died during the writing of this book

CONTENTS

ACKNOWLEDGEMENTS

The author wishes to thank the following who have kindly granted permission to use copyright material:

Advaita Ashrama for extracts from *The Complete Works of Swami Vivekananda* vols 5 and 7 (1973; 1972).

K.P. Bagchi & Company for extracts from *Marriage of Hindu Widows* by I.C. Vidyasagar, introduction by A. Podder (1976).

Cambridge University Press for extracts from *Women in Modern India* The New Cambridge History of India IV.2 by G. Forbes (1996) and from 'Introduction: Inventing Traditions' by E. Hobsbawm in *The Invention of Tradition* edited by E. Hobsbawm and T. Ranger (1984).

Carfax Publishing Limited of Abingdon, Oxfordshire for extracts from the article 'A Second Sita?' by Catherine Robinson in *Journal of Beliefs and Values* vol. 17 no. 1 (1996).

Ganesh & Company Publishers for extracts from *We Two Together* by J.H. and M.E. Cousins (1950).

Heritage Publishers for extracts from *Women and Social Change* by J.M. Everett (1981).

Madras Law Journal for extracts from 'Answers to a Questionnaire by His Holiness Sri Sankaracharya' (1941).

Manushi: A Journal About Women and Society for extracts from essays by Madhu Kishwar (a founder, editor and trustee of *Manushi*, a non-profit trust devoted to human rights, social justice and women's rights).

John Murray (Publishers) Ltd for an extract from *Lokamanya Tilak: Father of Indian Unrest* by D.V. Tahmankar (1956).

Orbis Books of New York for extracts from the essay 'Kali, the Savior' by Lina Gupta in *After Patriarchy: Feminist Transformations of the World Religions* edited by P.M. Cooey, W.R. Eakin and J.B. McDaniel (Copyright ©1991).

Oxford University Press of New Delhi for extracts from *The Inner World: A Psycho-Analytic Study of Childhood and Society in India* (Second Edition) by S. Kakar (1988) and from *The Social Dimensions of Early Buddhism* by U. Chakravarti (1987).

Oxford University Press of Oxford for an extract from *A Primer of Hinduism* (Second Edition) by J.N. Farquhar (London 1912).

Random House Inc. for an extract from the introduction to *Feminism: The Essential Historical Writings* edited by M. Schneir (Vintage Books 1972).

Random House UK Limited for extracts from *A Woman of India: Being the Life of Saroj Nalini* by G.S. Dutt (Hogarth Press 1929).

Sage Publications India Private Limited for extracts from essays 'Feminism: Indian Ethos and Indian Convictions' by S. Chitnis and 'Bride-burning: The Psycho-Social Dynamics of Dowry Deaths' by R. Ghadially and P. Kumar in *Women in Indian Society: A Reader* edited by R. Ghadially (1988).

The Theosophical Publishing House of Adyar, Chennai for extracts from *Ancient Ideals in Modern Life – Four Lectures Delivered at the Twenty-fifth Anniversary Meeting of the Theosophical Society at Benares December 1900* by A. Besant (London 1901), from *The Birth of New India: A Collection of Writings and Speeches on Indian Affairs* by A. Besant (Madras 1917) and from *The Besant Spirit: vol. 3 Indian Problems* by A. Besant (Madras 1939).

University of California Press for extracts from *Utopias in Conflict: Religion and Nationalism in Modern India* by A. Embree (Copyright © 1990 by The Regents of the University of California), from *Tilak and Gokhale : Revolution and Reform in the Making of Modern India* by S. Wolpert (Copyright © 1962 by The Regents of the University of California) and from the article 'Women and Movement Politics in India' by L.J. Calman in *Asian Survey* vol. 29 no. 10 (Copyright © 1989 by The Regents of the University of California).

University of Pennsylvania Press for extracts from the essay 'Deep Orientalism? Notes on Sanskrit and Power Beyond the Raj' by

Sheldon Pollock in *Orientalism and the Postcolonial Predicament: Perspectives on South Asia* edited by C.A. Breckenridge and P. van der Veer (1993).

University of Toronto Press for an extract from the essay 'The Subjection of Women' by J.S. Mill in *Essays on Equality, Law and Education* from The Collected Works of John Stuart Mill vol. XXI (1984).

Verso New Left Books Ltd for extracts from *The History of Doing: An Illustrated Account of Movements for Women's Rights and Feminism in India 1880–1990* by R. Kumar (London Verso 1993).

The Women's Press Ltd for an extract from the introduction to *Speaking of Faith: Cross-cultural Perspectives on Women, Religion and Social Change* edited by D.L. Eck and D. Jain.

Zed Books Limited for extracts from *Women and Right-Wing Movements: Indian Experiences* edited by T. Sarkar and U. Butalia (1995), from *In Search of Answers: Indian Women's Voices from Manushi* edited by M. Kishwar and R. Vanita (1984) and from *We Will Smash This Prison: Indian Women in Struggle* by G. Omvedt (1980).

The author is grateful for permission to reproduce copyright material but it has not always been possible to locate some of the owners of copyright, and in such cases information would be welcome.

The author would also like to express her thanks to all those who offered help and support during the writing of this book, and to give special mention to Anastasia Karaflogka, Jean Kennedy and Jane Underdown for their hard work.

Catherine A. Robinson, Bath

The Hindu Tradition and the Indian Women's Movement

There is a vast potential feminist literature from this period [the latter half of the nineteenth century and the first few decades of the twentieth] that is missing: the women of Eastern nations . . . – those multitudes who groaned under the heaviest yokes of bondage – created few writings.

No feminist works emerged from behind the Hindu purdah or out of the Moslem harems; centuries of slavery do not provide a fertile soil for intellectual development or expression. The insights that such writings from outside our own historical– cultural field might have offered can only be guessed at.

(Schneir 1972: xiv)

When I embarked upon this study, I read Miriam Schneir's comments, made in her introduction to *Feminism: The Essential Historical Writings*, in a secondary source. Her comments seemed to imply a denial of the very existence of the Indian women's movement at least until the middle of the twentieth century as well as giving an unfavourable impression of the Hindu tradition. This left me wondering about the history of the Indian women's movement which does in fact extend as far back as the middle of the nineteenth century and, in the course of that history, about the movement's representation of the Hindu tradition and itself in relation to it.

This study, then, examines the role of the Hindu tradition in the ideology and methodology of the Indian women's movement. In so doing, it demonstrates the process by which cultural and religious concepts and figures are accorded new meaning and significance under changing circumstances by different groups and individuals. It is to such a process of reinterpretation and reappropriation that Milton

1

Singer refers in his foreword to a collection of essays on the subject of contemporary India's 'rediscovery of the past as adaptation for the future' when he points to 'the cosmic mystery of how it is that the members of a "traditional" civilization can rediscover their pasts in the recurrent cycles of their history and yet invent new adaptations of their traditions for use in an indeterminate present and an open future' (Singer 1989: 14). By showing how leaders of the Indian women's movement have restated aspects of the Hindu tradition, this study provides some insight into the ways in which a women's movement can restate a religious tradition in a society where religion has been central to debate about the position of women and where opposition to the movement has frequently been rationalised in religious terms.

Clearly, 'in using the religious ideas and images offered within their cultures, women must choose carefully the religious symbols that effectively challenge and empower them rather than those that oppress and render them passive' (Miles 1987: 2). Yet a persuasive case can be made for this reinterpretation and reappropriation because 'the values and images of culture, the myths or stories it tells about reality, and the images and attributes with which it envisions the divine are of fundamental significance to the role, status and image of women in that culture' (Eck and Jain 1986: 4). When appealing to Hindu beliefs and values in order to improve the position of women while also allowing that the Hindu tradition has sanctified and sustained the position presently prevailing, the Indian women's movement has both asserted the actual adverse impact of the tradition and professed its potential positive impact.

Certainly, the Indian women's movement has a distinct identity, notwithstanding the significant degree of western influence which it has often been necessary to downplay. Such differences reflect the distinct social, political and economic as well as cultural and religious conditions in which the Indian women's movement has emerged and developed. One distinctive feature of the movement and one which indicates its independence, and, indeed, criticism, of the West is its frequent refusal to accept the application of the 'feminist' label to women's organisations in India. Earlier in the movement's history, this label tended to be rejected because it was thought to embody an antagonism towards men which was not evident in India where, it was claimed, Indian men supported Indian women's campaigns for change. More recently, this label tends to be rejected because it is thought to emphasise the sexual oppression of Indian women at the expense of the western oppression of all Indians regardless of their sex. In either instance, this shows that there are sensitivities about terminology although there is no widely used alternative to the 'feminist' label which, in any case, need mean no more than an awareness of how a person's sex determines her/his life-chances and an acknowledgement that this is unsatisfactory.

The Scope of this Study

Since this study concentrates on the relationship between the Hindu tradition and the Indian women's movement, women's organisations with a specific, non-Hindu, religious basis of membership have been excluded while the activities and achievements of Indian women of non-Hindu backgrounds and communities have been under-represented. For this reason, organisations such as the Stree Zoroastrian Mandal (Zoroastrian Women's Circle) which was established by Parsi women in 1903 and engaged in a variety of charitable endeavours (Desai 1977: 158) and the All India Muslim Women's Conference which was established by the Begum of Bhopal in 1916 and aspired to advance the educational and social interests of Muslim women (Everett 1981: 63) have been omitted. For the same reason, the contribution to the women's cause made by women such as Lady Tata, a Parsi, who was involved with the Bombay Presidency Women's Council, a founder of the National Council of Women in India and an active member of the All India Women's Conference (Natarajan 1932) and Jahan Ara Shahnawaz, a Muslim, who held a number of important posts in the All India Women's Conference (Shahnawaz 1971) have not been fully acknowledged. However, given that Hindu references tend to dominate the movement's mode of discourse, espoused by members with only a nominal affiliation to the tradition and even by those of a different heritage, it has not been necessary to determine the faith commitment, if any, of individual women. Certainly, the contribution made by western women to the women's cause in India has been included on the grounds that in identifying themselves with Indian women they tended to adopt a Hindu-oriented approach, be it positive or negative in tone.

3

The Methodology of this Study

The methodology of this study is multi-disciplinary, drawing upon historical, sociological and literary techniques in order to analyse the relationship between the Hindu tradition and the Indian women's movement. This methodology is appropriate to the subject under discussion, the creative interpretation of the Hindu tradition by the Indian women's movement, associated with its arguments for change and applied to its activities in society. The selection and arrangement of material is basically thematic, highlighting how the movement has appealed to Hindu beliefs and values, and, indeed, eschewed such appeal, in the light of the influence of the Hindu tradition over the status and image of women. Hence the coverage is consciously illustrative and as such focuses on what is only one , however important, feature of the Indian women's movement, its ideology and methodology with specific reference to the Hindu tradition. It does so with the purpose of coming to an understanding of the reasons for and against appeal to Hindu beliefs and values from the movement's point of view.

The Sources of this Study

A variety of sources have been consulted in writing this study on the relationship between the Hindu tradition and the Indian women's movement. In addition to a limited number of scholarly works on the position of women in the Hindu tradition and the Indian women's movement, the most significant of which are discussed in the next section, these sources consist mainly of the following (all in English which was the *lingua franca* of western-educated India): original contributions to, and contemporary records of, debate about the position of women; and the speeches and writings of leading members of the Indian women's movement. These sources are considered for the different ways in which the Hindu tradition has been interpreted in terms of its implications for women. Throughout, wherever possible, an effort has been made to allow participants in debate about the position of women and leading members of the Indian women's movement to express their views in their own words so that their arguments can be appreciated in a context appropriate to the protagonists themselves. In so doing, it becomes evident how these protagonists interpreted the Hindu tradition in the course of their campaigns.

4

This Study in the Context of Existing Literature

The distinctiveness of this study lies in its subject matter, the relationship between the Hindu tradition and the Indian women's movement, and its treatment of this subject matter, the integration of an awareness of modern discourse about the position of women in the Hindu tradition with an account of the Indian women's movement. Of course, there has been much writing on the subject of the position of women in the Hindu tradition. Similarly, there has been much writing on the subject of the Indian women's movement. However, writing on the position of women in the Hindu tradition tends not to consider the ways in which the Indian women's movement has conceptualised this position whereas writing on the Indian women's movement tends not to consider the ways in which the movement has appealed to Hindu beliefs and values in order to challenge the position of women in the Hindu tradition.

Nevertheless, two authors, Jana Matson Everett and Geraldine Forbes, both of whom have commented on the movement's appeal to Hindu beliefs and values, have been major influences on this study. Their work has been a springboard for the further more detailed discussion of such appeal to Hindu beliefs and values found in this study where such appeal is also located in the context of argument about the position of women in the Hindu tradition. These authors have been influential in suggesting important issues and identifying leading figures as well as locating some relevant primary sources and proposing theoretical and conceptual frameworks. Though reliance on particular ideas is indicated in the main text, it is necessary here to acknowledge a more general indebtedness to them in approach and direction for their work has informed and inspired this study in many ways.

Jana Matson Everett's *Women and Social Change in India* examines the Indian women's movement in a comparative perspective by reference to women's movements in Britain and America. She discusses what she regards as those characteristics of Indian life which have left their impression on the movement. She then gives a useful overview of the movement's emergence and development before offering an insightful analysis of its ideology and methodology. She also includes two case studies, the movement's campaigns for women's political and social rights, where she gives a critical assessment of its successes and failures. She concludes by comparing the Indian women's movement with its British and American counterparts, pointing to similarities and dissimilarities between these movements. This book has had a substantial impact on the structure and content of this study, however, this study has a different focus in which it develops one dimension of her thesis while for the most part ignoring the comparative material. In addition, this study includes a fuller version of reform and revival in nineteenth century India and extends the analysis by reference to contemporary events.

Although it is Geraldine Forbes' earlier conference papers and articles which have been more decisive in setting the agenda of this study, her recent book, *Women in Modern India*, has been valuable too. Here she examines the history of women in nineteenth and twentieth century India. She begins by considering male-led efforts at reform and pioneering attempts at female education. Next she chronicles the rise of women's organisations and then documents the campaigns for women's political and social rights. She also documents women's participation in the nationalist struggle for Indian independence and their contribution to the economy of imperial India. She covers the period from the mid-1930s to the mid-1940s which she terms transitional and the position of women in independent India including a brief overview of the contemporary women's movement. This book has had a substantial impact on various parts of this study, however, this study is more specialised in scope and does not try to offer a comprehensive account of Indian women over the last 200 years. Moreover, the way in which this study deals with reform and revival is very different as is the lengthier treatment of the contemporary movement.

Another book which has proven particularly useful is Radha Kumar's *The History of Doing: An Illustrated Account of Movements for Women's Rights and Feminism in India, 1800–1990*. This general survey of the Indian women's movement not only reproduces some significant primary sources such as legislation, petitions and resolutions but also incorporates an encyclopaedic record of the contemporary movement. In these respects, it has supplemented the work of Jana Matson Everett and Geraldine Forbes even if it has been less influential on the course of this study.

For the discussion of the Hindu tradition in terms of the position of women, Charles Heimsath's *Indian Nationalism and Hindu Social Reform* must be singled out for special mention. The interpretation of modern discourse about the position of women advanced in this study is shaped by his exposition and explanation of reform and revival in imperial India.

A wide range of other scholarly literature has been utilised in this study, most of it related to either or both the Indian women's movement and the Hindu tradition although some of it derives from other disciplines. This literature is important but, because its application is limited, it is acknowledged only in references in the main text.

In this connection, note should also be taken of Carol Sakala's *Women of South Asia: A Guide to Resources*. This remarkable, although now a little dated, bibliography contains entries on a broad range of topics relevant to women throughout South Asia from ancient up to modern times. Thus its compass clearly reaches far beyond the position of women in the Hindu tradition and the Indian women's movement with which this study is concerned. Yet for this and, indeed, for any other study on women in South Asia, this bibliography is an indispensable research aid, especially since most entries give a description of the source to which it refers and many of these sources have been examined.

Defining the Hindu Tradition

For the purposes of this study, the Hindu tradition is taken to signify what are now seen as strands of the one Hindu religion, some dating from the distant past (cf. Flood 1996: 8). It is also taken to signify other aspects of the Hindu way of life connected with the indigenous culture and civilisation which evolved on the sub-continent over millenia. This definition takes cognisance of the fact that the Hindu tradition is a modern creation, accepting that this nuances understanding of its meaning and implications as an academic and as an activist category.

The term Hindu derived from the Indo-Aryan word 'sindhu', this word employed by the Vedic people of the sub-continent to denote rivers in general and the River Indus in particular. Yet they did not use this word in an exclusively geographical sense to refer only to an area but also, in referring to themselves and their way of life thereby, used it in both ethnic and cultural senses. Though this word later became obsolete in indigenous sources, it was this word in various forms which passed into foreign use, as the Persian Hindu and hence cognate terms in other languages, where it retained its complex meaning and associations (Lipner 1994: 8–9). By the medieval period, in Muslim usage, Hindu had acquired a religious sense albeit a

7

negative one. That is, the term was used to differentiate between inhabitants of the sub-continent on the basis of their religious beliefs and practices where Hindu indicated those inhabitants who were neither Buddhists nor Muslims. Even so, Muslims did not view Hindu as indicating adherents of one religion; on the contrary, they mentioned many Hindu religions, none of which corresponded with the later concept of Hindu religion (Larson 1993: 181).

It was not until the modern period that Hindu acquired a positive religious sense in which it did indicate adherents of one religion. This one religion was regarded as the original and ancient Indian religion (Omvedt 1995: 7–9) and represented as a unified entity with a consistent internal structure (Jackson 1996: 88). Both of these are highly contentious claims: the former because it accords primacy to, as well as vesting authenticity and antiquity in, a specific construction of Indian religiosity; the latter because it assigns sectarian status within a diverse whole to distinct religious systems. Notwithstanding the number of western factors which contributed to this, reformers, revivalists and others also played an important part in the ongoing process of reification. Indeed, while such a concept of Hindu religion, however designated, has been subjected to intense scholarly scrutiny (e.g. von Stietencron 1991), this concept of the one Hindu religion originating in the Vedic scriptures which was developed during the modern period continues to dominate contemporary discourse in India as in the West (Frykenberg 1991).

The Hindu Tradition and the Position of Women

Contrasting characterisations of the impact of the Hindu tradition on the position of women were also evident during the modern period as part of the emergent, although contested, Hindu identity. The ensuing controversy was one in which competing versions of the position of women were produced taking different stances on the issue, including polemics against the tradition, apologetics for it, and a particular ambivalence in which it was depicted as having a dual nature, often expressed in terms of ancient splendour and present shame. This controversy has exerted a profound influence over understandings of the position of women, extending beyond clearly partisan and programmatic accounts, whether attacking or defending the tradition's treatment of women, even to ostensibly objective scholarly works. This influence has been such, therefore, that it has

8

largely determined the selection and interpretation of material, giving rise to a limited repertoire of 'facts and figures' and a conventional set of judgments and assumptions. Thus, through a complex and convoluted process of claim and counter-claim, the position of women in the Hindu tradition has been interpreted and reinterpreted. Consequently, some aspects of the Hindu tradition have been adduced again and again as points of reference in the course of arguments for a given stance, these arguments proceeding from one commonplace pronouncement about the position of women to another. For instance, based on the Vedic scriptures, it has frequently been declared that the position of women in ancient India was a favourable one, contrasting this with the adverse position of women in later times, perhaps reconstructed by reference to *Dharmaśāstra* literature, especially the work of the lawgiver Manu, or some other later texts, if not blamed on Muslim invasion or British rule.

Defining the Indian Women's Movement

For the purposes of this study, the Indian women's movement is taken to signify autonomous women's organisations which are formed by and for women. It is also taken to signify those organisations of women which, albeit not independent, pioneered women's extra-domestic and extra-familial involvement. Hence, this definition extends beyond the most narrow and restricted view of the Indian women's movement.

The term Indian women's movement is a convenient umbrella label for a movement far more complex and diverse than this rubric might indicate. It includes organisations dating from the mid-nineteenth century to the present day. It includes organisations with local, provincial and national constituencies. It also includes organisations with a particular religious- or community-based membership and those with a general membership as well as organisations founded on a single issue and those with a broader agenda. Including all of these, it thus includes the interrelationships between these organisations in both historical and contemporary perspective. Clearly, therefore, the movement has always been heterogeneous rather than homogeneous in its make-up, composed of many groups instead of a monolithic institution. This means that it is extremely difficult to take full account of the variety of views within the movement although it is possible to point to important and influential schools of thought such as different opinions about the impact of the Hindu tradition on the position of women.

The Indian Women's Movement and the Hindu Tradition

The Indian women's movement emerged and developed at the same time as controversy about the Hindu tradition and the position of women. Thus the movement was articulating its aims and aspirations for women in a milieu where certain ideas about the Hindu tradition were in common currency and where such ideas dominated debate about the position of women which was generally, if not universally, acknowledged to be poor and in need of improvement. This has meant that the movement has tended to refer to the Hindu tradition when protesting against beliefs and practices which have an adverse effect on women and when proposing ways in which such beliefs and practices could be changed for the better, whether these ways include or exclude appeal to the Hindu tradition. These references to the Hindu tradition, both positive and negative, have often been stereotypical, owing much in their nature and scope to already established protocols about what counted as evidence and, indeed, the proper construction to be put upon that evidence in terms of the position of women. That the movement has continued to refer to the Hindu tradition reflects the fact that it has been campaigning for women in a context still strongly influenced by earlier modes of discourse which accord primacy to particular portrayals of the Hindu tradition in relation to the position of women. To some extent, therefore, the movement has perpetuated previous epistemological and hermeneutic paradigms. It has done so by predicating its comprehensive rejection and its critical acceptance of the tradition on these premises.

The Ideology of the Indian Women's Movement

The ideology of the Indian women's movement has differed over time, the movement espousing different theoretical positions on the roles and responsibilities of women when pressing its case for change. These theoretical positions have often been indebted to western feminist ideologies of various kinds, in part at least because these ideologies have been well adapted to the somewhat westernised

10

conditions of imperial and post-imperial India, although they were further adapted to the otherwise dissimilar conditions of the subcontinent. An important dimension of these different theoretical positions has been the relationship in which each has stood with the Hindu tradition or some parts thereof. Notwithstanding, the movement has appealed to Hindu beliefs and values in promoting theoretical positions which have been congruous with, and those which have been contrary to, the norms and mores associated with the tradition. Moreover, in appealing to Hindu beliefs and values, the movement has made creative and constructive use of the tradition with which it has forged positive and productive links.

The ideology of the Indian women's movement is discussed here with reference to two typologies, Jana Matson Everett's account of 'First Wave Feminism' in terms of 'women's uplift' and 'equal rights' and Leslie Calman's account of 'Second Wave Feminism' in terms of 'rights' and 'empowerment' wings. The movement's ideology is discussed at the outset of this study to introduce the beliefs about women which have informed and inspired the movement's agenda and activities.

During the earlier years of the 'First Wave' Indian women's movement, the dominant ideology was one which Jana Matson Everett designates 'women's uplift' and defines as 'reform of social practices so as to enable women to play a more important and more constructive role in society' (Everett 1981: 82). She understands 'women's uplift' as a form of 'corporate feminism' which connotes for her a feminism 'claiming a larger role in politics for women on the ground that they have a special contribution to make as women' (Everett 1981: 18–19). Her more detailed description of 'women's uplift' emphasises that this ideology argued for women's entrance into public life on the basis of their domestic and familial responsibilities and the virtues inculcated in them, both of which were regarded as preparing women for their new public careers. This ideology also argued that it was imperative to improve the position of women in order to make the most of women's feminine talents which were seen as advancing the welfare of the nation. Accordingly, this ideology argued for many non-legislative educational and social measures to improve the position of women while also accepting ameliorative legislation where necessary to ban oppressive customs. As she explains:

> The potential of women in development, according to the women's uplift conception, involved expanding and strengthen-

11

ing female roles in society. Female roles – mother, wife, home-maker – and female values – sacrifice, loyalty, non-violence – were presented as relevant to the problems of development. In fact, the women's uplift argument was that women's role in development rested on her female roles and qualities. Women's movement leaders argued that debilitating social practices should be changed and women should be educated so that they might perform their roles in a more enlightened manner, and female values might have a more widespread impact on society. In the women's uplift conception, women's distinctive contribution to development was highly valued. The activities suggested by the women's uplift conception were primarily educational and social service in nature although legislation to abolish certain practices restricting women's potential was also implied.

(Everett 1981: 83)

This ideology was that which was advocated by leaders of the Indian women's movement in the first few decades of the twentieth century.

The origin of this ideology lay in the modern West where one school of thought had it that true womanhood, that is womanhood fulfilling its true familial and marital roles in the home, was characterised by moral and spiritual excellence. This was, for example, the opinion of John Ruskin who upheld the moral and spiritual excellence of true womanhood in his account of 'Man and Woman' first published during the 1860s. He believed that men and women were different in their natures and capacities with the sexes having complementary vocations in life and on this basis he rejected the notion 'of the "superiority" of one sex to the other' (Ruskin 1894: 264) because he denied that there was any means of comparing their relative merits. Insisting upon the incommensurability of the qualities of the sexes, he declared that 'each has what the other has not: each completes the other, and is completed by the other: they are in nothing alike, and the happiness and perfection of both depends on each asking and receiving from the other what the other only can give' (Ruskin 1894: 264). Thus he related that 'the man's power is active, progressive, defensive' whereas 'the woman's power is for rule, not for battle' (Ruskin 1894: 264). He indicated that the man was 'eminently the doer, the creator, the discoverer, the defender' in contrast to the woman who was the one who identified 'the qualities of things, their claims, and their places' (Ruskin 1894: 264). He further stated that the man's 'intellect is for speculation and invention' while the woman's 'intellect is not for invention or creation, but for sweet ordering, arrangement, and decision' (Ruskin 1894: 264).

John Ruskin's model of the relationship between the sexes located men and women in different spheres, the man in the extra-domestic, and the woman in the domestic, sphere. Associated with these different spheres were the different tasks allotted to the sexes in which man was to safeguard the woman from the trials and tribulations of society and woman was to provide the man with the comfort and consolation of home. He asserted that 'the man, in his rough work in the open world, must encounter all peril' as a consequence of which he allowed that 'often he [man] must be wounded, or subdued; often misled; and *always* hardened' (Ruskin 1894: 264). However, he maintained that woman 'by her office and place' was to be 'protected from all danger and temptation' so that, in reiterating the man's duty to ensure that the woman's purity was not corrupted by the brutalising influence of society, he added 'within his house, as ruled by her, unless she herself has sought it, need enter no danger, no temptation, no cause of error or offence' (Ruskin 1894: 264–5). His view was that the corresponding duty of the woman was to take care of the home wherein was to be found 'shelter, not only from all injury, but from all terror, doubt and division' (Ruskin 1894: 265). His concept of home, eulogised as 'a sacred place, a vestal temple, a temple of the hearth watched over by Household Gods' (Ruskin 1894: 265), was thus of a happy and harmonious place which was by definition to be separate from society.

The central theme of John Ruskin's concept of true womanhood was therefore that of moral and spiritual excellence. This excellence was an expression of the essential feminine identity when situated within the home and dedicated to home-making. The same excellence which he attributed to womanhood was for him a function of women being protected from society and charged with the running of the home as a holy trust. There was no question but that exposure to society and the forsaking of their homes in favour of participation in social life would detract from women's moral and spiritual excellence and 'unsex' them by divesting them of the ethical and religious virtues proper to their sex. John Ruskin's views were representative of the views of many others who shared his belief in the moral and spiritual excellence of true womanhood within the domestic environment of marriage and family.

Western feminists were able to adapt this ideology and turn it to their advantage. They did so by exploiting the consensus on the moral and spiritual excellence of true womanhood as an expression of the essential feminine identity but they took exception to the solely domestic setting and status with which this identity was associated and upon which it was thought to depend. Accordingly, western feminists challenged the widely held belief that women had to be kept safe from society within the home and that, were women to enter into society outside their homes, they would surrender their femininity by relinquishing their proper place and purpose. However, while western feminists were convinced that it was vital for women's virtues to be brought into social life, they considered that women's familial and marital roles in the home were what fitted women for assuming this responsibility. In this way, western feminists made the case that women should play their part in social life precisely because they possessed the particular virtues which were cultivated in women as wives and mothers, claiming that women would bring these values to bear on public affairs as their marital and familial concerns were extended to encompass issues external to their homes.

Ideas about the moral and spiritual excellence of true womanhood were accepted by many British people in India, both official and unofficial, while the feminist reworking of these ideas was accepted by many western women who lent their support to the Indian women's movement. Hence such ideas were accessible to the indigenous westernised population and in their feminist form available to the Indian women's movement. As the Indian women's movement had to address itself to a British as well as an Indian audience and as western women played an important part in its emergence and development, the pre-eminence of the ideology of 'women's uplift' was perhaps easily explicable.

Notwithstanding, in the revivalist climate of the time, another contributory factor to the pre-eminence of the ideology of 'women's uplift' may have been that it was consistent with certain aspects of elite Hindu culture which, in a manner analogous with the feminist reinterpretation of the cult of true womanhood, it extended and enlarged. These aspects of elite Hindu culture were very similar to the cult of true womanhood in that men and women were thought to be different in their natures and capacities with the sexes having complementary vocations in life. This culture also associated with distinct feminine roles distinct feminine virtues. Elite Hindu culture emphasised the feminine roles of wife, mother and mistress of the household and the feminine virtues of chastity, selflessness, piety and faithfulness. The ideology of 'women's uplift' accepted such stereotypical feminine roles and virtues. Yet while elite Hindu culture connected these feminine roles and virtues with the seclusion of women within the home, the ideology of 'women's uplift' urged that these feminine roles be extended beyond the privacy of the household to the public realm and that these feminine virtues be enlarged beyond the marriage relationship and family circle to the community and the nation (cf. Everett 1981: 65, 85–6).

These characteristics of the ideology of 'women's uplift', well suited as they were to the contemporaneous revivalist spirit in India, made it a comparatively easy ideology to espouse, especially as it lent itself to a methodology which appealed to Hindu beliefs and values. Yet its origins lay in the modern West, however much it was indigenised and archaised in the course of its adoption by new agents to advocate improvements in the position of women in a new social, cultural and religious context.

During the later years of the 'First Wave' Indian women's movement, the dominant ideology was one which Jana Matson Everett designates 'equal rights' and defines as 'the extension of the civil rights enjoyed by men in the political, economic, and familial spheres to women' (Everett 1981: 82). She understands 'equal rights' as a form of 'liberal feminism' which connotes for her a feminism 'claiming that the rights of men should be extended to women on the ground that women are equal to men and thus should have the same rights' (Everett 1981: 19). Her more detailed description of 'equal rights' emphasises that this ideology argues for women's entrance into public life on the basis of the utilisation of women's abilities. This ideology also argued that it was necessary to take action to eliminate any beliefs and practices which inhibited the utilisation of the abilities of those who were marginalised because by so doing there would be more people qualified for the work hitherto undertaken only by a minority of men. Accordingly, this ideology, accepting as it did the importance of such work being undertaken by as many people as possible, argued that women could make a significant contribution but that for them to make this contribution required the enactment of legislative measures to improve the position of women. As she explains:

> The equal rights conception argued that the potential of women
> – and of all groups – in development involved the realization of
> their full capacities. . . . The goal of equal rights concerned the
> removal of barriers – in the form of legal and social inequalities
> – which prevented various groups from realizing their full
> capacities. By removing these barriers, the achievement of equal

rights would expand the number of groups that could perform the roles previously restricted to urban educated men. Women leaders supporting the equal rights conception argued that these economic, political, and familial roles were crucial to development, and thus increasing the number of people able to perform these roles promoted development. This conception valued the capacity of women to perform roles crucial for development, those of educators, workers, citizens, and responsible family members. The activities suggested under the equal rights conception were focused around changing the legal status of women in the economic, political, and familial spheres.

(Everett 1981: 83)

This ideology was that which was advocated by leaders of the Indian women's movement in the middle decades of the twentieth century although it continues to be influential in contemporary 'Second Wave' feminism in India.

The origins of this ideology too lay in the modern West where another school of thought had it that the inequality of the sexes was solely a social phenomenon, neither inevitable nor innate because it was opposed to the natural equality of women. This was, for example, the opinion of John Stuart Mill who argued for the natural equality of women in his essay on 'The Subjection of Women' (1869). He was an exponent of the philosophy of utilitarianism, the foundational tenet of which was the greatest happiness of the greatest number, and it was to this notion of the public good that he referred when denouncing the prevailing inequality of women which he regarded as opposed to the public good. He claimed that it was unjust for women to be relegated to a status secondary to men by the legal system but, more than this, he saw the secondary status of women as contrary to the cause of humanity, declaring 'that the principle which regulates the existing social relations between the two sexes – the legal subordination of one sex to the other – is wrong in itself, and now one of the chief hindrances to human improvement' (Mill 1984: 261). For these reasons, he insisted that the inequality of women enshrined in law should be superseded by the equality of the sexes, 'a principle of perfect equality, admitting no power or privilege on the one side, nor disability on the other' (Mill 1984: 261). He was at pains to establish that whereas men were discriminated against on various pretexts, women were discriminated against simply on the grounds that they were women. His analysis was expounded as follows, that 'what, in unenlightened societies, colour, race, religion, or in the case of a conquered country, nationality, are to some men, sex is to all women' (Mill 1984: 340). In elaborating upon what this meant for all women as for some men, he indicated that it entailed their being allowed to perform only the tasks others were unable or unwilling to perform. This was because, in his view, discrimination amounted to 'a peremptory exclusion from almost all honourable occupations, but either such as cannot be fulfilled by others, or such as those others do not think worthy of their acceptance' (Mill 1984: 340) and this he deplored.

The central theme of John Stuart Mill's concept of the equality of women was thus that it was natural, even though in the society of his own day where the authority of men over women was assumed to be the norm it seemed otherwise. The subjection of women to men in law which informed the present patterns of social interaction between the sexes he condemned as immoral as well as counterproductive. On the grounds of ethics and expediency, then, he recommended that the laws were reformed so as to embody the equality of the sexes which would remove the legal advantages of men together with the legal disadvantages of women. He stressed that all women suffered from a disability arising from their sex and that this disability imposed limitations on their ambitions and activities. John Stuart Mill's views were representative of the views of many others who shared his belief in the natural equality of women irrespective of the inequality of the sexes in society.

Western feminists were able to appropriate this ideology for themselves because it had a direct bearing on the issues with which they were most closely concerned. They referred to the idea of the equality of women in nature in order to relativise the standards of the society in which they lived where the inequality of women was taken to be a fact of nature. They thus diagnosed the root cause of women's inequality as legal and so sought to have legal changes enacted which would uphold the equality of the sexes. Furthermore, the conclusion that the inequality of women was not only iniquitous but also antagonistic to the interests of everyone provided western feminists with a powerful principled and practical justification of their campaign for legal change. It allowed them to argue that attempts to abolish the legal superiority of men and the concomitant inferiority of women, whereby sex would no longer prove to be the severe disability for women which then it was, would serve the public good.

Ideas about the natural equality of women were also accepted by many British people in India, both official and unofficial, and the feminist application of these ideas was accepted by many western women who lent their support to the Indian women's movement. Again, such ideas were accessible to the indigenous westernised population and in their feminist version available to the Indian women's movement. Addressing a dual audience, both British and Indian, and admitting western women to its ranks, these factors conduced towards the espousal by the Indian women's movement of the ideology of 'equal rights' albeit at a later date than the ideology of 'women's uplift'.

The pre-eminence of the ideology of 'equal rights' was made possible by the changing climate in at least some influential sections of the community in which revivalism was less important. In these circumstances, the conflict between the ideology of 'equal rights' and certain aspects of elite Hindu culture was not as crucial. This conflict centred on the hierarchical nature of elite Hindu culture based on social duties determined by membership of groups contrasted with the ideology of 'equal rights' resting on the concepts of equality and the rights of the individual. Elite Hindu culture was based on hierarchy within society as a whole and within the family: within society, the hierarchy of castes where, the higher the position of the group, the stricter the requirements made on women's conduct; and within the family, the hierarchy of the sexes where women were subject to the authority of their male relations, initially in their natal and latterly in their marital homes. Also, in some significant senses, elite Hindu culture regarded women as members of one group, defined by sex, with the same duty which was distinguished by pure, loyal and selfless dedication to husband, family and household. This was completely at odds with the ideology of 'equal rights' which was predicated upon the equality of every individual with every other individual irrespective of their social status, including their sex, and which claimed for every individual a number of rights believed to be theirs by virtue of their common humanity (cf. Everett 1981: 36–40, 95).

Though these characteristics of the ideology of 'equal rights' clashed with elite Hindu culture, it too was sometimes legitimised by appeal to Hindu beliefs and values as, for example, when it was first introduced and when it was invoked in relation to the most controversial questions. Yet its dominance was a reflection of the liberal consensus which developed among the indigenous westernised elite who endorsed this ideology. The origins of the ideology of 'equal rights', like those of the ideology of 'women's uplift', lay in the modern West despite its tendency to self-present as neutral and value-free and as such independent of the tradition from which it emerged. In any case, if only to a limited extent, on occasion it too was indigenised and archaised as a means of advocating improvements in the position of women when being accorded a traditional justification. The 'Second Wave' Indian women's movement of the period beginning in the mid-1970s and continuing to the present is one in which Leslie Calman detects both a 'rights' and an 'empowerment' wing. Referring to the movement's heterogeneity at this time, she argues that 'it is a movement characterized by diversity' and that 'it is really many movements' (Calman 1989: 942). Further explaining this, she indicates that it does not have a monolithic unified structure, rather it is 'highly decentralized, . . . composed of countless organizations in . . . cities and rural areas' (Calman 1989: 942). This variety, according to her, is evident in the varied backgrounds, allegiances and affiliations of the women involved in it, including women 'who are wealthy, who are middle class, who are poor; who are communist, socialist, or resolutely nonideological; and those who are members of parties or who hold political parties in contempt for being elitist, opportunist, or corrupt' (Calman 1989: 942). Nevertheless, she pinpoints 'identifiable tendencies' for which she prefers the labels 'tendencies' and 'emphases' to 'divisions' and 'splits' on the basis that they are neither mutually antagonistic nor exclusive since 'the activities are in most respects complementary rather than conflictual' while 'there are many individuals and groups whose loyalties appear to crosscut the differences in emphasis' (Calman 1989: 942). She is able to classify two 'tendencies' or 'emphases' or 'organizational and ideological clusters' within the Indian women's movement (Calman 1989: 942). One of these 'organizational and ideological clusters', she describes as being concerned with 'issues of rights and equality', the other she describes as being concerned with 'empowerment and liberation' (Calman 1989: 942). Without underestimating the significant differences between these two, she also acknowledges that both are committed to changing attitudes in order to create a consensus supporting change whereby they 'seek to raise the consciousness of women and men, first to understand that women in contemporary India occupy an inferior position relative to men economically, socially and politically, and then to realize that this position is unjust and unacceptable' (Calman 1989: 942). She designates the two 'organizational and ideological clusters' within the Indian women's movement as the movement's 'rights' and 'empowerment' wings respectively.

Describing the 'rights' wing of the Indian women's movement, Leslie Calman observes that this wing campaigns for the rights of women and for their equality. This wing represents 'women's issues as issues of human rights within the secular democracy that India's constitution proclaims' in accordance with which its 'demands are most fundamentally for equality under the law' (Calman 1989: 943). This wing thus stresses the role of legislation as a mechanism for ensuring that women have equal rights. Accordingly, she states that among the objectives for which this wing works are the enactment and execution of laws enshrining the principle of the equal rights of women. She relates:

> The focus of this part of the movement is on moving the government to pass and administer laws that give women equality in those family matters subject to legislation (inheritance, marriage, divorce, and child custody), to act to improve women's health and access to education, to move toward equality in employment, and through both raised consciousness and the passage and implementation of legislation with regard to rape and dowry, to assure women freedom from violence.
>
> (Calman 1989: 943)

This primarily legal programme is very different from that found in the other wing of the Indian women's movement.

Describing the 'empowerment' wing of the Indian women's movement, Leslie Calman observes that this wing campaigns for the empowerment of women and for their liberation. This wing sets its sights on 'the personal and community empowerment of poor women' (Calman 1989: 945). This wing thus stresses a non-legislative solution to women's problems in which a 'bottom-up' rather than a 'top-down' model of initiative and enterprise is favoured. Accordingly, she states that this wing endeavours to enable women to become autonomous agents as it deems this to be a prerequisite of any real change. She relates:

> Here, if the emphasis is on rights, it is not on civil rights but on economic and social rights – the right to determine one's own future, which requires both political empowerment at the local level and access to the tools of economic well-being. The emphasis is on empowerment from below, not the conferring of rights or economic development from above.
>
> (Calman 1989: 945)

This wing of the Indian women's movement does not share the primarily legal programme of the 'rights' wing but instead seeks through other means to allow women to take charge of their own destinies.

As Leslie Calman makes clear, it is in advocating empowerment that the approach of the Indian women's movement is typical of the approach adopted by the non-party movement sector, that is 'empowering the grass roots' (Calman 1989: 946). Also typical of both the 'empowerment' wing of the Indian women's movement in particular and the nonparty movement sector in general is a lack of confidence in conventional state-centred methods to improve the position of marginalised groups, having in common 'a profound skepticism about the ability of contemporary party and electoral politics to broaden opportunities for political participation and economic development for those who by virtue of their sex, ethnicity, or caste have thus far been deprived of access' (Calman 1989: 946). It is this effective exclusion of women from political and economic processes on the grounds of their sex that the 'empowerment' wing of the Indian women's movement is trying to bring to an end.

Leslie Calman maintains that empowerment is important because of women's powerlessness in their homes and households which she attributes to 'mainstream religious and social traditions' (Calman 1989: 947). Influenced by such religious and social norms, women are subordinated to men in the family and, she insists, this domestic powerlessness and associated problems prevent women from assuming positions of authority and influence in society. As she contends:

> Women cannot hope to exercise public power so long as they are powerless over their own lives because of forced subservience to fathers, husbands, and in-laws; violence within the family; and limited educational opportunities. Nor can they exercise power over their own lives or public life if they are consumed with poverty, ill-health, and a lack of adequate food and clean drinking water.
>
> (Calman 1989: 947–8)

In her view, it is under these conditions that non-governmental action to empower women is necessary. She is clear that women are disempowered by cultural and religious beliefs and practices which do not lie within the competence of the state. On this basis, she acknowledges the imperative to use non-governmental means to advance the women's cause since neither cultural nor religious beliefs and practices are subject to ameliorative state action. What is required to combat these cultural and religious beliefs and practices and thereby empower women, she stresses, is the approach adopted by the non-party movement sector. Hence:

> Working outside of governmental channels to raise conscious-ness and self-esteem and to question social structures is critical for the obvious reason that there are many cultural and religious barriers to women's equality that are outside the realm of government action; thus transforming women's conscious-ness and building power at the grass roots is essential. This is activity that a movement, not a government, is best able to generate.
>
> (Calman 1989: 948)

An integral part of her argument for empowerment is, then, the idea that religion has promoted and perpetuated women's subordinate position in the family and, by extension, in society. Her account of this ideology makes no mention of religion in any context other than the negative one in which it is regarded as condemning women to their present powerless position.

Of the two wings of the 'Second Wave' Indian women's movement, the 'rights' wing represents a continuation of the ideology of 'equal rights' of earlier 'First Wave Feminism' in India. This is evident in the common reliance on legislation, although the development of this ideology is also apparent in the recognition that the promulgation of legislation granting women equal rights is not adequate in the absence of the ability to implement such legislation. Thus the 'rights' wing shares the modern western origins of the ideology of 'equal rights' and its relationship of conflict with parts of the Hindu tradition, albeit that appeal may be made to Hindu beliefs and values in its defence.

However, the 'empowerment' wing of the Indian women's movement is more innovative in nature and does not seem to stand in a direct line of descent from the movement of previous years. The origins of this ideology are difficult to determine despite the priority attached to grass roots activism which suggests wholly indigenous sources of inspiration. Yet the involvement in such grass roots activism of educated Indian women who are familiar with the ideologies of the modern West, if not also western women, does raise questions about whether it is possible to rule out other external influences, particularly in the light of parallel changes in emphasis in contemporary feminist praxis in the West.

The relationship between this ideology and the Hindu tradition is obvious at one level as this ideology regards religion as having a negative impact on women, a factor contributing to the powerlessness of women which it is attempting to overcome. Notwithstanding, the concept of power within the Hindu tradition, *śakti*, is feminine and, even if this is not the spring from which this ideology wells, it provides a potent symbolic resource for the empowerment of women in that it presents an image of free feminine strength and energy, deified in the form of many goddesses and especially in the form of the Great Goddess, which can be exploited. Again, this suggests that appeal may be made to Hindu beliefs and values in defence of empowerment. Certainly, such appeal has continued to feature in contemporary sources.

As the subject of this study is the relationship between the Hindu tradition and the Indian women's movement, it is important to investigate the ideological dimension of that relationship in order to contextualise discussion of the movement's methodology. It is the movement's methodology, in so far as it is possible to separate its ideology from its methodology, that is dealt with in the main text where appeal to Hindu beliefs and values, when, where and why, constitutes the major theme.

Summary

In chapter one, the 'Social Evils', prominent features of debate about the position of women in imperial India, are discussed. Notwithstanding western criticisms, these 'Social Evils', the performance of sati, the prohibition of widow remarriage, the institution of child marriage and the male monopoly over education, are shown to have been sacred to orthodox Hindus. The work of the Hindu reformers Ram Mohan Roy and Iswar Chandra Vidyasagar to improve the position of women is described, concentrating on Ram Mohan Roy's campaign for the prohibition of sati and Iswar Chandra Vidyasagar's campaign for the performance of widow remarriage. The extent of orthodox opposition to these campaigns which, in spite of this opposition, resulted in the criminalisation of sati and the legalisation of widow remarriage is noted. This opposition to social legislation on both religious and political grounds is further analysed in relation to the age of consent controversy provoked by Behramji Merwanji Malabari's denunciation of the practice of child marriage. The

23

religious opposition to legislation proposing to raise the age of consent is examined with reference to the debate between Ramkrishna Gopal Bhandarkar who rejected child marriage and Bal Gangadhar Tilak who accepted it. The political opposition to this legislation proposing to raise the age of consent is examined too, again with reference to the argument advanced by Tilak against legislative intervention in child marriage, in this instance contrasted with the argument advanced by Mahadev Govind Ranade who was in favour of legislative intervention. The revivalists' efforts to improve the position of women, arousing less orthodox opposition than those of the reformers, are also considered, indicating how Dayananda Saraswati and Swami Vivekananda advocated the extension of education to girls. This account of the 'Woman Question' through reform and revival in nineteenth century India sets the scene for the subsequent survey of the emergence and development of the women's movement.

In chapter two, the emergence and development of the Indian women's movement, influenced by both reform and revival, is outlined. Thus is demonstrated the way in which the women's movement evolved from early associations established by men into later organisations founded by women, the latter increasing in size and scope over the years. This process is illustrated by the biographies of two pioneers of the women's movement, Ramabai Ranade and Sarala Devi Choudurani. Ramabai Ranade's participation in women's associations established by men, beginning with the Arya Mahila Samaj, is contrasted with Sarala Devi Choudurani's founding of a women's organisation, the Bharat Stree Mahamandal. Recounting how she came to found the Bharat Stree Mahamandal, Sarala Devi Choudurani's critical comments about some parts of the Hindu tradition are used to introduce a discussion of the different stances of other pioneers of the women's movement. Pandita Ramabai Sarasvati's view that the Hindu tradition had a negative impact on women is analysed, indicating how she argued that it was essentially misogynistic and incapable of reinterpretation. Her censure of the Hindu tradition is juxtaposed with the approach adopted by Chimna-Bai, Maharani of Baroda, and Saroj Nalini Dutt who appealed to some aspects of the Hindu tradition in order to justify the aims and aspirations of the women's movement. Chief among the aspects to which they made appeal is shown to have been the position of women in ancient India personified by various women named in the scriptures. This discussion contextualises the discussion of the speeches and writings of Annie Besant and Sarojini

Naidu who also adopted this approach of appeal to aspects of the Hindu tradition.

In chapter three, the appeal to Hindu beliefs and values to justify the ideology of 'women's uplift' is considered by reviewing the speeches and writings of Annie Besant and Sarojini Naidu as leading figures of the women's movement. In so doing, the way in which they made use of the example of India's past is scrutinised, stressing that India's past was reconstructed in the light of the issues of their time as a means of legitimising the case for change. Their appeal to the example of India's past is seen in terms of the two interrelated themes of the 'Golden Age' of Indian civilisation and female characters in Hindu sacred literature which were regarded as representing both antique and indigenous norms. The 'Golden Age' of Indian civilisation is conceived as establishing the position of women in the model society where women played a full part in religious, social and political life. Accordingly, female characters in Hindu sacred literature are understood as exemplifying the ideals of womanhood while playing their part in all these areas of life. By appealing to these Hindu beliefs and values in support of 'women's uplift', Annie Besant and Sarojini Naidu are shown to have argued for modern Indian women to enjoy the high status and positive image they attributed to women in ancient India. Hence their justification of 'women's uplift' is recognised as being based on what were believed to be ancient Indian standards and principles. This self-same strategy of appeal to Hindu beliefs and values is also identified as having been employed to justify the ideology of 'equal rights'.

In chapter four, the different strategies employed to justify the ideology of 'equal rights' are documented by reference to the speeches and writings of influential members of the All India Women's Conference. These strategies are observed to have included both traditional and liberal justifications of the ideology. The early traditional justification of 'equal rights' is examined by enquiring into the opinions about the position of women expressed by Kamaladevi Chattopadhyaya, Lalit Kumari Sahiba, the Rani of Mandi, and Muthulakshmi Reddi when this ideology was first introduced. This strategy, it is emphasised, was one in which women's equality was authenticated by the assertion that women had been equal with men in ancient India. However, this strategy was later largely superseded by the liberal justification of 'equal rights' and this appeal to liberal beliefs and values is illustrated by commenting upon the views espoused by Margaret Cousins and Rameshwari Nehru.

Both Margaret Cousins and Rameshwari Nehru are considered as having looked to the example of the modern West, its humanistic and secular norms, to authenticate the equality of women which they also supported by appeal to the liberal credentials of the All India Women's Conference itself. This strategy is related to the liberal ideals widely-held among the westernised elite because it was consistent with the progressive convictions of this influential section of Indian society. Yet this strategy is described as being supplemented by the traditional justification of 'equal rights' when the issue with which the All India Women's Conference was concerned was most controversial. A case study is included of the conditions under which a traditional justification of this ideology continued to be offered, specifically the campaign for women's social rights.

In chapter five, the campaigns for women's political and social rights are chronicled, concentrating on the campaign for women's social rights in working for reform of Hindu personal law. The nature and scope of Hindu personal law is explained by outlining historical developments in British administration of that law whereby even the concept of personal law is seen to have derived from British sources. Moreover, the religious basis of that law in terms of its competence and constitution is stressed. The demand of the All India Women's Conference for reform of personal law to remove women's legal disabilities is discussed before sketching the main events of the period leading up to the eventual enactment of the Hindu Code Bill in the form of five separate acts. In the context of this controversy about reform of Hindu personal law, the way in which opponents and proponents of reform appealed to the Hindu tradition in support of their contrasting views is compared. Sri Sankaracharya's argument against reform of Hindu personal law is analysed in which he represented such reform as antithetical to the Hindu tradition because it rested on western egalitarian premises. That his orthodox objections were shared by many others is established by adducing excerpts from the evidence collected by the Hindu Law Committee. Renuka Ray's argument for reform of Hindu personal law when she contended that such reform was a means to restore to modern Indian women the equality experienced by their ancient Indian ancestresses is also analysed. Her argument as an All India Women's Conference activist that reform was consistent with the Hindu tradition is accounted for by the strength of opposition prompted by the Hindu Code Bill and its religious character. Thus the question of the conditions in which the women's movement has chosen to appeal to the Hindu tradition is raised.

In chapter six, the contemporary debate about the Hindu tradition is examined in the light of the position of women in independent India. The position of women in independent India is explored through a reading of the report of the Committee on the Status of Women in India which demonstrated that women's equality, a constitutional principle and object of government agencies and programmes, had not been achieved. The negative evaluation of the impact of religion on the position of women found in this report is assessed, wherein religion was regarded as an influence opposed to the achievement of equality despite also allowing that the Hindu tradition was ambivalent with favourable as well as unfavourable features for women. This report is acknowledged to have been one of the causes of the resurgence of the women's movement when it had become more moderate, even conservative, in its agenda and activities. Debate about the Hindu tradition in terms of the position of women is analysed as an important aspect of the resurgent women's movement. Cases of wholesale rejection of the Hindu tradition, both religious and secular in motivation, are discussed in which the possibility of reinterpreting the tradition in order to improve the position of women is excluded. However, other contributions to contemporary debate where the Hindu tradition is accepted in part and its ideals reinterpreted are also discussed. Among the Hindu concepts and characters appearing in examples of, and arguments for, such reinterpretation of the Hindu tradition in the interests of women are pre-Aryan India, heroines such as Sītā and Sāvitrī and the goddess Kālī which are considered here. The issues surrounding the reinterpretation of the Hindu tradition are then explored further.

In the conclusion, these issues surrounding the reinterpretation of the Hindu tradition are related to some of the problems now faced by the women's movement such as sati, dowry death and female foeticide, especially in view of the rise of the Hindu radical right in India. This is the springboard for a review of the continuing debate about the Hindu tradition in the contemporary women's movement.

CHAPTER ONE

The 'Woman Question' in India: Reform, Revival, and the Hindu Renaissance

This chapter examines the 'Woman Question' in India by exploring Hindu movements of reform and revival in relation to the roles and responsibilities of women. The analysis is set against the general attitudes and ideas characteristic of orthodox opinion contemporaneous with social, political, cultural and religious developments during the British period. Various beliefs and practices commended by orthodox Hindus but condemned by other Hindus are defined. The discussion of these 'Social Evils', central to the conduct of controversy in the British Raj, provides the starting point for an historical account of Hindu advocacy of change in the position of women which was a major theme of the Hindu Renaissance. Such advocacy is assessed in terms of the arguments advanced by reformers and revivalists whose different versions of the Hindu tradition were advanced when addressing the most momentous questions of the age.

The 'Social Evils'

It was in the modern era, which saw the foundation of British government and administration in India, that the 'Woman Question' attained prominence. Although the British presence in India began as a mercantile and commercial enterprise with the establishment of trading settlements in the seventeenth century, the British subsequently became the rulers of India exercising the powers and enjoying the privileges of government. This involved both an alteration in the character of British activities (marked by Shah Alam bestowing *diwani* or prime ministership upon Clive in 1765) and an expansion of the territories under British control (culminating in the annexation of the

Punjab in 1849). By the middle of the nineteenth century, the British ruled over the whole of the Indian sub-continent, withstanding even the Mutiny of 1857–8 which prompted the abolition of the East India Company and the appointment of a Secretary of State for India.

The British Raj engendered a variety of responses among Indians on social matters.[1] While some resisted changes in orthodox beliefs and practices, reformers urged the reformation of Hindu society in accordance with standards which were represented as Hindu and as consistent with western ideas, whereas revivalists urged the revival of Hindu society in accordance with standards which were also represented as Hindu but as independent of western corroboration.

One of the main subjects of contention, socially, religiously and politically, was the 'Woman Question'. Certainly, the criticisms of the Hindu tradition made by western observers and commentators frequently gave great emphasis to the manifold abuses, restrictions and miseries perceived to be the lot of Indian women. A famous example of this was in James Mill's *The History of British India*, first published in 1817, where, despite allowing that Hindus 'have some general precepts, recommending indulgence and humanity in favour of the weaker sex', he declared that 'nothing can exceed the habitual contempt which the Hindus entertain for their women' (Mill 1972: 283, 281). Moreover, he made a connection between the level of advancement and sophistication of a society and the position of women in that society, according to which the more advanced and sophisticated a society, the better the position of women within it, so that 'among rude people, the women are generally degraded; among civilized people they are exalted' (Mill 1972: 279). Both his description of the position of women in Hindu society and his definition of the relationship between that position and social progress, so much to the detriment of Hindus, proved to be extraordinarily persuasive and persistent.[2]

This negative portrayal of the position of women, located in the context of the wider significance commonly claimed for the position of women as an index of civilisation, informed and inspired the 'Woman Question' which, perhaps inevitably, tended to focus on what came to be known as the 'Social Evils'. The 'Social Evils' were also important in their own right as arguments for the continued supremacy of the British Raj, whether the 'Social Evils' were the measure by which the ineligibility of Indians to determine their own destiny could be established or the British Raj was the means by which the position of Indian women could be improved. Among the 'Social Evils' were the performance of sati, the prohibition of widow remarriage, the institution of child marriage and the male monopoly over education which orthodox Hindus insisted were important and integral to their religion. Clearly, as has often been pointed out, these issues addressed only aspects of women's lives, mainly sexual aspects, and did not reflect the fullness of women's experiences. Again, also as has often been pointed out, the concept of the position of women was defined in terms of the high caste lifestyle and did not acknowledge the extent to which it ignored very striking differences of lifestyle between women belonging to different groups.

Orthodox Opinion in Imperial India

The British regarded Hindu orthodoxy as normative and thus as setting the standard for Hindu conduct. This concept of orthodoxy clearly derived from the self-image of the Brahmans as sacred specialists; however, in the light of critique of 'Orientalist' constructions of Hindu culture and civilisation (cf. Said 1995), it may be questioned whether British acceptance of the Brahmans' estimation of their own importance led them to misunderstand the scope and application of orthodoxy as both universal and uniform. The British identified Brahmans as occupying the principal place in Indian society and accorded orthodoxy the status of primary indigenous ideology but the prestige and influence ascribed to Brahmanic orthodoxy was perhaps as much part of the phenomenon of imperialism as the way in which the British subsequently went about redefining the role they had assigned to the Brahmans and hence to orthodoxy. Irrespective of whether the British actually approved of orthodoxy, by proceeding on the premise that it epitomised the Hindu way of life, they endorsed claims of orthodox dominance, even to the extent that they often enforced (as much as they could) what they considered to be orthodox beliefs and practices.

The British privileging of orthodoxy had obvious implications for debate about the position of women in imperial India since it entailed the prioritisation of orthodox opinion in this debate, at least in so far as that opinion was represented and rehearsed at that time. By thus privileging orthodoxy in the way that they did, it was the British who effectively dictated the agenda for campaigns to change the position of women and determined that the purported religious basis of that position was of fundamental significance.[3] Furthermore, Hindus who campaigned to change the position of women were henceforward compelled to challenge the ascendancy of orthodox opinion in the religious terms which came to characterise debate about the position of women in imperial India. Moreover, 'the conception of tradition' which both orthodox Hindus championed and other Hindus criticised was 'specifically "colonial"' in that under British rule 'women become emblematic of tradition, and the reworking of tradition is conducted largely through debating their rights and status in society' whereby 'both "tradition" and "modernity" . . . are contemporaneously produced' (Mani 1987: 121–2, 151).[4]

Orthodox Hindus proclaimed their teaching on women as timeless truth in what they professed to be an eternal and unchanging tradition. Accordingly, when engaged in debate about the position of women in imperial India, they advocated the performance of sati, the prohibition of widow remarriage, the institution of child marriage and the male monopoly over education as religiously important, indeed, in some instances imperative.

Orthodox Hindus regarded the performance of sati, a wife's self-immolation in the fire in which her husband's body was cremated, as blessed and praiseworthy. Great rewards were promised to the woman who ascended her husband's funeral pyre to join him in death as this was acknowledged to be the supreme and perfect expression of her constancy and faithfulness to a beloved husband. In comparison with the moral excellence of the act and the glorious destiny it presaged, the conduct of a chaste widowhood was adjudged, at best, an adequate alternative and, at worst, a poor substitute.

Failing the performance of sati, therefore, orthodox Hindus insisted on the prohibition of widow remarriage. They did so on the grounds that marriage was indissoluble and inviolable for the wife, a conjugal commitment which continued to bind her to her husband after his death for as long as she lived. On becoming a widow, a woman mourning her husband was required by them to live simply in a spirit of self-denial.

Orthodox Hindus also upheld the institution of child marriage whereby a very young girl became a bride, her groom maybe a boy of about the same age, maybe a man many years her senior. Pre-pubertal marriage was believed to guarantee feminine chastity while maximising the possibilities of conception. Given that both virginity and the procreation of children, especially sons, were highly prized, such early marriage was pronounced to be an absolute necessity.

Moreover, orthodox Hindus maintained the male monopoly over education. For them, education was a privilege and prerogative which only a boy might enjoy since he alone was eligible to receive instruction in sacred knowledge. Consequently, they allowed a girl no access to learning which, in any case, was deemed incompatible with her future domestic and familial duties as wife and mother.

In the unique milieu of imperial India, those Hindus who were dismissive of practices which orthodox Hindus defended, and even extolled, disputed the religious justification which sanctified them. In so doing, these other Hindus denied the religious authority and authenticity attributed to such practices as ancient precepts with contemporary power. This is not to imply that the Hindu tradition lacked creativity and vigour in the pre-imperial period nor that religion was the sole or even the main factor sustaining the 'Social Evils', only to indicate that the characteristics of the imperial period were distinctive and different, influencing orthodox and other Hindu contributions to debate, and that in this climate the 'Social Evils' derived legitimacy, albeit bitterly contested, from receiving a religious rationale.

The Reformers

The reformers, among them Ram Mohan Roy (1772–1833) and Iswar Chandra Vidyasagar (1820–91) who worked for the prohibition of sati and the performance of widow remarriage respectively, characterised change as commensurate with the humanitarian, rational and liberal principles which they not only shared with many westerners but which they believed also typified the 'true' or 'real' Hindu tradition. In so doing, they criticised orthodox norms and values while commending reform of the position of women by reference to religion.

Ram Mohan Roy

Ram Mohan Roy was committed to improving the position of women. He argued that women should be able to inherit property as this right had been recognised by ancient lawgivers and abrogated only by later commentators. He denounced Kulinism, a form of polygyny, as a contravention of scriptural rules which governed when a second marriage could take place.[5] However, he was most famous for his prolonged and determined campaign for the prohibition of sati, a campaign which provoked considerable religious controversy.[6]

This campaign was conducted in the context of earlier British efforts to legislate on this matter (Dhagamwar 1988). In 1812, the British authorities had attempted to regulate the practice according to principles they had been advised were enshrined in Hindu law. Thus sati was banned if it was seen as inauthentic or illegitimate by Hindu standards, that is, if it was the product of coercion or intoxication, or if it was performed by a woman carrying or nursing a child. The government circular of 1817, which amended the provisions of five years previously, had even dared cast doubt upon the religious basis of the practice. Clearly, in this context, the obvious outcome of a successful campaign was the promulgation of additional legislation to criminalise sati, eventually enacted in 1829, although Ram Mohan Roy himself was at one stage ambivalent about the expediency and effectiveness of legislation.[7]

A central concern of Ram Mohan Roy's campaign was the rehearsal and refutation of arguments for the religious nature and importance of sati. Indeed, after sati had been criminalised, he wrote the 'Abstract of the Arguments regarding the Burning of Widows Considered as a Religious Rite' (1830), its purpose described as being 'so that enquirers may . . . be able to form a just conclusion, as to the true light in which this practice is viewed in the religion of Hindus' (Roy 1906: 367). In this abstract, he declared that sati had no status in the Hindu religion, emphasising that a widow was not required to perform sati, that a chaste widowhood was superior in any case and even that the rules for the performance of sati had never been followed correctly.

Ram Mohan Roy began his review of these religious arguments by remarking:

> The first point to be ascertained is, whether or not the practice of burning widows alive on the pile and with the corpse of their husbands, is imperatively enjoyed [sic] by the Hindu religion?
>
> (Roy 1906: 367)

He denied that it was compulsory for a woman to mount her husband's funeral pyre, referring to Manu and Yājñavalkya as writers who recommended that a widow live austerely and virtuously and so endorsed an alternative to sati.

Roy continued:

The second point is, that in case the alternative be admitted, that a widow may either live a virtuous life, or burn herself on the pile of her husband, it should next be determined whether both practices are esteemed equally meritorious, or one be declared preferable to the other.

(Roy 1906: 368)

He claimed that the *Vedas* were opposed to sati and dismissed claims to the contrary as unfounded and inconclusive.[8] He recalled his earlier account of Manu and Yājñavalkya on widowhood and, although he mentioned certain writers, Aṅgiras, Vyāsa, Viṣṇu and Hārīta, who, he admitted, favoured sati, insisted that in these instances sati was counselled for the achievement of personal gain. He commented that those actions motivated by such a prospect were traditionally regarded as base, a teaching he attributed to the *Bhagavad Gītā* and Manu. Further, he stated that the respective standing of these scriptures led the author of the *Mitākṣara* (who discussed the views of different writers) to pronounce sati suitable for a widow who did not seek the supreme goal. He asserted that a modern authority concurred with this judgment, categorising sati with those actions motivated by the prospect of personal gain. Thus an appropriately conducted widowhood was represented as more praiseworthy than sati.

Roy then stated:

The third and the last point to be ascertained is whether or not *the mode* of Concremation prescribed by Harita and others was ever duly observed.

(Roy 1906: 371)

He stressed that in order to comply with these conditions, a woman had to have chosen freely to perform sati and to have the capacity to withdraw from the rite, should she have changed her mind, so long as she atoned for this in some way. For him, the failure to comply with these conditions meant that sati amounted to suicide on the part of the woman while it was tantamount to murder on the part of those who supported it. Moreover, he contended that these conditions had never been fully observed. Accordingly, he concluded that advocates of sati resorted to prevailing custom and practice to condone the suicide and murder of women.

In closing, Roy urged:

We should not omit the present opportunity of offering up thanks to Heaven, whose protecting arm has rescued our weaker

sex from cruel murder, under the cloak of religion, and our
character, as a people, from the contempt and pity with which it
has been regarded, on account of this custom, by all civilised
nations on the surface of the globe.

(Roy 1906: 372)

Nonetheless, it was due in no small measure to his own campaigning,
coupled with the pro-reform climate of British opinion and especially
the pro-reform convictions of the then Governor-General, William
Bentinck, that sati was prohibited.

In a manner reminiscent of Ram Mohan Roy, the regulation which
criminalised sati presented this prohibition as consistent with Hindu
religious teaching on the grounds that sati was neither compulsory for
a wife on the death of her husband nor superior to a chaste
widowhood. This prohibition was also presented as being in
agreement with the views of Hindus, whether because they did not
perform sati or because they did not approve of associated abuses, as
well as the dictates of morality. Hence the preamble of the regulation
proclaimed:

> The practice of suttee, or of burning or burying alive the
> widows of Hindus, is revolting to the feelings of human nature;
> it is nowhere enjoined by the religion of the Hindus as an
> imperative duty; on the contrary a life of purity and retirement
> . . . is more especially and preferably inculcated, and by a vast
> majority of that people throughout India the practice is not kept
> up, nor observed: in some extensive districts it does not exist; in
> those in which it has been most frequent it is notorious that in
> many instances acts of atrocity have been perpetrated which
> have been shocking to the Hindus themselves, and in their eyes
> unlawful and wicked.

(Regulation XVII of the Bengal Code 1829)

Notwithstanding, orthodox Hindus were unconvinced by these
arguments about the religious justification of the prohibition of sati
and consequently protested against the measure.

In a petition raised in the same month, December 1829, that the
prohibition of sati became law, orthodox Hindus appealed to custom
together with scripture as authority for the sanctity of sati which, they
reiterated, was the voluntary act of a pious widow. Moreover, they
portrayed the prohibition as an infringement of religious freedom
while warning that it would be counter-productive. In this way,

orthodox Hindus contested both the premise that sati had no religious basis and that its prohibition had popular support:

> Under the sanction of immemorial usage as well as precept Hindu widows perform of their own accord and pleasure and for the benefit of their husbands' souls and for their own the sacrifice of self immolation called suttee – which is not merely a sacred duty but a high privilege to her who sincerely believes in the doctrine of her religion – and we humbly submit that any interference with a persuasion of so high and self annihilating a nature is not only an unjust and intolerant dictation in matters of conscience but is likely wholly to fail in procuring the end proposed.
>
> (Petition against the Prohibition of Sati 1829)

Despite such representations, the request for the reinstatement of sati was rejected by the Privy Council in London in January 1830, although in any case the legislation neither prevented satis being performed nor put an end to legislative deliberation about whether all satis, irrespective of the distinction earlier drawn between types thereof, were to be subject to the same ban (Dhagamwar 1988: 36).

Throughout, because the religious credentials of sati were taken to be crucial, religious issues figured prominently, although not exclusively, in the debate concerning the prohibition of sati as was reflected in the religious rationale with which the statute was prefaced. Ram Mohan Roy, arguing on the basis of scripture that sati was neither religiously necessary nor valued, and also that it had never been executed properly in any event, made a religious case for the prohibition of sati, a prohibition which orthodox Hindus opposed by insisting that sati was indeed a religious act.

Iswar Chandra Vidyasagar

Iswar Chandra Vidyasagar was also committed to improving the position of women. Sharing many of Ram Mohan Roy's interests and concentrating on related issues, after the prohibition of sati, he focused public attention on the plight of surviving widows. Whereas Ram Mohan Roy had endorsed a chaste widowhood in the context of his condemnation of sati, Iswar Chandra Vidyasagar took the view that there was an acceptable alternative to widowhood, namely widow remarriage.

In the 'Marriage of Hindu Widows' (1855), Iswar Chandra Vidyasagar acknowledged that widow remarriage was a practice 'which has not Prevailed [sic] among Hindus for many ages' and accordingly set out to demonstrate its legitimacy 'for if it be otherwise, no man, having any regard for religion, would consent to its introduction' (Vidyasagar 1976: 2). The way in which he went about this was to provide a scriptural precedent because 'it will not be admitted by our countrymen that MERE reasoning is applicable to such subjects' (Vidyasagar 1976: 2). On the contrary, as he explained, this practice 'must have the sanction of the Sastras' because 'in matters like this, the Sastras are the paramount authority among Hindus and such acts only as are conformable to them are deemed proper' (Vidyasagar 1976: 2). Consequently, he commented:

> It must . . . first be settled, whether the marriage of widows is a custom consonant or opposed to the Sastras.
>
> (Vidyasagar 1976: 2)

Addressing this issue, he upheld the authority of the *dharmaśāstras* in which category he located the *Parāśara Saṃhitā*, the scripture upon which, in the light of traditional Hindu chronology, he based his defence of the performance of widow remarriage.

The key to his interpretation of the nature and importance of this scripture was the theory of the four ages of increasing decline and degeneration, in which, he stated, the human capacity for virtue was lessened and with it the capacity to discharge the duties of previous ages. This left him with the question of which duties were obligatory in the present age when this process of decline and degeneration had run its course. For an answer to this question, he turned to the *Parāśara Saṃhitā* from which he quoted a verse associating different *Dharmaśāstras* with the different ages and itself with the present age. On this basis, he concluded 'that as Parasara has prescribed the Dharmas of the Kali Yuga, the people of the Kali Yuga ought to follow the Dharmas prescribed by him' (Vidyasagar 1976: 4). Having thus sought to show the contemporary relevance of this scripture, he then examined the *Parāśara Saṃhitā*'s judgment on widow remarriage.

Vidyasagar quoted this judgment as follows:

> On receiving no tidings of a husband, on his demise, on his turning an ascetic, on his being found impotent or on his degradation – under any one of these five calamities, it is canonical for women to take another husband.
>
> (Vidyasagar 1976: 7)

According to him, the *Parāśara Saṃhitā* permitted a widow to remarry, to live chastely or to immolate herself on her husband's funeral pyre. Continuing, he stated that, after the British prohibition of sati, a widow could only choose between remarrying or living chastely. However, in his opinion, the *Parāśara Saṃhitā* permitted widows to remarry because in the present age a widow would find it very hard to live chastely. He concluded:

> Be that as it may, what I wish to be clearly understood is this – that as Parasara plainly prescribes marriage as one of the duties of women in the Kali Yuga under any one of the five above enumerated calamities, the marriage of widows in the Kali Yuga is consonant to the Sastras.

> (Vidyasagar 1976: 8)

His central thesis, that in the present age the performance of widow remarriage was sanctioned by the scriptures, specifically the *Parāśara Saṃhitā*, provoked much debate and many objections were made to his argument.

In order to meet these objections, Vidyasagar wrote a second, more detailed pamphlet, 'Marriage of Hindu Widows: The Rejoinder' (1855), in which he rebutted allegations that his understanding of scripture, including and especially the *Parāśara Saṃhitā*, was faulty. Among the points he disputed were that widow remarriage conflicted with both the *Vedas* and *Manu's Dharmaśāstra* and that the *Parāśara Saṃhitā* either referred to ages other than the present age or to other ages as well as the present age, moreover that it allowed only for the marriage of betrothed girls, not the remarriage of widows. He lamented:

> Unfortunately man, the stronger sex, arrogates to himself rights which he is not willing to accede to weak woman. He has taken the Sastras into his own hands and interprets and moulds them in a way whieh [*sic*] best suits his convenience; perfectly regardless of the degraded condition to which woman has been reduced through his selfishness and injustice.

> (Vidyasagar 1976: 102)

Even so, his argument failed to convince orthodox Hindus and, so far as legislation was concerned, what appears to have been decisive in persuading the British to set aside orthodox objections to the measure was the permissive nature of its provisions which meant that it merely allowed but did not compel widow remarriage.

The bill which proposed to legalise widow remarriage thus began by relating that there were Hindus who regarded the performance of widow remarriage as religiously approved, notwithstanding its customary prohibition, and justified the measure as enabling Hindus who accepted widow remarriage to practise it. The preamble declared:

> Many Hindoos believe that this imputed legal incapacity, although it is in accordance with established custom, is not an [sic] accordance with a true interpretation of the precepts of their religion, and desire that the Civil law administered by the Courts of Justice shall no longer prevent those Hindoos who may be so minded from adopting a different custom, in accordance with the dictates of their own conscience.
>
> (A Bill to Remove All Legal Obstacles to the
> Marriage of Hindu Widows 1855)

However, in reality, very few Hindus were to take overt advantage of the opportunity afforded them by the bill when it became law in July 1856 such were the strictures against widow remarriage among higher social groups. Furthermore, in addition to failing to secure the performance of a substantial number of widow remarriages, this legislation may even have had a negative impact on women in those communities where widow remarriage was common (Carroll 1983).

Irrespective of its permissive character, orthodox Hindus were outraged by this bill and, while it was under consideration, submitted petitions to the Legislative Council of India protesting against the legalisation of widow remarriage. Such petitions rejected the scriptural argument opposing the prohibition of widow remarriage, instead this prohibition was presented as ordained by the scriptures. For example, a petition submitted by 'Professors of the Hindu Law, Inhabitants of *Nuddea, Trebeni, Bhatparah, Bansbariah,* Calcutta, and other places' stated that the prohibition of widow remarriage was indeed scriptural. This petition contended that the scriptures which were seen as supporting widow remarriage had been misinterpreted since they did not apply to widows in the present age and maintained that the scriptures with jurisdiction over Hindu social life specifically prohibited widow remarriage. Thus the petitioners testified:

> That the Marriage of Hindu Widows is prohibited in the Veda, the Puranas, and other Shastras. . . . For the texts pointed out by the former [advocates of widow marriage] as sanctioning widow marriage, have invariably been explained and asserted by

the latter [Hindu legal compilers and commentators] to refer to betrothed girls, and to widow sin [sic] in past yogas (ages). And in truth all the digests of the Hindu Law which have regulated Hindu manners, customs, and religious practices, from time immemorial, not only no where authorize widow marriage, but on the contrary expressly discountenance it.

(Petition against the Legalisation of Widow Remarriage 1856?)

The ineffectiveness of the legislation when enacted may be attributed, at least in part, to the depth of opposition evident in this and other petitions as those Hindus antagonistic towards widow remarriage also exercised a powerful influence over sections of Hindu society. Within this social context, their disapproval proved to be a disincentive to the performance of widow remarriage even on the part of those who favoured them.

Again, as in the case of the debate concerning the prohibition of sati, discussion was not conducted on purely religious lines but religious issues were the fundamental features of the controversy over the performance of widow remarriage. Iswar Chandra Vidyasagar identified a scripture, the Parāśara Saṃhitā, which he construed as allowing widow remarriage and insisted on its authority in spite of the hostile reaction of orthodox Hindus for whom the prohibition of widow remarriage was presented as an article of faith.

Both Ram Mohan Roy and Iswar Chandra Vidyasagar challenged the meaning and significance which orthodox Hindus attached to scripture and advocated reform by appeal to various texts. They did so in an effort to counter opposition to reform on the religious grounds claimed by orthodox Hindus. Their approach was by no means incontrovertible within this frame of reference, as witnessed by the Hindu Dharma Sabha (Hindu Religious Society) and the Hindu Dharma Vyavasthapak Sabha (Society for the Preservation of the Hindu Religion) which opposed the prohibition of sati and performance of widow remarriage respectively. However, it was important in offering a religious justification of the campaigns against sati and for widow remarriage in a context where this justification was seen as crucial.

The Religious Implications of Social Legislation

In such a context, opponents of social legislation including the measures which criminalised sati and legalised widow remarriage frequently founded their opposition on its religious implications, deploring the relativisation, if not outright rejection, of orthodox beliefs and practices which this legislation involved. The debate over the religious implications of social legislation, reflecting the centrality of religion in discourse about various social practices subject to legislative proposals, was perhaps most clearly displayed in the age of consent controversy which centred on the institution of child marriage.

Behramji Merwanji Malabari (1853–1912), an eminent Parsi journalist, was a leading figure in the age of consent controversy and, indeed, one of those responsible for publicising this issue at a time when the age of consent was 10 years as laid down by earlier legislation. In the course of his campaign, he urged the recognition that child marriage was the cause of many other social problems and so stressed the detrimental effects of this institution. In his Note I on 'Infant Marriage in India' (1884), he asserted that the only justification offered for child marriage was scriptural while expressing his view that the scriptures did not, as was so often claimed, command child marriage. He went as far as to say that any practice for which no other justification could be offered was justified in religious terms, thereby rendering it invulnerable to criticism. He remarked:

> I have never heard an argument in favour of infant marriage as a national institution, except that it is enjoined by the Shastras. But so far as I have been able to see, no Shastra enforces marriage proper on a girl under 12 years of age, when presumably the boy must be between 15 and 20. So much as to the social or so-called religious aspect of the practice. In India every custom that is unintelligible, or actually indefensible, becomes a religious question, the merits of which we are not supposed to appreciate in this *Kaliyuga*.
>
> (Malabari 1888: 3)

Although, as befitted a Parsi, his argument against child marriage was not primarily a religious one but concentrated on its adverse biological and also moral, social and economic consequences, he was repeatedly compelled to address the subject of its religious status as he did in a letter 'to the Shastris of Poona' (1886). Here he restated his position that the scriptures, far from prescribing child marriages as orthodox Hindus presumed, in reality proscribed such marriages, writing:

> I submit that religion not only does *not* sanction *infant* and *unequal* marriages, but it absolutely forbids them. . . . Go to the

noble *Grihasutras*, to the admirable *Smritis*, to the moral code of Manu and the medical code of Dhanvantar – throughout the entire range of the Hindu Shastras there is not a line to be found in favour of infant marriages.

(Malabari 1888: 190)

However, the remedies he proposed were not legislative. He suggested, for instance, that educational materials should warn against child marriage, that married men should be barred from sitting university examinations and that unmarried men should be accorded priority over their married counterparts in obtaining employment. It was when other reformers took up the issue that the proposal to amend the extant legislation and raise the age of consent from 10 to 12 years was made. This more modest and practical proposal was one of the considerations which persuaded the British authorities to proceed with legislation despite having previously declined to take any action, at least until they were convinced of both the necessity and support for it.

For all Malabari's efforts to refute its religious basis and, on the contrary, represent it as irreligious, as the age of consent controversy intensified, it was child marriage as 'a religious question' which was hotly debated, notably by Ramkrishna Gopal Bhandarkar and Bal Gangadhar Tilak. Their debate about child marriage, if, as Malabari contended, it was in fact contrary to Hindu religious teaching, the position espoused by Bhandarkar, or if, as orthodox Hindus maintained, it was an important and integral part of Hindu life, the position espoused by Tilak, concentrated on the celebration of the sacrament of *garbhādhāna* or rite of impregnation. What was at issue was the proposition that a Hindu marriage had to be consummated, at which time the sacrament of *garbhādhāna* was to be celebrated, as soon as the bride attained puberty with her first menstruation. Bhandarkar denied that the scriptures specified the precise timing of the celebration of the sacrament and hence the consummation of marriage, further he advanced a scriptual argument against the unitary nature of the sacrament which likewise allowed him to advocate delaying the consummation of marriage. Tilak, however, rejected Bhandarkar's theory on the timing and nature of the sacrament, stressing that the scriptures did specify when the sacrament was to be celebrated and scorning the suggestion that the sacrament was composed of two separate elements, thereby also rejecting Bhandarkar's case for the legitimacy of the later consummation of marriage.

In 'A Note on the Age of Marriage and its Consummation according to Hindu Religious Law' (1891), Ramkrishna Gopal Bhandarkar (1827–1925), a scholar of Sanskrit and professor of Oriental languages, posed the problem of 'whether intercourse immediately after maturity is necessary according to the Hindu religious law' (Bhandarkar 1891: 3). He held that the scriptures did not oblige the celebration of the sacrament of *garbhādhāna* and the consummation of marriage after the bride's first menstruation. Rather, he considered that there was no clear ruling on this subject, declaring:

> The texts prescribing the Garbhâdhâna ceremony and intercourse do not provide that they should come off on the occasion of the first monthly course, but leave the matter indefinite.
>
> (Bhandarkar 1891: 19)

In accounting for the different attitudes taken towards the bride's first menstruation, he appealed to the *Āśvalāyana Gṛhya Pariśiṣṭa*, to which scripture he ascribed the subdivision of the sacrament of *garbhādhāna* into two separate elements 'called Prâjâpatya and Garbhalabhana respectively' (Bhandarkar 1891: 13). In his view, the former, comprising only religious ritual, was to be celebrated after the bride's first menstruation; the latter, culminating in the consummation of the marriage, was to be celebrated after a menstruation, not necessarily the first. He explained:

> The author of the Parisishta looks upon these ceremonies as distinct from each other, and directs that the first, consisting of the consecration of the fire and the oblations, should be performed on the occasion of the first course; but the second, which must be followed by intercourse, on the occasion of *a* course.
>
> (Bhandarkar 1891: 14)

By thus subdividing the sacrament of *garbhādhāna*, he indicated that the consummation of marriage was not inextricably linked to the bride's first menstruation, but only to a menstruation.[9] These findings, which ran counter to orthodox convictions, were bitterly contested by Tilak with whom Bhandarkar conducted a public correspondence.

In a letter to the Editor of the *Times of India*, Bhandarkar invited his detractors to adduce authentic and authoritative scriptural evidence that the celebration of the sacrament of *garbhādhāna* after the bride's first menstruation was mandatory. Bal Gangadhar Tilak (1856–1920) exploited this opportunity in a characteristically robust and forthright manner. A prominent nationalist and champion of Hindu orthodoxy, he identified the Hindu religion as the basis of national unity and stalwartly supported its orthodox interpretation.[10] Accordingly, in his reply to Bhandarkar's letter, also addressed to the Editor of the *Times of India*, he defended the orthodox understanding of when the sacrament was to be celebrated, deploring what he characterised as Bhandarkar's innovative hypothesis which, he insisted, misrepresented the Hindu heritage. Hence, in 'The Express Texts of the Shastras Against the Age of Consent' (1891), he commented:

> Howsoever plausible the learned Doctor's new interpretation might be, his view . . . was in direct conflict with the almost unanimous opinion of the great Hindu divines. . . . In the face of these high authorities, who have been regulating our ceremonial law for some centuries past, no amount of quibbling, no modern "grammar and propriety," and I may say, no leaders in English dailies, will make us believe that our ceremonial law is otherwise than what the greatest and the most learned of our divines have stated it to be.
>
> (Tilak 1891: 3)

He rejected Bhandarkar's subdivision of the sacrament of *garbhādhāna* into two separate elements, referring to the scriptures to corroborate his conclusion that it was imposssible to accept Bhandarkar's argument 'that a preliminary part of an essentially one whole ceremony can be performed to-day, while the principal part thereof can be put off almost *sine die*' (Tilak 1891: 7). Closing his summary of scriptural evidence, he asserted that the scriptures did dictate the celebration of the sacrament of *garbhādhāna* after the bride's first menstruation. He was unimpressed by Bhandarkar's exposition of the *Āśvalāyana Gṛhya Pariśiṣṭa*, the recent provenance of which he contrasted with the weight of tradition, pronouncing the opinion:

> These are enough to shew that Dr. Bhandarkar's interpretation of the *parishista* is a modern invention, and that all our *smriti* and *prayoga* writers clearly and expressly enjoin *garbhadhana* to be performed on the occasion of the *first* course. . . . Without fear of any contradiction I may therefore state that from the earliest times of the *Sutras* down to the present day, a period extending over not less than 2500 years, this has been our *shastra* and practice.
>
> (Tilak 1891: 10)

The significance of his insistence on the celebration of the sacrament of *garbhādhāna* after the bride's first menstruation was its consequences for the consummation of marriage which, for him, was governed by the bride's attainment of puberty. On this basis, he portrayed the attempt to raise the age of consent from 10 to 12 years as jeopardising the sanctity of Hindu marriage since a bride's first menstruation might be before her twelfth birthday and, if so, the discharge of a religious duty would be deemed an act of rape.

The Political Implications of Social Legislation

Opponents of social legislation were also, and increasingly, exercised by its political implications, casting doubt upon the probity and expediency of accepting the role of the imperial power in legislating on social questions, let alone appealing to the British authorities for a legislative answer to these questions which was at variance with orthodox beliefs and practices. This concern about the political implications of social legislation, indicating that a wider agenda was involved in what were often treated as essentially religious issues, was evident in the age of consent controversy when conflicting opinions were expressed as to whether the agitation for, even assent to, the enactment of such legislation constituted a concession of the incompetence of Hindus to order their own affairs.

Tilak, who presented the religious case against social legislation, also presented a powerful political argument against such legislation during the age of consent controversy. At an early stage of this debate in 1881, and perhaps atypical of his polemic on the subject of child marriage in not denouncing reform outright, writing in the *Mahratta* he indicated his antipathy towards any British involvement in social questions, irrespective of whether such involvement would prove advantageous. Though he described child marriage as 'this evil custom' (Tilak 1881:1) and despite encouraging Hindus to adopt voluntary measures against its ills, he contended that Hindus needed to demonstrate an independence of the British appropriate to their aspirations for political autonomy, especially when, in his view, legislation was not the remedy. He explained:

> If we want that we should be proficient in the art of self-government, the first qualification we should show is the *ability*

to manage our own business which will be better regulated by
ourselves than by the passing of an act or resolution.

(Tilak 1881: 1)

Clearly, on this line of reasoning, it was counterproductive for Hindus
to ask the British to legislate on their behalf since such recourse to the
imperial power undermined their campaign for freedom.

It was Mahadev Govind Ranade (1842–1901), a member of the
Bombay judiciary, who defended the decision to look for legislative
solutions from the British. In his essay on 'State Legislation in Social
Matters' (1885), written in response to Malabari's 'Notes', he set out
to show that the demand for social legislation was conducive to the
nationalist cause. Maintaining that the specification of the age of
marriage was a matter for the government, he rejected the suggestion
that, because those most adversely affected, the women themselves,
had not protested against their plight, there were no grounds for
government action – after all, he argued, it was common for the
oppressed to identify with the ideology of their oppressors. Moreover,
while Tilak predicated his objection to social legislation on nationalist
principles, excluding the possibility of simultaneously seeking British
support in social areas while struggling for political liberty, Ranade
gave social legislation a nationalist rationale.

Ranade did this by minimising the part played by the British
authorities, emphasising the extent to which Hindus determined the
direction of change and conceiving the British contribution in purely
procedural terms for the purposes of enactment. He insisted:

> The initiation is to be our own, . . . dictated by the sense of
> the most representative and enlightened men in the commu-
> nity, and all that is sought at the hands of the foreigners is to
> give to this responsible sense, as embodied in the practices
> and usages of the respectable classes, the force and the
> sanction of law.

(Ranade 1915: 80)

Addressing the central issues raised by Tilak, his approach was to
assert that in reality the enactment of social legislation ran counter to
continued British political dominance, since:

> In this case . . . the foreign rulers have no interest to move of
> their own accord. If they consulted their selfish interests only,
> they would rather let us remain as we are, disorganized and

demoralized, stunted and deformed, with the curse of folly and wickedness paralyzing all the healthy activities and vital energies of our social body.

(Ranade 1915: 80)

Far from regarding social legislation as damaging or detrimental, it was the present parlous state of Hindu society which he considered to mitigate against political progress. Indeed, the claim that social and political advance were interrelated and interdependent so that the one could not be achieved in the absence of the other was a major theme of his public career. However, notwithstanding his and like-minded campaigners' efforts, social legislation was still problematic for political as well as for the religious reasons which referred to a specific practice's supposed religious character.

The Revivalists

In a climate where social legislation was criticised as inimical to the Hindu religion and to the political integrity of the Hindu community, the reformers' espousal of such legislation as the means whereby the position of women would be improved made them suspect. This dilemma, how to avoid charges that any advocacy of change in this area inevitably entailed a negative evaluation of the Hindu way of life, was resolved by the revivalists who, eschewing social legislation as a strategy, justified improvements in the position of women by locating them in a revivalist context. Thus, they articulated their agenda in a manner acceptable to the national cultural and religious revival, and thereby with indigenous sentiments and sensibilities, circumventing some of the opposition which the reformers aroused on religious and on political counts.

The revivalists, including Dayananda Saraswati (1824–83) and Swami Vivekananda (1863–1902) both of whom opposed the male monopoly over education, characterised change as restoration and renewal of ancient beliefs and ideals which, for them, constituted the 'true' or 'real' Hindu tradition contrasted with the western model of progress.[11] Like the reformers, they criticised orthodox norms and values, however, they also criticised the reformers' objectives and methods, commending revival, not reform, of the position of women by reference to religion.

Dayananda Saraswati

Dayananda Saraswati constantly called for a return to the *Vedas*, deploring what he considered to be aberrations which debased, and accretions which obscured, Vedic truth. Taking the *Vedas* as the touchstone of his iconoclastic monotheism, he condemned as superstitious and corrupt many current religious and social customs prized by orthodox Hindus. On the same basis, he condemned the reformers because they did not accept the special status of the *Vedas*, accusing them of being unpatriotic in their admiration for the West and alienated from their own history, and alleging that this meant they were unable to bring about decisive change.

So far as women were concerned, he opposed the prohibition of widow remarriage and the performance of child marriage together with polygamy and the seclusion of women.[12] Given the importance he attached to the *Vedas*, he insisted that women, as well as those men traditionally denied sacred knowledge, should have access to the scriptures through a Vedic education. In the *Satyārth Prakāś* (*Light of Truth*) (1875), he responded to the declaration that 'it is a precept of the Veda that woman and the servant should not be allowed to learn' (Saraswati 1970: 72). Maintaining that 'all human beings, whether men or women have a right to study' (Saraswati 1970: 72), he rejected as false and fraudulent the evidence adduced in favour of this injunction against universal Vedic education. Instead, he cited another verse which he regarded as genuine and interpreted as a Vedic endorsement of access to the scriptures for everyone irrespective of social divisions. Summing this up, he stated:

> See, the Lord himself saith: We have revealed the Vedas, for, the Brahmanas, Kshatriyas, Vaishyas, Shudras and our servants, and very low castes, that is, for all the people, who should read and teach the Vedas, listen to and read them to others, so as to improve their knowlege [*sic*], to adopt the virtuous course of conduct, to eschew vicious habits, to get rid of distress and to obtain happiness.
>
> (Saraswati 1970: 72–3)

Accordingly, he argued that 'it is a proof of your ignorance, selfishness and stupidity that you prohibit women from studying' (Saraswati 1970: 73) and, again, quoted from the *Vedas* to establish the validity and veracity of his view on female education which was that girls, like boys, should undergo a period of studentship when they would be instructed in sacred knowledge.

In answering the question 'should women study the Vedas?' (Saraswati 1970: 73), he justified female education in religious and other subjects. He did this by citing examples of educated women drawn from the scriptures as the basis of his evocation of an ancient India where women were educated. He emphasised the wife's role in Vedic ritual, a responsibility for which, he was convinced, she required a Vedic education, commenting:

> If she has not studied the Vedas and other scriptures, how can she read the Vedic verses with fluent pronunciation and proper annotation and converse in Sanscrit on the occasion of worship? Gargi and other ladies, the jewels of women of ancient India, became eminently learned by the study of the Vedas and other scriptures.
>
> (Saraswati 1970: 73)

He also endorsed an education where women would be taught what was appropriate to the traditional occupation of their class, whether priest, warrior, merchant or serf. As proof of this, he proclaimed:

> The wives of kings and nobles of Aryavarta (ancient India) knew the military art and laws of chivalry very well. If they did not know it, how could Queen Kekayee and others accompany King Dashrath and others to the battle field and take part in fighting?
>
> (Saraswati 1970: 74)

Among the advantages of female education, the curriculum of which was to include 'grammar, religion, medicine, arithmetic, hardicraft [sic], as a matter, of course' (Saraswati 1970: 74), he listed the development of moral sensibility, the promotion of marital and familial harmony, the loving care of children and the efficient management of the household. In these ways, Dayananda Saraswati made a case for female education on the pattern of his portrayal of India's past, a cause taken up by the Arya Samaj which he founded. That this was a religious argument for female education addressed to religious arguments against female education again demonstrates the religious nature of debate about the position of women.

Swami Vivekananda

Swami Vivekananda, the foremost disciple of the mystic Sri Ramakrishna and exponent of a version of Vedantic philosophy with a social conscience, stressed the significance of religion since, for him, a religious resurgence was a precondition of social as all other change and hence the key to India's return to greatness. He denounced the way in which orthodox Hindus insisted upon a statement of their religion in terms of social practices, to the extent that any regulation of such practices was represented as endangering religion itself. He was equally unimpressed by the reformers whose negative tactics he blamed for much of the orthodox reaction, asserting that in a century of campaigning the reformers had made no real impact and arguing that their approach was dependent on the West and, therefore, inappropriate and ineffective in India.

Aware of the difficulties experienced by women but, at best, ambivalent about earlier efforts at amelioration, he expressed impatience about being asked what was to be done for women. He emphasised that women should be setting their own priorities rather than having them set by men, proposing education as the means by which women would be enabled so to do.[13] Thus, when commenting 'On Indian Women – Their Present and Future' (1898), he explained:

> Our right of interference is limited entirely to giving education. Women must be put in a position to solve their own problems in their own way. No one can or ought to do this for them. And our Indian women are as capable of doing it as any in the world.
>
> (Vivekananda 1973: 229–30)

Consequently, in 'Conversations and Dialogues 18' (1901), while he criticised existing female education, attributing its shortcomings to the fact that it was 'not founded on a religious basis' (Vivekananda 1972: 220), he did not reject female education as such, only its present form. In its stead, he recommended an approach to female education 'with religion as its centre' (Vivekananda 1972: 220). Moreover, he challenged the contention that female education was somehow suspect for religious reasons.

Denying that the scriptures denigrated women's abilities, he held the priests accountable for having debarred other groups from a Vedic education and 'deprived the women . . . of all their rights' (Vivekananda 1972: 214) during what he characterised as the age of decline. He contrasted this priestly exclusivity with his depiction of ancient India. To this end, he named educated women whose participation in philosophical debates was related in the scriptures and asked why their modern counterparts should not, in like manner, be allowed to acquire sacred knowledge, claiming:

You will find that in the Vedic or Upanishadic age Maitreyi, Gârgi, and other ladies of revered memory have taken the places of Rishis through their skill in discussing about Brahman. . . . Since such ideal women were entitled to spiritual knowledge, why shall not the women have the same privilege now?

(Vivekananda 1972: 214–15)

In order to allow women to acquire such knowledge and, indeed, to correct the contemptuous attitude towards women which he represented as the major factor responsible for India's descent from past glories, he approved the establishment of a *math* or monastery for women and, associated with it, a girls' school. Consistent with his insistence upon the role of religion in female education, he set out a syllabus of 'religious scriptures, literature, Sanskrit, grammar, and even some amount of English' in which 'Japa, worship, meditation, etc. shall form an indispensable part of the teaching' although subjects 'such as sewing, culinary art, rules of domestic work, and upbringing of children, will also be taught' (Vivekananda 1972: 217). Further, describing the pupils' maxim as 'spirituality, sacrifice, and self-control' and social service as 'the vow of their life' (Vivekananda 1972: 218), he suggested that, were women to be educated in this wise, worthy successors of scriptural figures would be seen. He predicted:

If the life of the women of this country be moulded in such fashion, then will there be the reappearance of such ideal characters as Sitâ, Sâvitri and Gârgi.

(Vivekananda 1972: 218)

Thereby Swami Vivekananda promoted female education on the precedent of his interpretation of Indian past practice and this became a central concern of the Ramakrishna Mission which he formed. This too was a religious argument for female education addressed to religious arguments against female education, re-emphasising the religious nature of debate about the position of women.

Thus Dayananda Saraswati and Swami Vivekananda supported female education by appealing to an idealised vision of ancient India which they had in common with orthodox Hindus. In this way, they legitimised improvements in the position of women by presenting them as religiously proper without provoking similar levels of orthodox opposition when the religious status of any measure was the major issue.

Reformers and revivalists were important, however, not only for advocating change in the position of women but also for fostering a new (or renewed) consciousness on their part. This phenomenon called the 'Awakening' of Indian women was evident when, initially under the patronage of men and the auspices of male-sponsored societies, later independently and in autonomous organisations, women began to work on their own behalf.

CHAPTER TWO

The 'Awakening' of Indian Women: The Emergence of the Women's Movement

This chapter examines the 'Awakening' of Indian women by describing the emergence of the women's movement. The development of the women's movement is charted in order to demonstrate how the movement evolved from societies dependent on male support into organisations founded by, as well as for, women. This account raises the issue of the extent of male support for the women's cause once women took to acting on their own initiative and not in accordance with male guidance. Facing opposition even from some supposedly sympathetic men, the way in which women sought to legitimise their activities is also discussed. Particular attention is paid to the appeal to aspects of the Hindu tradition as a means of justifying women assuming unaccustomed public roles and responsibilities.

The Development of the Women's Movement

Influenced by movements of reform and revival, some women in nineteenth century India found themselves in a very different position from previous generations. New experiences, especially education, had encouraged women to expand their horizons beyond their homes and domestic duties. As well as inspiring women with the motivation to make contact with other women, education also furnished them with the means to share ideas and to foster a maturing sense of identity. As Geraldine Forbes explains:

> For the first time in India's history women began to communicate with women outside their families and local communities. On the one hand there was a small group of

women who shared English as a common language. This made
possible communication across language barriers. On the other
hand, there were growing numbers of women literate in the
vernaculars which enabled them to learn about women's issues
in the new women's journals. Both groups, marginalized by
more traditional society, sought the companionship of women
like themselves.

(Forbes 1996: 64)

These were the conditions in which the women's movement could
develop as women now had the aspiration and ability to participate in,
even establish their own, associations.

The process by which the women's movement developed has been
sketched as follows: early societies founded by men for women, and,
later, organisations founded by women for women, growing over the
years from small district to large national bodies.[1] However, this
process of development was by no means a simple and straightforward
sequence in which women's associations under the charge of men gave
rise and gave way to others which could undertake autonomous
activities. In practice, the former were not only or, indeed necessarily,
prior to and preparatory for the latter while the latter often existed
independently of and concurrently with the former. Nor were all
women's associations progressive in character and constitution. On
the contrary, many were conservative groups which proved to be
powerful bastions of opposition to the women's movement and its
agenda for change. Notwithstanding such complexity and ambivalence, a process of development is evident extending from the
nineteenth into the twentieth century.

Pioneers of the Women's Movement and Early Associations

Ramabai Ranade (1862–1924) was the second wife of Mahadev
Govind Ranade and, as his protegée, helpmate and companion, she
took an interest and involved herself in improving the position of
women.[2] It is clear from her autobiography, *Himself: The Autobiography of a Hindu Lady*, that, in contrast to her later contribution to
the cause, her background was orthodox. Declaring that 'the girls of
our family were carefully guarded from any modern ideas' (Ranade
1938: 2), she related the story of her paternal aunt whose husband's
death was interpreted as punishment for his having taught his wife

Sanskrit. This story she used to explain why 'in our family any sort of education for girls was considered unpropitious' (Ranade 1938: 2). Her orthodox girlhood came to an end with her marriage, aged 11 years. Notwithstanding, both the example of her mother and the advice given her by her father on her conduct in the marital home impressed her greatly. She explained that her mother 'understood that the god or *guru* of every wife is her husband' and that her father's advice was that 'whatever trouble comes, endure it silently and don't talk back' and 'never repeat tales to your husband' (Ranade 1938: 6, 20). Indeed, it was her devotion to her husband which led her to comply with his wishes even when what he wanted her to do was at odds with her upbringing. Moreover, her obedience to his will brought her into conflict with the women of her husband's family whose suspicion and hostility towards the lifestyle her husband expected her to lead she bore with fortitude.

The marriage between the 31 year old reformer and supporter of widow remarriage and his child bride had already provoked controversy. On the death of his first wife, it was anticipated that Ranade would marry a widow. That he did not do so disappointed his colleagues who were doubly disappointed that his bride was so young, especially given his opposition to child marriage. However, while a grief-stricken Ranade sought to decline the match or at least postpone it, he eventually acceded to his father's authority as head of the household, thereby discharging his filial duty at the cost of damaging his relations with fellow reformers. Ramabai thus found herself married to a reformer but at the behest of his orthodox father. Her future father-in-law had regarded with horror the prospect of his son contracting an alliance with a widow or an adult woman and, to avert this catastrophe, acted so quickly that Ramabai's marriage to his son was performed only a month after the death of his first daughter-in-law.

Consistent with his convictions, immediately on marriage Ranade began his young wife's education. He also encouraged her participation in activities intended to promote female education more widely such as speaking at a girls' school prizegiving and, most notably, her association with Pandita Ramabai, an advocate of education for women whose learning had won her the honorific Sarasvati. Ramabai went to Pandita Ramabai's women's club while living in Bombay and when she moved to Poona resolved to form her own women's club on the same lines which, in her own words, was 'an appointed place and time when the educated women could gather to discuss simple subjects under the direction of some respectable gentlemen of experience' (Ranade 1938: 67). Subsequently, Pandita Ramabai came to Poona and, together with Ranade and other prominent members of the Prarthana Samaj, she founded the Arya Mahila Samaj (Noble Women's Society) based on Ramabai's local women's club.[3] This women's society scandalised orthodox opinion including Ramabai's mother-in-law who, Ramabai recounted, gave credence to the most scurrilous and inaccurate report of Pandita Ramabai's teachings, for instance, that she asked 'why should women submit to men?' and exhorted women 'free yourselves from the control of such oppressors' (Ranade 1938: 78). This placed Ramabai in an extremely difficult position since her husband endorsed her friendship and frequent visits with Pandita Ramabai while the women of his household tried to dissuade her from attending meetings of the Arya Mahila Samaj.

This division within the family was evident in Ramabai's report of the reaction of her mother-in-law to her conspicuous appearance before a public meeting held to promote female education. On this occasion, Ramabai was charged with the responsibility of reading a speech in English before a large mixed audience and, given her inexperience, her husband had written the speech for her and drilled her in its delivery. Whatever satisfaction Ramabai felt at her successful part in proceedings was overshadowed by the antipathy with which her speech-making was received at home. Her husband was reproached for imperilling his honour and endangering his family's reputation by an open demonstration of what had hitherto been a more private challenge to convention. Angrily reprimanding Ranade for his complicity in his wife's outrageous behaviour, Ramabai's mother-in-law compared the orthodox ideal of wifely virtue, shy, submissive and observing the social segregation of the sexes, with the 'new woman', educated, self-confident and enjoying the company of her husband. She complained:

Day by day men are growing more careless of their good name. Formerly women would not even stand in the presence of a man. Then how should they speak to them! Its [sic] only at the time of *punyaharachan* [auspicious day of marriage] that wives may sit near their husbands in the presence of a few people, and even then only with bent head and without courage to lift their faces! Weren't such wives appreciated? Was there no love between such wives and their husbands? Nowadays, love means for a woman boldly to wrap her garment about her and be near her husband, to sit on a chair, to read and write like a man – to such a state have we come! Until today, we have kept this state of affairs within the house; but today's affair is beyond that! Aren't you ashamed to have her read an English speech in front of such a great crowd? Did your turban remain on your head?

(Ranade 1938: 83–4)

Despite the fact that her husband did not admit that she had only been doing as he bid her and that this exacerbated her problems with the women of the household, Ramabai testified that she 'continued to do the things Himself wanted me to do' (Ranade 1938: 85).

So pervasive and persistent was his influence over her that, when Ranade died, Ramabai did not permanently withdraw from the world and adopt the traditional way of life of an orthodox widow. Instead, still in tandem with male reformers, she carried on with the enterprise she had embarked upon under her husband's tutelage. In 1908, with Behramji Malabari and Dayaram Gidumal as well as with Begum Nawab Misra, she founded the cross-community organisation for social service, the Seva Sadan, which included among its aims the practical education of women, preparing them to take their place in public life and inspiring them to share the ethic of social service. Four years previously, in 1904, she attended the first meeting of the Bharat Mahila Parishad (Indian Women's Conference), the women's section or auxiliary of the National Social Conference. The National Social Conference had been co-founded by Ranade in 1887 when the Indian National Congress of which he was also a founder decided to concentrate on political issues and exclude the discussion of social questions from its deliberations. The male leadership of the National Social Conference later chose to convene an ancillary annual meeting for women where they could debate those social questions which most concerned them. Ramabai addressed the first meeting of this women's auxiliary, characteristically urging her audience to labour alongside men for India's welfare and recommending that her listeners volunteer for social service.

Throughout her career, Ramabai was associated with societies, the Arya Mahila Samaj, the Seva Sadan and the Bharat Mahila Parishad, dependent on male support. Though she had deviated significantly from orthodox norms of feminine conduct, her major motivating factor had been her husband's favour and approval. Initially joining with him in his work to improve the position of women and latterly working with other male reformers to achieve this end, her experience had been of men's espousal of the women's cause and assistance in women's efforts to contribute towards their own betterment. She proposed a partnership between men and women and stated her belief in the capacity of the sexes to co-operate in the pursuit of a common objective. Her outlook differed markedly from the views expressed by Sarala Devi Choudurani who was not prepared to accept what she saw as women's subordinate role in reform associations or concede that the reformers' benevolence extended to a voluntary abdication of their dominance over women.

Unlike Ramabai Ranade, Sarala Devi Choudurani (1872–1945?) was born into a family committed to reform.[4] She was the granddaughter of Debendranath Tagore, a leader of the Brahmo Samaj, and the daughter of Swarnakumari Devi, a poet and novelist who founded her own women's society, the Sakhi Samiti, financed by women's craft fairs, mahila silpamelas. She was well educated but her family objected nevertheless when she left home to become a teacher at a girls' school. Returning home, she assisted her mother in her work for women; later her nationalist activities, concentrated on physical culture and martial courage, made her famous. In 1905, she was persuaded to marry a fellow nationalist, a member of the Arya Samaj, with whom she was to have one son. After her marriage, though, she devoted more of her energies to improving the position of women and in due course she established the Bharat Stree Mahamandal (Great Circle of Indian Women).

In an article entitled 'A Women's Movement' in which Sarala Devi set out her own version of events surrounding the establishment of the Bharat Stree Mahamandal, she identified the limits of male support when women attempted to form their own organisation without reference to men. She related how the motion to found the Bharat Stree Mahamandal as 'a permanent association of Indian ladies . . . for the amelioration of the condition of Indian women' was endorsed by the 1909 session of the Bharat Mahila Parishad, one of the 'men-manoeuvred women's meetings' of which she was so critical (Choudurani 1911: 344, 345). Plans were made for the new organisation's inaugural assembly, however, those men whom she termed 'the so-called social reformers' (Choudurani 1911: 345) disparaged this development. Portraying as patronising the reformers' attitude towards women, she related how women's issues featured in their rhetoric and how the reformers even prevailed upon women to voice their opinions. However, she contrasted the self-image of the reformers as advancing the cause of women with their resistance to women taking charge of their own future, in this case, by forming their own organisation. According to her:

They advertise themselves as champions of the weaker sex; equal opportunities for women, female education and female emancipation are some of their pet subjects of oratory at the annual show [National Social Conference]. They even make honest efforts at object lessons in the above subjects by persuading educated ladies to come up on their platforms and speak for themselves. But woe to the women if they venture to act for themselves.

(Choudurani 1911: 345)

She noted that the new organisation was a product of the National Social Conference, observing that despite this 'the members of that body which professed to have as its goal the raising of women through education to the altitude of self-help' (Choudurani 1911: 345) did not support women when they had acquired the necessary self-confidence and self-reliance to strike out on their own. Instead, these 'avowed champions of the sex' made every effort to prevent the Bharat Stree Mahamandal being a success, 'insisting on a man-manipulated meeting of women just as usual' (Choudurani 1911: 345). In consequence, two women's meetings were held in 1910 when both the Bharat Mahila Parishad and the Bharat Stree Mahamandal met. Characterising the Bharat Mahila Parishad meeting as under the control of men with 'the women on the stage acting as mere puppets in a show of marionettes' (Choudurani 1911: 345), she presented a contrasting picture of the Bharat Stree Mahamandal as managed by women for women with the aid of those men who were prepared to help. Thus, for Sarala Devi, the Bharat Stree Mahamandal not only represented a significant advance on those societies which were dependent on male support, but the strong and sustained opposition to it also demonstrated that there was a divorce between the declared policy of reformers and their demeanour in practice.

The purpose of the Bharat Stree Mahamandal, one of the first autonomous women's organisations, was defined as being:

The creation of an organisation by means of which women of every race, creed, class and party in India may be brought together on the basis of their common interest in the moral and material progress of the women of India; and in and through which organisation they may work in association and in a spirit of mutual helpfulness for the progress of humanity through that of their own sex.

(Choudurani 1911: 347)

In order to achieve this, the Bharat Stree Mahamandal's programme included the following: to educate women within their own homes and promote the production of vernacular reading materials through which women could be informed about relevant subjects; to market women's handicrafts for them so as both to preserve their personal and family honour and to persuade them to employ their time gainfully; to facilitate women's access to medical care; and to provide the financial resources to underwrite these activities. In many ways, these objectives were very similar to those of other societies whose members' deference to men Sarala Devi so deprecated. Moreover, her insistence upon the need for women to organise independently, restricting membership of the Bharat Stree Mahamandal to women though 'irrespective of nationality, race, class or creed' (Choudurani 1911: 347), did not extend to embracing the proposition that men's and women's interests conflicted. Stating that 'in India more than anywhere else the woman's cause is the man's cause' (Choudurani 1911: 350), she expressed the hope, even expectation, that men would be moved to lend their aid.

One of the most striking features of Sarala Devi's critique of the reformers was her comment on the real reason why they were reluctant to relinquish their power over women. Her argument was that the reformers' refusal to allow women to exercise leadership in their own right was influenced by Manu, the most famous of the Hindu lawgivers whose law-book occupied a pivotal position in modern polemic. She interpreted his teaching as inspiring men's distrust of women even then and she attributed to it men's continued tendency to exert control over women. Somewhat sarcastically, she remarked:

Surely traditions die hard – even among social reformers of India. So they are not to blame if the shade of Manu still haunts them and actuates them in their want of faith in the capacities of Indian women and prompts them to follow the usage long established of keeping them under thraldom at every stage of their growth.

(Choudurani 1911: 345)

Notwithstanding, on other occasions she referred to different aspects of the Hindu tradition, such as the position of women in ancient India,[5] which she viewed in a positive light as a precedent for change.

This then points to how women involved in early associations interpreted and evaluated the Hindu tradition in terms of its impact on and implications for women. This also relates to how they went about offering rationales for their organisations and the enterprises in which they were engaged for the welfare of women, including how they represented the Hindu tradition in this regard. While the Hindu tradition was subject to intense criticism, many women did appeal to Hindu beliefs and values which they could adduce as evidence that their activities were worthy of acceptance in traditional terms.

The Early Women's Movement and the Hindu Tradition

Pandita Ramabai Sarasvati (1858–1922) was the author of one of the most well known books on the position of women, *The High-Caste Hindu Woman*, which contained a thorough-going condemnation of Hindu attitudes towards women. She had been educated by her parents who had not arranged her marriage when she was a child.[6] When they died, she and her brother continued their father's work, travelling from place to place and speaking for female education. On her brother's death, she married one of his friends with whom she had a daughter but she was widowed shortly afterwards. This did not deter her from campaigning for improvements in the position of women which she did as leader of the Arya Mahila Samaj with its commitment to the promotion of female education and by testifying before the Hunter Commission on education in India when she made a strong case for women teachers and doctors. Given this need, she decided to learn English so that she could acquire further knowledge and wrote a book, *Stri Dharma Neeti* (*Women's Religious Law*), to subsidise her journey to England. In England, while staying with Christian nuns, she converted to Christianity and both she and her daughter were baptised. She studied hard at Cheltenham Ladies' College before resolving to go to America to attend her cousin, Anandibai Joshee's, graduation as a doctor of medicine. It was in order to raise the money for her travels that she wrote *The High-Caste Hindu Woman* which was also intended to raise the awareness of western women about the way of life of their Hindu counterparts.

In *The High-Caste Hindu Woman*, Pandita Ramabai began by insisting that 'in order to understand the life of a Hindu woman, it is necessary for the foreign reader to know something of the religion and the social customs of the Hindu nation' (Sarasvati 1890: 1). Referring to the proportion of the population whom she classified as 'professors of the so-called Hindu religion in one or the other of its forms', she argued that 'among these the religious customs and orders are essentially the same' while 'the social customs differ slightly in various parts of the country, but they have an unmistakeable [*sic*] similarity underlying them' (Sarasvati 1890: 1). What followed was a brief overview of 'the religion of the Hindus' in general terms, at the conclusion of which she explained that 'the principal customs and religious institutes of the Hindus' derived from the law-books, according special status to *Manu's Dharmaśāstra* described as being 'believed by all to be very sacred' (Sarasvati 1890: 1, 6). Her account of the position of women, illustrated by many quotations from *Manu's Dharmaśāstra*, was thus introduced in the context of 'Manu and other law-givers' and 'sacred law' (Sarasvati 1890: 6). In particular, her account was predicated on what she understood to be the consensus between these lawgivers in their teaching about women and structured around a threefold division of a woman's life, childhood, marriage and widowhood, which she also attributed to Hindu law as expounded in their law-books.

Pandita Ramabai emphasised that the birth of a daughter, unlike the birth of a son, was not attended by joy and celebration but by sadness and worry. For all that a girl was not as welcome as a boy, she characterised childhood as the best years of a woman's life when she could amuse herself, playing and having fun without being compelled to go to school or undertake other onerous tasks. However, as she was at pains to point out, these happy years of childhood came to an abrupt end with the girl's marriage when still very young and her transfer to her husband's home where she would be expected to do housework under the strict tuition and rigorous supervision of her mother-in-law. Indeed, she stressed that the new bride was not only placed in unfamiliar surroundings under the authority of often critical strangers, but also suggested that the norms of the joint family made it difficult for her to find comfort and consolation in her relationship with her husband. Further, whatever the trials and tribulations of a wife, she made clear that the plight of a widow was far more pitiable since it was seen as a penalty for the woman's own transgressions and as such she was treated with harshness and contempt. So glorious were the rewards promised to the woman who committed sati, in contrast to the terrible prospect of widowhood, that she claimed women would even be prepared to end their lives in torment to avoid the restrictions and humiliations of widowhood.

Moreover, although Pandita Ramabai did indicate that in the past women had not been subjected to all these rules and regulations, she did not subscribe to the widely held belief that the position of women in ancient India, albeit more favourable in some respects, represented the ideal to which modern India should aspire. Thus, for instance, with reference to widowhood, she argued in what had come to be conventional terms among those who advocated change in the position of women that in the past widows had been able to remarry. Her argument was that widows were permitted to remarry in ancient India, in her own words 'when the code of Manu was yet in the dark future, and when the priesthood had not yet mutilated the original reading of a Vedic text' (Sarasvati 1890: 40). Hence, in her opinion, which again was in conformity with the tenor of much critical thought, both lifelong widowhood and sati arose later: the former prescribed in *Manu's Dharmaśāstra*; the latter, since it was not so prescribed, requiring a Vedic justification which it was anachronistically and illegitimately accorded. Even so, ancient India was not for her, as it was for so many others, a model and exemplar of the proper position of women. This was because she did not follow the line of reasoning about the loss of earlier freedoms to the conclusion generally reached, namely that some earlier period set the standard. Certainly, her understanding of the relative merits of past and present when judged by the welfare of women was more equivocal than was common. Such an outlook was perhaps evident in her backdating of female seclusion which, though admittedly more prevalent and more strict once the Mughals had established their dominion over India, she traced to the pre-Mughal period, even to before the common era, in any event, identifying its origins in Hindu misogyny.

This rejection of the notion that there were aspects of the Hindu tradition to which women could appeal was demonstrated in her discussion of Hindu scriptures where her censure of *Manu's Dharmaśāstra* was not contrasted with acclaim for an alternative text. Instead of making distinctions between types of scripture on the basis of their statements about women as was the usual strategy of those who shared her concerns, she took Manu's tenets to be not only authoritative for Hindus but also representative of those communicated in the canon as a whole. Hence, she summarised the lawgiver

Manu's teaching about women on the basis that 'all Hindus, with a few exceptions, believe implicitly what that law-giver says about women' (Sarasvati 1890: 28), including warnings that women were neither temperate nor trustworthy. In so doing, she asserted that he was expressing views typical of those contained in the canon as a whole. Consequently, she observed that he was but 'one of those hundreds who have done their best to make woman a hateful being in the world's eye' (Sarasvati 1890: 30), declaring:

> I can say honestly and truthfully, that I have never read any sacred book in Sanscrit literature without meeting this kind of hateful sentiment about women. True, they contain here and there a kind word about them, but such words seem to me a heartless mockery after having charged them, as a class, with crime and evil deeds.
>
> (Sarasvati 1890: 31)

Her judgment was, therefore, that the canonical assessment of the character and capabilities of women was profoundly negative.

Pandita Ramabai also contended that the Hindu tradition differentiated between the duties of the sexes to the extent that 'religion . . . has two distinct natures in the Hindu law; the masculine and the feminine' (Sarasvati 1890: 32). Defining the religious duty incumbent on a woman in terms of reverence for her husband, consecration of her life to his service and compliance with the relevant rules of conduct, she stated that its 'sum and substance' was:

> To look upon her husband as a god, to hope for salvation only through him, to be obedient to him in all things, never to covet independence, never to do anything but that which is approved by law and custom.
>
> (Sarasvati 1890: 32)

Clearly, in her estimation, there was no equality between the sexes in their treatment by the Hindu tradition because it required a woman to submit to her husband upon whom her religious destiny rested.

Despite acknowledging that there were 'a handful of Hindus entertaining progressive ideas . . . doing all they can to reform the religious and social customs of Hindustan' (Sarasvati 1890: 65), the logical outcome of Pandita Ramabai's argument was that it was not possible to restate the Hindu tradition in favour of women. This would certainly make sense of her conversion to Christianity but this act alienated her from many Hindus who would otherwise have been her allies in attempting to improve the position of women. Her ambivalence was evident in the way in which she couched her call for western sympathizers to provide the necessary financial resources to support her educational endeavours. Though she pledged that her future pupils would not be 'disturbed in their religious belief', she urged the recognition that 'to prepare the way for the spread of the Gospel by throwing open the locked doors of the Indian zenanas' initially required making female education a priority (Sarasvati 1890: 63, 65).

Pandita Ramabai's conversion to Christianity, and associated with it the contentious question of whether she would proselytise her pupils, was to have a significant effect on her subsequent career. On her return to India, she founded the Sharada Sadan (Home of Wisdom) as a school for widows; however, allegations were made that she was converting widows which led to the loss of the support of some prominent Hindus as well as the withdrawal of a number of pupils. Notwithstanding the veracity or otherwise of these allegations, when she founded the Mukti Sadan (Home of Liberation) and was not constrained by the need to observe a policy of religious neutrality, she set about openly and actively converting her charges. Her rejection of Hinduism and allegiance to Christianity nevertheless proved problematic in many ways. Undoubtedly, it distanced her from many would-be colleagues. It also made her approach very different from that of other women, including Chimna-Bai, Maharani of Baroda, and Saroj Nalini Dutt, who appealed selectively and critically to aspects of the Hindu tradition in defence of their objectives and organisations. Although their strategies for improving the position of women were not the same, the Maharani and Saroj Nalini both sought to show how their schemes were in fact in accordance with the position of women in ancient India, in support of which claim they cited women named in the scriptures.

Chimna-Bai, Maharani of Baroda, (dates unknown) was the wife of the Gaekwad of Baroda, a princely kingdom of west-central India which enjoyed a reputation as one of the most progressive native states, a reputation which her activities further enhanced.[7] Something of the esteem in which she was held was evident in her presidency of the first All India Women's Conference in 1927. One of her major contributions to the cause was the book *The Position of Women in Indian Life* written in collaboration with a like-minded co-author which, in her own words, was produced in the 'hope that something tangible may be effected to raise woman's position in Indian public life' (Baroda and Mitra 1912: xvi).

In her preface, the Maharani outlined how her journeys in the West had made her aware that western women participated in public life whereas Indian women played no part in extra-domestic and extra-familial life, reflecting that 'the co-operation which exists between Western men and women in public affairs is practically unknown in India' (Baroda and Mitra 1912: ix). This near male monopoly over Indian public life she blamed on the almost complete absence of philanthropic bodies in which men and women worked together for the common good and claimed that the few such bodies already found in India had in any case made little impression. Recalling that 'I often wondered whether I could do anything to awaken my Indian sisters from the lethargy of ages, to enable them to take their proper place in Indian public life' (Baroda and Mitra 1912: ix-x), she related how she resolved to study western society and to make available the information she gathered as it was most relevant to women. In so doing, it was her purpose to stimulate debate among Indian women about these issues with the aim that certain western institutions could be modified to meet Indian needs. Although she believed that there was much which India could gain from the West, she was anxious 'to guard against too slavish an imitation of Western notions' (Baroda and Mitra 1912: xv). Clearly concerned to prevent the loss of India's unique identity and to ensure that due regard was given to its heritage and environment, she insisted that each people, like either sex, must retain its own nature and disposition and thus stated that 'there should be no hasty adoption of customs essentially foreign to our habits' (Baroda and Mitra 1912: xv).

In the main text, therefore, the Maharani and her co-author tried to prove that there was an Indian paradigm for their advocacy of a public role for women. They did so by composing a history of humanity from the beginning of time, concentrating on the position of women. In this history, they narrated the origins of marriage and the associated differentiation of the responsibilities of husband and wife where, in their version of events, the wife was responsible for the home and children while the husband was responsible for external matters. They allowed that the transition from a nomadic to a settled lifestyle was beneficial to the wife 'but she still remained the property of her husband, who had absolute right over her in every way' (Baroda and Mitra 1912: 4). However, they also emphasised that 'amid the bygone civilizations of the world, an era of glory dawned for women' (Baroda and Mitra 1912: 4). They explained that this was a period when women were treated with the greatest respect and, employing the Hindu scriptures as evidence, corroborated their theory by referring to what they interpreted as the public roles held by the women of ancient India.[8] They commented:

> In the ancient literature of India, dating from centuries before European culture began, in the great epics of the Ramayana and Mahabharata, woman took distinguished part in her husband's work, aiding him with her love and counsel, accompanying him, like Sita and Draupadi, even into exile. She shared in the public ceremonies, and was accorded the highest rank and dignity.
>
> (Baroda and Mitra 1912: 4)

Sharing the widespread belief that the position of women in India had worsened over the millenia, they described women's previous participation in public life which they contrasted with later developments, thereby throwing into bold relief women's exclusion from public life in modern times.

Remarking upon this process of decline and deterioration in the position of women, the Maharani and her co-author asked:

> But how has it fared with the woman of India through the long centuries since civilization dawned upon her land? We have seen that in the early ages of the world . . . she enjoyed the highest public honour, and was a participant in all the wisdom and activities of her day. . . . But succeeding years in India checked woman's glory.
>
> (Baroda and Mitra 1912: 13, 14)

They also shared the widespread belief that such decline and deterioration in the position of women was prompted, at least in part, by the arrival of foreign conquerors, a contention strengthened by their discussion of the preferential property rights given women in ancient India which, in their opinion, 'have hardly yet been excelled by any laws in any country in the West' (Baroda and Mitra 1912: 14). They complained that India 'became a prey to external invasion and internal strife' and, in the consequent violent turbulence, 'the cause of learning, and with it that of woman, was forced to the wall' (Baroda and Mitra 1912: 14). Continuing in the same vein, they deplored that 'the arts of peace had no room to expand' and, attendant on the conflict of recent centuries, added that 'woman's interests and education fell into a depth of miserable neglect and suppression, from which they are only now recovering' (Baroda and Mitra 1912: 14).

The Maharani and her co-author were insistent that modern Indian women were to be the main, if not sole, contributors to improving their own position but justified any such improvement on the basis of ancient Indian practice where, as inspiring examples of women of the past indicated, women were not merely concerned with domestic and familial matters but played a full part in society. They even espoused the view that the best mothers were those whose care was not limited to their own household, thereby enlarging the scope of the maternal role and the concept of the family so that women became the mothers of the nation 'who feel it their duty to act as true parents in endeavouring to redress any wrong they see in the world around them' (Baroda and Mitra 1912: 349). In this way, they paid homage to a domestic institution regarded as sacrosanct by Hindus while arguing that it found its fullest expression in public life where the woman as 'the mother of that great public family – the nation – should let no abuse exist which she can possibly help to remove' (Baroda and Mitra 1912: 349). Their appeal to aspects of the Hindu tradition to legitimise women's participation in public life was typical of the approach taken by many who wished to improve the position of women. Indeed, this was the approach taken by Saroj Nalini Dutt when speaking up for mahila samitis (women's institutes) which she formed throughout rural Bengal, the first at Pabna in 1913. She too looked to ancient India and women of the past to show that there was no contradiction between the mahila samiti movement and the Hindu tradition.

Saroj Nalini Dutt (1887–1925) was the daughter of one of the first Indians to enter the Indian Civil Service and grew up in a westernised family with the benefit of education.[9] When she married, her husband was also a member of the Indian Civil Service and it was as she accompanied him to his different postings that she founded mahila samitis with educational, vocational, medical and charitable aims.

In his biography of Saroj Nalini, *A Woman of India: Being the Life of Saroj Nalini*, her husband recalled that 'she had realised that to make the country advance, the first and foremost work was the awakening of its women' (Dutt 1929: 89). He further recalled that, though she appreciated the help and support of men, she thought that this awakening was dependent on women's own commitment to the cause which 'was why she yearned to stir up the women themselves to wake up and join in a united effort for their own emancipation' (Dutt 1929: 89). Inspired by the prospect of Indian women working together for the benefit of India, she saw mahila samitis as a means by which this could be brought about. For instance, when challenged concerning women's capabilities to join such institutes, she emphasised not only that women possessed the potential to progress but also that they would be enabled to make a practical contribution towards the welfare of the nation, exhorting the sceptical:

> Give them the opportunity, put them in touch with other women in social life and let them take part in some kind of activity for the amelioration of social and national life, and you will find that they will have plenty of things to talk about and also to carry through in action.
>
> (Dutt 1929: 90)

However, her founding of mahila samitis was often fraught with difficulty because members of the local community were opposed to them, fearing their impact on the character and expectations of women and hence on the Hindu family and home.

This opposition and how she chose to meet it were both evident in her husband's report of a conversation between Saroj Nalini and 'a very reactionary old gentleman of Birbhum' (Dutt 1929: 98) where she founded the second mahila samiti in 1916. This man asked her whether 'this attempt to interest our women in affairs outside the home' was 'alien to the civilisation of our country' and whether it would 'denationalise our women' (Dutt 1929: 98). She responded by denying these accusations and by naming women of ancient India renowned for their learning. Taking her examples from Hindu scripture and history,[10] she asked:

> In ancient India did not women take a leading part in the intellectual life of the country? Who has not heard of Maitreyi, Gārgi, Lilāvati, and the illustrious wife of Mandana Misra, to mention only a few typical among them?
>
> (Dutt 1929: 98)

Having thus demonstrated the validity of women's education, a major goal of the mahila samitis, she went on to argue that in ancient India women had been interested and involved in public affairs. She did so on the grounds that the term used by a Bengali housewife to denote her tasks was 'ghar-saṇśar', meaning home and world respectively. For her, this term showed that women had not always been excluded from the public role for which the mahila samitis were now preparing them and she even went as far as to blame Indian men for restricting women to their current private concerns. Commenting on the implications of the term *'ghar-saṇśar'*, she declared:

> This conclusively proves . . . that in the old times the woman's legitimate sphere of work in our country was considered to be not the home alone but the world as well as the home, neither of which can be neglected without great detriment to the other. In the course of time the men of our country, in their blind and shortsighted selfishness, persuaded the women to believe that their world was synonymous with their homes and to confine their activities and their outlook within the four walls of their home alone, to the utter neglect of all that appertains to the outside world.

> (Dutt 1929: 99)

Moreover, making the common connection between the position of women and the condition of the nation, she maintained that the limitations placed on women had been damaging to India and that only women would be able to remedy the situation.

The need felt by Saroj Nalini to show that the mahila samitis were compatible with the Hindu tradition, irrespective of allegations to the contrary, was reflected in the way in which she was portrayed in her biography where her husband went to great lengths to present her as faithful to traditional virtues. For instance, he stressed that 'she took a particular pride in building up her life in accordance with the ideals of ancient Hindu womanhood' and suggested that her success in winning over her fellow Indian women 'lay in her own fondness for the Hindu woman's innate simplicity and modesty of manner and her deep and loving respect for the old customs of the country' (Dutt 1929: 30, 82). Yet notwithstanding these attempts to portray her as embodying the moral and spiritual qualities prized in women, the mahila samiti movement did meet with resistance from those who were worried that its work to improve the position of women threatened the Hindu religion. Clearly, this made it imperative to address the issue of the relationship between the activities of the mahila samitis and the prevalent view of Hindu teaching about women in order to overcome this opposition. What was more, at least in its own estimation, the movement was able to achieve wider acceptance for its work. Thus Indira Ghosh, Secretary of the Malda Mahila Samiti, having observed that when this institute was founded some 'were of the opinion that Hindu rites and customs of ages would be trampled down in the very near future', concluded that 'with intense patience, faith, perseverance, and self-sacrifice our members have now, through the grace of God, convinced our critics that the Samiti is not a revolutionary organisation, inconsistent with religion and the social system' (Dutt 1929: 138). This was certainly the impression which Saroj Nalini herself had tried to convey by appealing to aspects of the Hindu tradition as precedents for the programme of the mahila samitis.

In much the same way and for much the same reason, Annie Besant and Sarojini Naidu who were leading figures of the women's movement also appealed to Hindu beliefs and ideals, in particular to the 'Golden Age' of Indian civilisation and to female characters in Hindu sacred literature. This appeal to the position of women in the model society and to the ideals of womanhood likewise involved the selective reinterpretation and critical reappropriation of the Hindu tradition as it had been described and delineated hitherto.

CHAPTER THREE

'Women's Uplift':
The Appeal to Hindu
Beliefs and Values

This chapter examines the way in which 'women's uplift' was justified by appeal to Hindu beliefs and values, especially the example of India's past in terms of the 'Golden Age' of Indian civilisation and female characters in Hindu sacred literature. This appeal to Hindu beliefs and values is discussed with specific reference to the speeches and writings of Annie Besant and Sarojini Naidu who came to prominence as advocates of the women's cause in the late nineteenth and early twentieth centuries respectively. The way in which they employed the example of India's past to legitimise their aims and objectives for modern Indian women is analysed. Accordingly, this account focuses on how, when campaigning on behalf of women in modern India, they reconstructed India's past as a time when women had enjoyed a high status and a positive image and represented it as the pattern or prototype for their own endeavours. Their appeal to the 'Golden Age' of Indian civilisation and to female characters in Hindu sacred literature is thus shown to have reappraised the position of women in the model society and restated the ideals of womanhood.

Annie Besant and Sarojini Naidu

Annie Besant (1847–1933) was an important and influential figure in both the women's movement and the nationalist struggle in India.[1] However, she became famous while still in Britain where her varied career took her from the atheism of the Free Thought Society to the socialism of the Fabian Society before she joined the Theosophical Society with its eclectic esotericism and particular interest in Eastern religions, including Hinduism. Drawn to Theosophy by reading

Madame Blavatsky's *The Secret Doctrine*, it was in this capacity that she travelled to India where she was to live and work. She expressed great admiration for Indian culture and civilisation, nevertheless, she was concerned about Indian social practices, many of which adversely affected women. She was also active in nationalist politics, her interest in which led the British to intern her during the First World War. She was president of the Theosophical Society (1907–33) and founder of the Home Rule League (est. 1916). In 1917, she was awarded the presidencies of the Women's Indian Association, established by women theosophists drawing upon the Theosophical Society's organisation in India, and the Indian National Congress. In the post-war period, she was eclipsed by Gandhi and increasingly marginalised from Indian opinion by her opposition to non-co-operation. Although for some years she continued to work for constitutional change, including the enfranchisement of women, at the end of her life she was no longer a major public figure.

Sarojini Naidu (1879–1949) was another important and influential figure in both the women's movement and the nationalist struggle in India.[2] Famous for her poetry, which won her the title of 'Nightingale of India' and fellowship of the Royal Society of Literature, she was also committed to improving the position of women and changing the political status of India. She campaigned on behalf of women in respect of social and political issues. For example, she moved a resolution promoting the welfare of Hindu widows at the National Social Conference in 1908 and she urged the enfranchisement of women at the head of a deputation appearing before the Secretary of State for India in 1917. She was president of the Women's Indian Association and the All India Women's Conference, the latter initially envisaged by members of the former as a one-off assembly to discuss the subject of female education but subsequently developing a permanent structure as a forum for debating a variety of social and political issues. A close associate and colleague of Gandhi, she exercised a leadership role in nationalist activity as one of his most trusted friends and followers. In 1925, she became president of the Indian National Congress; in 1931, she attended the Second Round Table Conference; and, after independence, in 1947, she became governor of United Provinces (Uttar Pradesh).

Before the formation of national women's organisations such as the Women's Indian Association (est. 1917) and the All India Women's Conference (est. 1927) and/or in addition to the platform provided by these organisations, leaders of the Indian women's movement,

including Annie Besant and Sarojini Naidu, debated and communicated ideas through involvement with various bodies and by
exploitation of various media. Annie Besant's participation in the
Theosophical Society, the Home Rule League and the Indian National
Congress enabled her to advance her views. She also wrote pamphlets
and articles for journals. Likewise, Sarojini Naidu's participation in
the National Social Conference and the Indian National Congress
enabled her to advance her views. She also addressed local women's
associations and meetings sponsored by student and youth groups.
Thus the speeches and writings of Annie Besant and Sarojini Naidu
were not only diverse in intention, circumstance and date but also in
occasion, audience and location. Since they were speaking and writing
for different purposes, on different pretexts, under different
conditions, to different people, as well as at different times and in
different places, a number of factors apart from their own opinions
influenced the tone and content of particular pronouncements.

The Example of India's Past

When Annie Besant and Sarojini Naidu appealed to Hindu beliefs
and values to legitimise 'women's uplift',[3] they looked to the example
of India's past as they envisioned it, thus claiming inspiration from
age-old native norms. Their account of India's past was both
descriptive and prescriptive: in describing the 'Golden Age' of Indian
civilisation, they prescribed the position of women in the model
society; and in describing female characters in Hindu sacred
literature, they prescribed the ideals of womanhood. However, despite
declaring them to be old in origin and indigenous in derivation, the
way in which Annie Besant and Sarojini Naidu redefined these
concepts and qualities was both modern in date and western in
influence. In so doing, they portrayed the innovative and alien as
ancient and Indian, thereby accommodating and underwriting
conduct which challenged orthodox opinion by appeal to Hindu
beliefs and values.[4]

Moreover, this process of redefinition occurred in the context of
imperial rule. The contours of India's past were thus shaped by
British attitudes as Indians remade their heritage in an image which,
by laying claim to what the British admired, was best suited to
achieving their ends. They reproduced the past, therefore, in a
manner which prepared it to meet the needs of the present under the

Raj, in which circumstances 'the value system, the mores of the colonial rulers are seen as a norm, and the subjugated people argue that they earlier had a system exactly like that of the colonial rulers' (Thapar 1987: 13). Clearly, such versions of the past were prompted by British polemic and propaganda and resulted from a reading back into India's past of those attributes which had become highly prized precisely because they were what the British themselves regarded as important.[5] This phenomenon can be classed as 'invented tradition' , 'symbolic expression of community' and 'past-as-wished-for' , theories which analyse how the past is understood and used in the present. Eric Hobsbawm's account of 'invented tradition' emphasises that 'all invented traditions, so far as possible, use history as a legitimator of action and cement of group cohesion' and that 'they are responses to novel situations, which take the form of reference to old situations, or which establish their own past by quasi-obligatory repetition' (Hobsbawm 1984: 12, 2). Similarly, Anthony Cohen's account of 'symbolic expression of community' stresses that 'the past is being used here as a resource' and that 'although the re-assertion of community is made necessary by contemporary circumstances, it is often accomplished through precisely those idioms which these circumstances threaten with redundancy' (Cohen 1985: 99). Or again, Stuart Piggott's account of 'past-as-wished-for' draws attention to inspired and imaginative recreations of the past 'in which a convenient selection of the evidence is fitted into a predetermined intellectual or emotional pattern' (Piggott 1974: 3). Seen in this light, the appeal to the 'Golden Age' of Indian civilisation and to female characters in Hindu sacred literature was an attempt to authorise modern ideas and activities by reference to the past. Furthermore, this attempt was made at a time when imperial rule was challenging the relevance of the religious legacy inherited by modern Indians. Indeed, the resultant reinterpretation and reappropriation of the Hindu tradition was driven by conviction and imbued with sentiment.

Whether viewed as a case of 'invented tradition', 'symbolic expression of community' and/or 'past-as-wished-for', when Annie Besant and Sarojini Naidu appealed to the 'Golden Age' of Indian civilisation and to female characters in Hindu sacred literature, they looked to the example of India's past where India's past was seen to determine criteria for change which were regarded as neither novel nor foreign. By looking to this example, they simultaneously stressed the discontinuity which emphasised the need for, and the continuity which allowed of, a return to the standards and principles of ancient India as they represented them to have been. Their appeal to the 'Golden Age' of Indian civilisation, as establishing the position of women in the model society, both rested on the disparity between an idealised ancient India and a degenerate modern India, and regarded past accomplishments as assurance of present capacity and promise of future success in improving the position of women. Similarly, their appeal to female characters in Hindu sacred literature, as exemplifying the ideals of womanhood, both contrasted the virtues epitomised by these characters of ancient Indian scripture with contemporary beliefs and practices, and affirmed that modern Indian women could realise such ideals once again.[6]

Throughout, Annie Besant and Sarojini Naidu were propounding a version of India's past set within a framework in which its importance derived from a particularly favourable and powerful vision of its nature and implications. In practice, the nature of India's past was conditioned by current concerns and causes and its implications by the manner in which present problems were addressed and purposes advanced by recourse to it. Furthermore, Annie Besant and Sarojini Naidu linked India's fate with the destiny of Indian women by correlating the degree of civilisation achieved with the status of women. Accordingly, they associated the greatness of India's past with the qualities displayed by the women of ancient India and thus argued for change as a condition of national renewal and recovery.

'Women's Uplift' and the Example of India's Past

During their careers, Annie Besant and Sarojini Naidu looked to the example of India's past in speaking and writing about their aims and objectives for modern Indian women. The following discussion focuses on two interrelated themes, the 'Golden Age' of Indian civilisation and female characters in Hindu sacred literature, which were integral parts of the argument they advanced for 'women's uplift'.[7]

The 'Golden Age' of Indian Civilisation

The appeal to the 'Golden Age' of Indian civilisation in support of 'women's uplift' was a call to return to what were promoted as being the standards and principles of ancient India. The 'Golden Age' was informed by conventional perceptions of the past, albeit that these were already influenced by various western ideas and assumptions. These perceptions included especially the Vedic period, envisaged as a long-lost era of greatness, and the theory of the four ages, whereby the first age of purity and perfection was succeeded by ages of ever-growing corruption and vice. Both inculcated a nostalgic and romantic attitude towards the past and, at least in comparison, a negative and critical attitude towards the present, attitudes which were also attributes of the ideology of the 'Golden Age'. Moreover, Annie Besant and Sarojini Naidu reinterpreted the 'Golden Age' as a 'Golden Age' for women where they were not subject to those latter-day customs and practices which restricted them to the domestic sphere and limited their interests to the family and household but instead participated fully in religious, social and political life. Thus the appeal to the 'Golden Age' of Indian civilisation established the position of women in the model society.

Consequently, when Annie Besant and Sarojini Naidu appealed to the 'Golden Age' of Indian civilisation as establishing the position of women in the model society, they contrasted this position with the position of women in modern India. On the other hand, by looking to the example of India's past, they asserted that the position of women in modern India could be changed to comply with ancient Indian standards and principles.

Appealing to the 'Golden Age' of Indian civilisation, Annie Besant remarked:

> In those days the Aryan woman was free, dignified, and strong; she stood beside her husband at the altar, for without her he could not discharge his priestly duties in the home; she stood beside him in life, through death, in the gladder life beyond; she was not separable from him, but a part of his very self.
>
> (Besant 1917: 303)

Having related the religious role of women in ancient India as partners in religious ritual, she denied that the prohibition on women's access to the Vedic scriptures dated from antiquity, pointing out that certain Vedic hymns were credited to women composers and also that the tradition remembered women who participated in sophisticated philosophical debates on the same terms as men. Similarly praising the achievements of women in ancient India, Sarojini Naidu asserted:

> At the beginning of the first century [India] was already ripe with
> civilization and had contributed to the world's progress radiant
> examples of women of the highest genius and widest culture.
>
> (Naidu 1918a: 17)

This situation, she reasoned, made it all the more ironic that, so many
centuries later, it was 'necessary for us to stand upon public platforms
and pass resolutions in favour of what is called female education in
India' (Naidu 1918a: 17). These descriptions of ancient India as the
'Golden Age' were idealised, in the sense that ancient India was taken
as the touchstone by which modern India could be judged, and
anachronistic, in the sense that ancient India was a reification of the
hopes and aspirations of modern Indian women.

One issue which assumed great importance for the Indian women's
movement was political representation. This helps to explain why
descriptions of the position of women in ancient India were sometimes
cast in terms of female suffrage and sought to support the case for the
extension of fundamental political rights to women. In her statement
to the Joint Select Committee on the Government of India Bill in
1919, Annie Besant denounced the proposed legislation because, she
insisted, 'it introduces a sex disability into Indian life that is alien to
its whole spirit', claiming that discrimination between men and
women was not part of Indian political practice where 'in the elected
Councils which have marked Indian civilisation from the dawn of
history, women were not barred, and the idea of sex as a barrier only
came with Western systems' (Besant 1921: 430). She highlighted
Indian support for the enfranchisement of women and, although she
acknowledged 'that there might be some objection from orthodoxy or
conservatism', characterised the source of this opposition as 'modern
orthodoxy and modern conservatism' on the basis that, according to
her, no such opposition existed in ancient India (Besant 1921: 431).
Thus she explained that opponents of women's enfranchisement
'object to the revival of the old Hindu custom of recognising women's
place in public life' (Besant 1921: 431). Therefore, when the decision
whether to enfranchise women had been delegated to the Presidencies
and Provinces, she praised those legislatures which 'led the way in
restoring to Indian women one of their ancient privileges' (Besant
1921: 465).

Sarojini Naidu's view was much the same when she gave evidence
before the Joint Select Committee. She pointed to 'the ancient and
historic Indian tradition of woman's place and purpose in the civic and

spiritual life of the nation' (Naidu 1995: 162). She did so in order to counter the complaint that the enfranchisement of women was neither appropriate for nor acceptable to present-day India and to confirm her claim that enfranchisement was, in fact, the unfolding of ancient Indian norms and values under modern conditions. Substantiating her statement about the part played by women in the India of the past, she cited woman's 'contribution to the national achievement by her wit and wisdom, her valour, devotion and self-sacrifice, as scholar and statesman, soldier, saint, queen of her own social kingdom and compassionate servant of suffering humanity' (Naidu 1995: 162). This she considered to be the means by which she could both disprove 'the reiterated argument of the illiberal or uninstructed opponent of women's suffrage as being too premature or too novel and radical a departure from accepted custom' and prove 'that the Indian woman . . .[,] so far from demanding an alien standard of emancipation, . . .desires that her evolution should be no more than an ample and authentic efflorescence of an age-long ideal of dedicated service whose roots are deep hidden in the past' (Naidu 1995: 162). It is apparent that such portrayals of ancient India as the 'Golden Age' were influenced by present-day needs and expectations and addressed issues of real and practical importance for modern Indian women.

Annie Besant and Sarojini Naidu often stressed that women were valued members of ancient Indian society who occupied an honoured position in public as well as private life. Annie Besant thought that in ancient India women possessed 'a wide and deep education and a dignified liberty' in which the nature of the marital union, somewhat surprisingly defined as 'that complete unity, which we find in India alone, and a complete subordination of the wife to the husband', by no means entailed an exclusively domestic role for women (Besant 1901: 121). On the contrary, she maintained that the wife's relationship with her husband 'did not prevent woman from exercising lofty functions, from playing her part in the family and in the world' (Besant 1901: 121). Indeed, Sarojini Naidu, referring to the 'legitimate place [of Indian womanhood] in the secular and spiritual counsels of the nation', specified 'the classic position' of Indian woman 'held in a happier epoch of our country's story' as 'symbol and guardian alike of the hearth-fires, the altar-fires and the beacon-fires of her land' (Naidu 1925b). Likewise, though more prosaically, proceeding on the assumption that women in ancient India had been interested and involved in wider social and political activities, she recalled Indian woman's 'rightful place as a co-sharer . . . in civic responsibility and a comrade . . . in re-building the ancient glory of your land' which she regarded as conforming with 'the old ideals of Indian civilization' (Naidu 1925a). This emphasis upon the co-operation between men and women in ancient India, and the contribution then made by women to public life, was significant as setting a precedent for the public role modern Indian women were now adopting.

As Annie Besant declared when comparing the status of Hindu women in ancient and modern India:

> In the revival of religion, men's minds are turned to the earlier conditions of Hindu social life, . . . and they see . . . how much the dignity and position of the Hindu woman . . . excelled in those days the social condition of to-day. That study of ancient ideals leads necessarily to the desire to apply them to modern life, and a wish grows up for the restoration of social happiness on the old lines and in consonance with national ideals, rather than for reforms based on western ideas.
>
> (Besant 1921: 175–6)

Having indicated that ancient India was the indigenous inspiration for efforts to improve the position of women, she listed some such efforts, among more general measures, adding that 'all these attempts to restore old ideals in the place of modern abuses grow naturally out of the religious revival' (Besant 1921: 176). Thus she hailed 'the Awakening of the Women to claim their Ancient Position' which position she called 'a very noble one', and considered to sanction both marriage and renunciation as life styles for women (Besant 1921: 313, 334). She stated:

> The great majority married, becoming, as Manu said, the Light of the Home; some took up the ascetic life, remained unmarried, and sought the knowledge of Brahman.
>
> (Besant 1921: 334)

Sarojini Naidu also welcomed the way in which contemporary events evinced the influence of ancient India. She speculated that the willingness of a large audience to attend to her address was 'the first augury of the hope of to-morrow that India has returned – . . . inevitably – to that first ideal of the Devi' (Naidu 1918a: 208). She interpreted India's 'old ideal of wisdom' as the insight 'that woman is an embodied deity of Lakshmi and Saraswati', referring to 'the Devi aspect of Indian woman' (Naidu 1918a: 208). Continuing, she posed a question intended to contrast the extra-domestic role of ancient

Indian women with the exclusively domestic role of women in modern India:

> Women who, according to your tradition, should have been your comrades, your equals sharing, according to the old Shastraic teaching, your spiritual and civic life, what are they to-day?
>
> (Naidu 1918a: 209)

Glowing testimonials to India's early glories as the 'Golden Age' were, then, of no mere antiquarian or academic interest; rather they articulated an ancient Indian agenda for change in modern India which attempted neither to undermine national pride nor acknowledge the superiority of western culture.

On these grounds, Annie Besant and Sarojini Naidu were able to express their views in a manner which appeared to enhance, not undermine, national prestige. They espoused change but represented it as a recovery of the pure practice of the past, not western-inspired innovation. Therefore, the means envisaged to ameliorate existing conditions and remove modern abuses, deplored as indicative of a degeneration from earlier Indian norms and values, was a return to the past and not an acceptance of alien mores. Implicit in the appeal to the 'Golden Age' of Indian civilisation was the view that antiquity was authoritative and relevant and so invested with continuing significance for modern life. Consonant with this approach, and similarly implicit in the appeal to the 'Golden Age' of Indian civilisation, was the avowed reliance on Indian, and not western, ideals and institutions.

On the subject of an ancient standard for the improvement of the position of women, Annie Besant announced:

> I look to ancient India for the model and ideal, in order to give reason and inspiration why modern India should change her ways in some very definite respects.
>
> (Besant 1901: 108)

Discussing how best to fulfil the potential of Indian women, she summed up her advice in this manner, 'that you should study and realise the old Ideal, and that you should then see how it may be re-introduced; . . . so that in the future, as in the past, there may be great, heroic, strong, pure, and devoted women in India' (Besant 1901: 135). In like fashion, before giving an extremely favourable account of different aspects of ancient India including the position of women which she defined in terms of having a 'lofty and legitimate place and function'(Naidu1995: 149), Sarojini Naidu commented:

[India] endures once more the poignant travail of her destined renascence, and her imminent *tomorrow* can seek no lovelier inspiration than the chronicle of her immortal *yesterday.*

(Naidu 1995: 148)

Thus she counselled men to 'restore to your women their ancient rights' (Naidu 1918a: 20). In putting forward such views, Annie Besant and Sarojini Naidu claimed to be motivated by ancient principles and not by new ideas.

On the subject of an Indian standard for the improvement of the position of women, Annie Besant commented upon 'the ancient self-respect, dignity, and liberty' which, on the whole, Hindu women had retained in regions beyond Muslim hegemony where they were 'not under the very narrow seclusion system which is the characteristic of those parts of the country where the Mussalmân has ruled for long' (Besant 1901: 125). By laying the blame for India's problems on the forfeiting of India's own values, she was able to advocate the ending of female seclusion as a readoption of those values, arguing:

For if it were possible, however slowly and however gradually, to enlarge these restrictive limits, to gradually widen out the life of the woman, you would not be following the West, but following your own ancestral custom; you would only be giving back to the modern women what the ancient Indian women continually enjoyed.

(Besant 1901: 125)

Again, when expressing her ambitions for Indian women, that women be afforded the opportunity 'to develop our body and spirit and mind' which, in turn, would restore 'an ideal womanhood that will make noble wives who are helpmates, strong mothers, brave mothers', Sarojini Naidu contended:

We ask for nothing that is foreign to our ideals, rather we ask for a restoration of those rights, the rights that are the immortal treasures.

(Naidu 1918a: 96h)

In so doing, Annie Besant and Sarojini Naidu claimed to be motivated by Indian principles and not by western ideas.

Thus, when Annie Besant and Sarojini Naidu appealed to the 'Golden Age' of Indian civilisation, they appeared to pose no threat to patriotic sentiments or nationalist aspirations since they considered ancient India provided the corrective to modern Indian beliefs and practices. Indeed, the evocation of India's past splendours which was an integral part of the appeal to the 'Golden Age' of Indian civilisation was also a simultaneous recollection of the high status and positive image of women with which these splendours were associated.

This correlation of the character of civilisation with the position of women was explicitly acknowledged by Annie Besant who, vindicating ancient India's claims to greatness in these terms, remarked:

> It has been said that the position of woman in any civilisation shows the stage of evolution at which that civilisation has arrived; and if that maxim be taken as accurate, then there can be no kind of doubt as to the height of civilisation attained in ancient India, when we contemplate the position which there was held by women, and study the types that then were found in the land.
>
> (Besant 1901: 107)

This was explicitly acknowledged by Sarojini Naidu too who, stating that ancient India's 'womanhood enjoyed a freedom and franchise unknown in the modern world', described this as 'highest proof of a country's civilization' (Naidu 1995: 149). Further, she suggested that India's past greatness had been established on the basis of women's place and role, declaring:

> Ancient Hindu India laid the foundation of her civilisation on the position and responsibility of woman.
>
> (Naidu 1918a: 167)

Not only was it affirmed, therefore, that the position of women in ancient India demonstrated the greatness of India at that time, but also that the latter was dependent on the former, indicating the importance of women for India's well-being. Among the means by which women could make a positive contribution to their country, in the opinion of Annie Besant and Sarojini Naidu, were by influencing their families and by their maternal qualities.

Emphasising the extent of women's influence over their husbands and children, Annie Besant asserted:

> The wife inspires or retards the husband; the mother makes or mars the child. The power of woman to uplift or debase man is practically unlimited.
>
> (Besant 1917: 155)

Sarojini Naidu made much the same point about women's influence, describing women as 'the real nation-builders' and proclaiming:

> For it is true to-day as it was yesterday and will be to the end of human life that the hand that rocks the cradle is the power that rules the world.

> (Naidu 1918a: 20)

Moreover, Annie Besant pointed to the existence of a special relationship between Indian women as mothers and the condition of the Indian nation:

> It was the mothers of India in the past who made the great India of the past – the great women of India who made India what she was in the ancient days.

> (Besant 1917: 235)

One reason for this was the belief that maternal values had implications beyond the home for the state of the nation, a belief which Sarojini Naidu expressed when she professed:

> The true standard of a country's greatness lies not so much in its intellectual achievement and material prosperity as the undying spiritual ideals of love and service and sacrifice that inspire and sustain the mothers of the race.

> (Naidu 1918a: 32)

Attributing a nation's standing to the influence and qualities of its women, Annie Besant and Sarojini Naidu gave an account both of how India came to fall from, and how to ensure her rise to, greatness.

Annie Besant, reflecting on the position of modern Indian women, remarked 'how great, how saddening, is the change' (Besant 1901: 122). Or, again, she referred to the modern Indian woman as 'a dwarfed and mutilated copy of the ancient model' (Besant 1939: 114). Explaining how modern Indian women lacked the learning and no longer exercised the extra-domestic role of their ancient foremothers, she observed:

> While the woman remains eastern, she is not eastern of the older type. She has lost her knowledge while retaining her devotion; she has lost her share in public life while retaining her authority in the home.

> (Besant 1939: 114)

The significance of this definition lay in her understanding that women had an essential part to play in India's progress, in her own words, 'that a high type of womanhood is as necessary for the national welfare as a high type of manhood' (Besant 1939: 113).

Sarojini Naidu made it clear that men's mistreatment of women had serious consequences, not just for women, but also for men. Speaking on the education of Indian women, she discussed the 'national ideal' and the necessity of addressing 'the woman question' for its achievement (Naidu 1918a: 18). She condemned the way in which many men failed to support female education, either opposing it outright or seeking to restrict what was taught, asking:

> How then shall a man dare to deprive a human soul of its immemorial inheritance of liberty and life? And yet, my friends, man has so dared in the case of Indian women. That is why you men of India are to-day what you are: because your fathers, in depriving your mothers of that immemorial birthright, have robbed you, their sons, of your just inheritance.
>
> (Naidu 1918a: 19–20)

In another speech where once more she focussed on the vital role of women, she insisted that 'the real test of nationhood is the woman' (Naidu 1918a: 98). According to her:

> If the woman has taken her proper place in the society then the central problem is solved. The goal of society depends upon the unit of the woman. . . . When women lost their self-reverence, degeneration came in.
>
> (Naidu 1918a: 98, 99)

As a corollary of this account of India's fall, predicated as it was on the fall of Indian women, Annie Besant and Sarojini Naidu suggested that India could regain her ancient glory only when there was an improvement in the position of women.

Annie Besant and Sarojini Naidu painted a gloomy picture of India's prospects if Indian women were not provided with the means to promote national regeneration. Issuing a warning, Annie Besant announced:

> Indian greatness will not return until Indian womanhood obtains a larger, a freer, and a fuller life, for largely in the hands of Indian women must lie the redemption of India.
>
> (Besant 1917: 155)

In the same vein, Sarojini Naidu argued:

> Unless and until they raise the fallen condition of women in this country and make their voice heard, India's salvation was only a distant dream.
>
> (Naidu 1918a: 27)

Consequently, women's participation in every area of activity, not merely in family and domestic matters, was regarded by both as essential to India's restoration. Annie Besant advised:

> For India's uplift, then, her daughters must come out from their seclusion, and take back their place in the common life, out of which they have slipped . . ., to the sore detriment of the Motherland.
>
> (Besant 1939: 115)

Indeed, when endorsing a resolution on Self-Government for India, Sarojini Naidu contended:

> If I stand before you as a chosen representative of united India it is only because the womanhood of the Nation stands by you to-day and you require no proof more worthy, more convincing of your evidence for responsible and complete Self-Government than the sense of instinctive and fundamental justice you show in letting the voice of Indian womanhood to [sic] speak and confirm the vision, the demand, the endeavour, the ambition of Indian manhood.
>
> (Naidu 1918a: 241–2)

Failing the rise of Indian women, India would not rise, just as the fall of Indian women had encompassed the fall of India.

Accordingly, Annie Besant and Sarojini Naidu stressed the importance of the contribution to be made by women since, without their co-operation, India's future could not be assured. Annie Besant expressed this view that women's role was crucial, stating:

> For India's uplift, the woman must have an open field, unfettered hands, and unimpeded activity. . . . Womanhood as well as manhood must be consecrate to the Motherland, for in their union lie the strength, the stability, the freedom of India.
>
> (Besant 1939: 117, 118)

Sarojini Naidu also took the same view about the role of women as being necessary for India's deliverance:

For, no man lives for himself and no woman lives unto herself and no nation can be single-handed. You want the two hands of a nation to uplift itself and together we shall carry the soul of India to the heights of her eternal glory.

(Naidu 1918a: 198)

Consistent with an understanding of the complementary character and conduct of the genders, the nature of women's contribution to their country tended to be represented in conventional terms; for instance, feminine virtues were to be applied to, and feminine roles were to be performed in, the national setting.

Annie Besant pointed to the unique and selfless qualities exhibited by a woman in the discharge of her domestic duties, and predicted that those qualities would still be in evidence when she became conscious of, and committed to, extra-domestic concerns:

> Sacrifice is so essentially a part of her daily life as a wife, a mother, a mistress of her household, that she does not calculate it as does a man. It comes to her by habit, and the good of her unit, the family, so dominates her mind that it never strikes her to put her individual comfort in conflict with her devotion to those she loves. When that is extended to the country, when she makes the larger interests her own, the same characteristic comes out.

(Besant 1939: 116–17)

Or again, using the domestic image of the household, Sarojini Naidu described her policy as president of the Indian National Congress as particularly suited to a woman, and, outlining her aims as a daughter of Mother India, elaborated on this theme by speaking of ensuring the harmony and unity of her Mother's house and family:

> Mine, as becomes a woman, is a most modest, domestic programme, merely to restore India to her true position as the supreme mistress in her own home, the sole guardian of her own vast resources, and the sole dispenser of her own hospitality. As a loyal daughter of Bharat Mata, therefore, it will be my lowly though difficult task, through the coming year, to set my Mother's house in order, to reconcile the tragic quarrels that threaten the integrity of her old joint family life of diverse communities and creeds, and to find an adequate place and purpose and recognition alike for the lowest and the

mightiest of her children and foster children, the guests and the strangers within her gates.

(Naidu 1925b)

So women could play their part in India's recovery by bringing their feminine virtues to bear on, and exercising their feminine roles in, public life, but an improvement in their position was a prerequisite of this by which women would be equipped and enabled to make their contribution to India. The emphasis was not upon women's rights for their own sake, but upon fitting women for their national responsibilities.

In appealing to the 'Golden Age' of Indian civilisation, as establishing the position of women in the model society, Annie Besant and Sarojini Naidu looked to the example of India's past as the guide and inspiration for modern India. In so doing, they located 'women's uplift' in a national context whereby advocacy of change, represented as neither innovative nor alien, was regarded as conducive to India's restoration to greatness.

Female Characters in Hindu Sacred Literature

The appeal to female characters in Hindu sacred literature in support of 'women's uplift' was also a call to return to what were promoted as being the standards and principles of ancient India. These characters were drawn from ancient Indian scripture, namely the Epics (the *Rāmāyaṇa* – Sītā and Kausalyā – and the *Mahābhārata* – Draupadī, Kuntī, Gāndhārī, Sāvitrī, Damayantī and Śakuntalā) and the *Upaniṣads* (specifically, the *Bṛhad Āraṇyaka Upaniṣad* – Maitreyī and Gārgī). However, in certain cases, their stories were also communicated through a variety of other media in both popular and elite culture, including well-known vernacular versions. Such variants, whether directly or, as in some instances, mediated by western sources, may well have been as, or even more, powerful influences on their characterisation by Annie Besant and Sarojini Naidu.[8] In appealing to these characters, they were engaged in a process of reappropriation which, adopting as it did a selective and critical approach, introduced a number of crucial changes into the conventional biographies of these characters by means of different emphasis and scope.

Sītā was the wife of Prince Rāma whom she insisted upon accompanying when he was exiled to the forest at the behest of his

91

stepmother. She endured not only the privations of life in the forest, but also abduction and imprisonment by Rāvaṇa, the demon king. Resisting Rāvaṇa's advances, her husband nevertheless required her to prove her constancy and chastity on two occasions: once, immediately after she was liberated by Rāma and his allies, when she emerged unharmed from a burning pyre; and then, some time later, as a condition of her return from the banishment Rāma had imposed on her, when she returned to mother earth. Kausalyā was Sītā's mother-in-law and the chief queen of King Daśaratha although she had been displaced in his affections by her co-wife, Kaikeyī, who schemed to secure her own son's accession to the throne in preference to Kausalyā's son, Rāma, who was the crown prince.

Draupadī was the joint wife of the five Pāṇḍavas whose marriage to the brothers was celebrated during their exile in a bitter dispute over the succession with their cousins, the Kauravas. She was central to the brothers' adventures in exile and their efforts to recover their kingdom. Kuntī was the wife of King Pāṇḍu who had renounced his throne because of a curse and the mother of the Pāṇḍavas, the natural mother of the three eldest sons and the adoptive mother of the two youngest, all of whom were conceived by the use of a boon given her as a maiden. She joined her sons in their exile and, among other things, insisted upon their polyandrous union with Draupadī. Gāndhārī was the wife of Pāṇḍu's blind elder brother, Dhṛtarāṣṭra, in deference to whose disability, which meant that the throne had passed first to Pāṇḍu, she bound her own eyes. She was the mother of the Kauravas who, led by her eldest son, Duryodhana, grew up envious of their cousins and so brought about their own downfall, leaving her to grieve their deaths in the great war with the Pāṇḍavas.

Sāvitrī was the wife of Satyavat whom she chose as her husband despite the prediction that he would die within the year. Having held her husband in her arms as he died, she refused to relinquish him to Yama, god of death, who arrived to collect his soul. Her persistence persuaded Yama to offer her a series of boons, excluding only her husband's life, culminating in his granting her wish that she might have one hundred sons. This, she pointed out, was impossible without her husband whereupon Yama released Satyavat and restored him to his wife (*Mahābhārata* 3.42.277–83). Damayantī was the wife of Nala but their marriage aroused divine jealousy and the desire for revenge led to Nala's ruin in a game of dice. She remained loyal to her husband but Nala abandoned her in the hope that she would return to the comfort and security of her parental home which finally, after many ordeals, she did. The couple were eventually reunited due to her own efforts, principally her ruse of planning remarriage (*Mahābhārata* 3.32.50–78). Śakuntalā attracted the attention of Duḥsanta Paurava when he visited the hermitage where she lived. Pressing his suit by appeal to the *gāndharva* rite of marriage (marriage by mutual consent), she consented to his proposal on the condition that their son should be his heir. When their son was old enough, she took him to his father's court but his father denied all knowledge of him until the intervention of a celestial voice prompted him to acknowledge his son and honour Śakuntalā as his queen (*Mahābhārata* 1.7.62–9).

Maitreyī was the religiously-inclined wife of Yājñavalkya who, when he announced his intention to renounce the world and divide his property between his two wives, questioned him about what would be gained by the possession of riches and asked him to teach her about spiritual matters (*Bṛhad Āraṇyaka Upaniṣad* 2.4.1ff; 4.5.1ff).[9] The philosophically-gifted Gārgī was among those who examined Yājñavalkya after he had claimed to be the most learned of sages and whose questions led him to warn her to enquire no further. Examining him on another occasion, she pronounced him to be without superior in sacred knowledge (*Bṛhad Āraṇyaka Upaniṣad* 3.6.1ff; 3.8.1ff).

Among the heroines of the Epics were some dear to the heart of the Hindu and conventionally viewed as paragons of feminine virtue, notably Sītā and Sāvitrī. Others, although familiar names in much-loved tales, perhaps even those to whom paeans of praise were addressed, were, for whatever reason, overlooked or overshadowed. Of the figures from the *Upaniṣads*, neither Maitreyī nor Gārgī conventionally assumed the status of a role model for women. Notwithstanding, Annie Besant and Sarojini Naidu represented these characters as worthy of esteem and emulation, both those conventionally regarded with reverence, idealised as faithful and devoted wives, and those not held in such renown, maybe because there was something irregular or unusual about their marriage and family life or because they followed another lifestyle altogether.[10] In respect of the former, they revalued aspects conventionally admired and reaccentuated aspects conventionally ignored. In respect of the latter, they identified aspects which were consistent with traditional attitudes concerning women and endorsed aspects which were inconsistent with these attitudes. Throughout, they drew the most constructive and comprehensive conclusions from partial and limited evidence whereby unfavourable statements were not taken into consideration and sweeping generalisations were made on the basis of isolated events. According priority to what was portrayed as the religious, social and political part these characters played, no loss of feminine qualities was conceded in the resultant recasting; on the contrary, it entailed an enrichment and enlargement of the range of qualities deemed to be feminine. While the prestige of these characters was, then, if anything, enhanced, what these characters symbolised and sanctioned underwent a significant shift towards extra-domestic interests and involvements.[11] Thus the appeal to female characters in Hindu sacred literature exemplified the ideals of womanhood.

Consequently, when Annie Besant and Sarojini Naidu appealed to female characters in Hindu sacred literature as exemplifying the ideals of womanhood, they contrasted these ancient Indian ideals with the ideals of womanhood in modern India. On the other hand, by looking to the example of India's past, they asserted that the ideals of womanhood in modern India could be changed to comply with ancient Indian standards and principles.

Appealing to female characters in Hindu sacred literature, Annie Besant identified significant differences between the conditions of ancient and modern women, to the detriment of the latter, and thus legitimised modern women's aims and goals by reference to an ancient standard. Declaring that it was her intention to present 'certain definite facts as regards the life of woman in ancient India' (Besant 1901: 117), she went to some lengths to demonstrate that the various forms of discrimination against modern Indian women derived neither sanction nor precedent from the lives of ancient Indian women. Not only had there been women who 'wore the sacred thread, had the right of kindling the sacrificial fire, studied and taught the Vedas, and lived unmarried in their own houses', but 'women of the household – the wives and mothers – also enjoyed a large amount of liberty and took their part in a number of public ceremonies' (Besant 1901: 118, 119). In support of such points concerning the roles and responsibilities of women in ancient India 'in the home and outside the home' (Besant 1901: 117), she cited Gārgī together with Kausalyā, Draupadī, Sītā and Gāndhārī. Illustrating the lifestyle of unmarried women who were committed to the acquisition of sacred knowledge, she described Gārgī as 'a knower of Brahman . . . who questioned Yâgnyavalkya in the great assembly of sages, being given her place there to put questions as she would' (Besant 1901: 119). Further, illustrating the lifestyle of married women, who, she stressed, were not confined to family and household, she commented that Kausalyā was 'the officiating priestess at a great sacrifice', Sītā and Draupadī 'showed knowledge of the world, understood the ways in which things went on in the external world, were able to give wise counsel to their husbands', and Gāndhārī 'addressed her son in words of remonstrance, reproof and counsel' (Besant 1901: 119, 120).[12] Having outlined the position of women in ancient India with reference to such scriptural figures, she asserted:

> You find . . . how in those days women were really wise and great, that their counsel was highly valued, that their advice was respectfully listened to and followed, because knowledge gave them the power to speak, and learning and wisdom gave them the authority to pronounce their opinion.
>
> (Besant 1901: 120–1)

Thus she juxtaposed 'the ancient and wise way' with 'the modern and foolish way', comparing what she adjudged to be the ancient Indian approach of 'training, educating, raising the woman, putting her more and more on a high level, and then giving her a reasonable and dignified liberty' with what she maintained was the modern Indian approach of 'keeping her ignorant and undeveloped, childish and irrational, and then shutting her in within a narrow environment' (Besant 1901: 133).

Annie Besant also commended 'the ideal women of ancient India' as 'cast in heroic mould' (Besant 1939: 114). Recalling the heroism of Damayantī, Sītā, Gārgī, Kuntī and Gāndhārī, she recounted:

> Damayanti was consulted by ministers and nobles of her husband's kingdom, and appealed to against his folly; Sita remained fearless, although alone and surrounded by enemies, and, pressed too far to repeated self-justification, went away in quiet dignity; Gargi faced great Sages in argument, and outargued the greatest; Kunti was the brave adviser of her sons; Gandhari entered a council of warriors and chiefs to rebuke her arrogant son.
>
> (Besant 1939: 114).

In line with this chronicle of the virtues of these scriptural figures, she condemned the position of modern Indian women as 'abnormal and transitional', for as men had become divorced from spiritual matters, women had become divorced from social and political affairs, with the result that, in her opinion, 'religious life has been narrowed by the loss of intellectuality; public life has been coarsened by the loss of idealism' (Besant 1939: 113–14).

95

Sarojini Naidu appealed to female characters in Hindu sacred literature in order to raise the consciousness of Indian women and so to justify their assumption of different roles and responsibilities by reference to an Indian standard. She referred to scriptural figures to impress upon 'the mind of Indian woman that she is not a toy, nor a chattel, nor an instrument of pleasure or amusement, but the inspirer of the spirit' (Naidu 1918a: 99). She queried why Sītā, Sāvitrī and Damayantī were held in such high esteem by Indians and exercised so powerful an influence over them. Answering her own question, she explained:

> They had no stupidity, quarrelsomeness, idleness, timidity, and so on. Damayanti had no terror of death though she was separated from her husband. It was spiritual understanding and intellectual development that made them great.
>
> (Naidu 1918a: 99)

Indeed, when president of the Indian National Congress, she modestly protested her own inadequacies and shortcomings as an exponent of the excellence which such scriptural figures epitomised, but expressed the hope that her tenure as president might be informed by a little of the greatness of Sītā and Sāvitrī:

> Poignantly conscious as I am of my own utter unworthiness to interpret so exquisite, so austere an ideal of wisdom, devotion, and sacrifice, as embodied through the ages in the radiant heroines of our history and legend, I trust, that to the fulfilment of the lofty task you have allotted me, even I might bring some glowing ember of the immortal faith that illumined the vigil of Sita in her forest exile, and bore the feet of Savitri undaunted to the very citadels of Death.
>
> (Naidu 1925b)

In this way, Annie Besant and Sarojini Naidu regarded appeal to female characters in Hindu sacred literature as both relevant and rewarding. As ideals attributed to ancient India through its scripture, therefore principles nominally neither new nor western, these characters were considered to be important and instructive for modern Indian women, the issues with which they were concerned, and the changes for which they campaigned.

Annie Besant articulated her ambition for modern Indian women by appealing to female characters in Hindu sacred literature. After making suggestions as to how 'Indian girlhood' might become 'noble womanhood' (Besant 1917: 161), she alluded to the greatness of women in ancient India, noted the virtues of modern women, notwithstanding the difficulties they faced, and asked what Indian women yet might be. She expressed her aspirations for the future in terms of the qualities exhibited by Gārgī, Sāvitrī, Sītā, Damayantī and Śakuntalā, testifying:

> We hope for, we dream of, a Womanhood that shall blend into one perfect whole the wisdom of Gargi, the tameless courage and wit of Savitri, the unchanging love of Sita, the proud endurance of Damayanti, the unwavering fealty of Shakuntala.
>
> (Besant 1917: 162)

Or, again, Sarojini Naidu cited these scriptural figures to encourage the development of women's latent abilities. She observed that modern Indian women continued to be true to 'those living ideals that make the names of the women of our country and literature so immortal' and even speculated that they had the capacity not only to equal but to exceed the achievements of women in ancient India:

> There is not a single home in the length and breadth of India, no matter rich or poor, where womanhood is not as great to-day as in the days of Sita and Savitri, greater perhaps in potential powers because we have gathered a great deal of world experience, of high civilisation and growing responsibility.
>
> (Naidu 1918a: 69–70)

On these grounds, she charged men with the obligation, hitherto unacknowledged and unaccepted by them, to enable women to make the most of their talents. Although she allowed that 'they [modern Indian women] are backward', according to her, they were not to blame for this because, in her figure of speech, men 'will not give them what is called the daily oil – the opportunity that brings that flame to the lamp' (Naidu 1918a: 71).

There can be no doubt of the respect and admiration in which Annie Besant and Sarojini Naidu held the female characters in Hindu sacred literature to whom they appealed. For example, Annie Besant extolled Sītā who kept 'her faith unsullied and her courage undaunted through bonds and in face of death', Sāvitrī 'who wrenched her husband from the icy grip of death', Śakuntalā 'who, according to Goethe, is the one whose name we utter to express all that is best in womanhood', and Kausalyā 'ideal mother', adding that she 'might run through a long list of names and not exhaust the wealth of noble women that India has borne to the race' (Besant 1917: 303). Eulogising these scriptural figures, she remarked:

> Literature can show no grander types of womanhood than are to be found in the great epic poems of India, types sketched in by master hands from noble models, and uniting in a few heroic figures all that is at once strongest and sweetest, most lofty and most devoted in humanity.
>
> (Besant 1917: 303)

Yet respect and admiration for these scriptural figures was often conceived in national terms, endowing them with a significance for India as representing its values. For instance, Sarojini Naidu praised the purity, selflessness and bravery of scriptural figures, lauding 'that greatest Sita, that unconquerable Savitri, that faithful Damayanti and that Sakuntala who made her name famous' as 'embodiments of the nation's ideals' (Naidu 1918a: 112). This assisted Annie Besant and Sarojini Naidu when they appealed to female characters in Hindu sacred literature to express their opposition to present-day practices, and their support for measures intended to improve the position of women. They were also assisted by the implicit or explicit connection made between the standing of India and the position of Indian women because, as ideals attributed to ancient Indian scripture, these characters were associated with India's past glory. The recovery of this long-lost glory was, then, conditional on the reinstatement of the lifestyle and the reactualisation of the qualities of these characters, for and by modern Indian women.

Annie Besant referred to these characters as proof that there had been no child marriage in ancient India. She believed that a national revival was dependent on a religious revival as 'a spiritual impulse' was required 'to reawaken the eager self-sacrifice which is the essence of public spirit, and the sense of unity which is the life-blood of a Nation' (Besant 1939: 103). Consistent with her claim that the Hindu tradition was 'the most potent lever for raising India into National Self-Consciousness', she confided that her initial work in India had been to bring to the attention of Hindus 'the supreme value of their National religion', her subsequent objective being to argue for 'a National education which should recognize religion and morals as an integral part of the teaching of youth' (Besant 1939: 104, 105). However, she insisted that child marriage was a major obstacle to the achievement of her educational aims, attributing to it, and the associated occurrence of early parenthood, the untimely end to the all too brief education of girls. Asserting that 'these child marriages were no part of the older Hindu religion in the days of its virility', she argued that scriptural figures had not been married as children, on the contrary:

> Damayanti was no child when she loved Nala; Savitri was no child when she went forth from her father's house, found and pledged her maiden faith to Satyavan, and held to her word against parents and Narada.
>
> (Besant 1939: 105)

Exercised by the adverse physical and other consequences of child marriage for both boys and girls, she intimated that as Damayantī and Sāvitrī had married as adults, so should modern Indian women.

Sarojini Naidu referred to these characters to convey her hostility towards the system of indentured labour.[13] In forthright language, she urged her countrymen to take action against this system which had caused women so much suffering:

> Let the blood of your hearts blot out the shame that your women have suffered abroad. The words that you have heard . . . must have kindled within you a raging fire. Men of India, let that be the funeral pyre of the indenture system.
>
> (Naidu 1918a: 121)

While she contended that Indian men might be moved by the plight of their womenfolk, she announced: 'I feel the dishonour offered to me in the dishonour to my sex' (Naidu 1918a: 121). Connecting her plea with the courage of Sītā and Sāvitrī, she claimed to speak for the wives of indentured labourers when she said:

> I have travelled far . . . to raise my voice . . . for those women whose proudest memory is that Sita would not stand the challenge to her honour but called upon mother earth to avenge her and the earth opened up to avenge her . . . I come to speak on behalf of those women who, like Savitri, have followed their men to the gates of death and have won back, by their indomitable love, the dehumanised soul of their men in the colonies abroad.
>
> (Naidu 1918a: 121–2)

Thus she gave impact to her address by quoting the qualities of these scriptural figures. In so doing, she stated that modern Indian women were inspired by Sītā and, what was more, in their colonial context, she identified them with Sāvitrī. Drawing out the wider implications of such an issue, she enquired 'how shall the wealth and power and glory of a nation be founded save on the immutable honour of its womanhood?' (Naidu 1918a: 123).

Annie Besant referred to these characters as part of her argument in favour of female education. She outlined a varied curriculum for the education of an Indian girl, including reading, writing, arithmetic and domestic science but in which 'above all else must the Indian girl be trained in the devotion and piety to which her nature so readily responds' (Besant 1917: 115). She therefore proposed:

> All the great heroines of Indian story should be made familiar to her, with their inspiring example and elevating influence. The Indian ideal of womanhood should be made living to her in these heroic figures, and she should be taught to regard them as her exemplars in her own life.
>
> (Besant 1917: 115)

Moreover, invoking Sītā, Sāvitrī, Gārgī and Maitreyī, she advocated female education as a means of ensuring that the virtues of these scriptural figures would be manifest once more. She commented of educated Indian girls:

> Among them we may hope to see revived the glories of the past, the tenderness and fidelity of Sita and Savitri, the intellectual grandeur of Gargi, the all-sacrificing spirituality of Maitreyi.
>
> (Besant 1917: 115)

In similar vein, considering that 'the national movement for girls' education . . . must accept the general Hindu conceptions of women's place in the national life, not the dwarfed modern view but the ancient ideal' (Besant 1917: 150), Annie Besant instructed:

> Reading-books should be provided consisting of stories of all the sweetest and strongest women in Indian story, so that the girls may feel inspired by these noblest types of womanhood as compelling ideals, and may have before them these glorious proofs of the heights to which Indian women have climbed.
>
> (Besant 1917: 152)

She contrasted 'the very narrowness of their present lives, their triviality and frivolity' with this 'broad and splendid type' which was to stand 'as a model for their uplifting', facilitating female education 'along lines purely national and in consonance with immemorial ideals' (Besant 1917: 152). She denied that the purpose of what she labelled 'the national movement for girls' education' was to produce 'girl-graduates, educated for the learned professions'; instead, she emphasised that its goal was to prepare women to be 'nobly trained wives and mothers, wise and tender rulers of the household, educated teachers of the young, helpful counsellors of their husbands, skilled nurses of the sick' (Besant 1917: 150). This was because, in her view, 'the *national* movement for the education of girls must be one which meets the national needs' (Besant 1917: 150), and hence an education suited to women's domestic duties was preferred to higher education for professional employment. Notwithstanding, she did recommend that provision be made for an advanced religious education for those who could benefit from it, stating:

> Where any girl shows capacity for deeper thought, philosophical studies and explanations should not be withheld from her, so that opportunity may be afforded for the re-appearance of the type of which Maitreyi and Gargi and the women singers of the Vedas were shining examples.
>
> (Besant 1917: 151)

By stressing that scriptural figures should feature prominently in the syllabus of female education, and by describing the desired outcome of this education as bringing about the return of such figures, she attempted to advance the cause of education for modern Indian women.

Sarojini Naidu characterised Sāvitrī as the 'glorious type of virtue, courage, wisdom, truth, among women' (Naidu 1918a: 138). Yet she used the imagery of Sāvitrī's redemption of her husband to highlight how modern Indian women were deprived of the wherewithal to redeem their country by being deprived of education. In a lecture on the 'National Education of Women', she explained:

> You talk of Indian womanhood, you talk of the courage and devotion that took Savitri to the very realms of death to win back her husband's soul, yet to the Savitris of today you deny that power to win back the national life from the depths of death.
>
> (Naidu 1918b)

In this way, she concentrated on the benefits which would be conferred upon the nation by the participation of modern Indian women who were represented as following in the footsteps of Sāvitrī.

Indeed, praising the distinguished and distinctive contribution made by Indian women to nationalism 'who bring to its helping the uncalculating heroism, the endurance, the self-sacrifice, of the feminine nature' (Besant 1921: 337), Annie Besant implied that the example of female characters in Hindu sacred literature was a stimulus to patriotism:

> Indian women, nursed on her old literature, with its wonderful ideals of womanly perfection, could not remain indifferent to the great movement of India's liberty.
>
> (Besant 1921: 336)

Moreover, remarking that 'the womanhood of India was beginning to awake' (Naidu 1918a: 96d), Sarojini Naidu explained that this was effected by the same force which had produced Gārgī, Maitreyī, Sāvitrī and Sītā:

> The women themselves, have begun to realise the cause of a new spirit which is nothing but a renaissance of the old spirit which gave to India those Gargis, Maitrayis, those Savitris and Sitas . . .
>
> (Naidu 1918a: 96b)

Changes, which were themselves validated by reference to these scriptural figures, were endorsed in terms of national progress and emphasised women's duties, rather than their rights, as citizens. Thus measures which favoured women were promoted as favouring India's development and progress.

In appealing to female characters in Hindu sacred literature, as exemplifying the ideals of womanhood, Annie Besant and Sarojini Naidu looked to the example of India's past recorded in ancient Indian scripture as the guide and inspiration for modern India. In so doing, as in the case of appeal to the 'Golden Age' of Indian civilisation, they located 'women's uplift' in a national context whereby advocacy of change, represented as neither innovative nor alien, was regarded as conducive to India's restoration to greatness.

The appeal to the 'Golden Age' of Indian civilisation, as establishing the position of women in the model society, and to female characters in Hindu sacred literature, as exemplifying the ideals of womanhood, was an appeal to Hindu beliefs and values by Annie Besant and Sarojini Naidu in support of 'women's uplift'.[14] Another way in which their contemporaries and successors went about asserting their own aims and objectives for modern Indian women, contrasted with continued appeal to constructions of tradition, was appeal to liberal beliefs and values.

CHAPTER FOUR

'Equal Rights': The Appeal to Liberal Beliefs and Values

This chapter examines the alternative approaches adopted in order to justify 'equal rights'. It is demonstrated that this ideology was initially accorded a traditional rationale by reference to the example of India's past. It is also shown that this strategy was later largely superseded by appeal to the liberal beliefs and values associated with the modern West. Such change is studied through a survey of selected speeches and writings by leading members of the most powerful and influential of the women's organisations, the All India Women's Conference, during a period running from the late 1920s to the early 1940s. Moreover, the reasons for this change are considered as well as an analysis offered of the conditions under which activists continued to offer a traditional justification of 'equal rights', in addition to or in place of the explicit espousal of liberal norms.

The All India Women's Conference

The All India Women's Conference was founded in reaction to an address by Mr E. F. Oaten, Director of Public Instruction in Bengal, during a prize-giving at Bethune College, a women's college in Calcutta which had been opened in 1849 as a school for girls.[1] On this occasion, Mr Oaten urged women to make their views known on the subject of female education and to press for their demands to be met. Following this address, Mrs A. L. Huidekoper, a former principal of Bethune College, wrote articles on the subject which were published in the Women's Indian Association journal, *Stri Dharma*. In the light of these articles, the secretary of the Women's Indian Association sent out a letter in which she reiterated that it was imperative for women to produce their own authoritative response to the issues raised by female education. It set forth the practical arrangements proposed which consisted of a series of regional conferences to be held before a national conference was convened. This plan met with a significant measure of support as regional conferences were held throughout India in the autumn and winter of 1926 and the national conference, convened in Poona in January 1927, was attended by 2,000 people.

A number of resolutions were passed about female education. However, it was clear from the outset that it was not possible to promote female education in isolation from other goals, notably raising the age of marriage and ending the practice of female seclusion, which had obvious implications for the accessibility and availability of educational opportunities to girls and women. It was also clear that the preparation of a memorandum on female education had not exhausted women's enthusiasm but that, on the contrary, there was sufficient impetus to sustain further sessions of the same sort. Thus, the All India Women's Conference widened its scope beyond educational issues to include first social and then political questions and acquired the institutional machinery of a permanent organisation.

Many of the most prominent women of a whole generation were involved with the foundation of the All India Women's Conference. Of those women whose selected speeches and writings are to be discussed in detail, though they may have occupied other positions of responsibility, all became presidents of the organisation in due course: Kamaladevi Chattopadhyaya (1903–88) became president in 1944 but had earlier served for some years as honorary general secretary; the Rani of Mandi (dates unknown) became president in 1929 though the previous year she had headed up the organisation's delegation campaigning for the age of consent to be raised; Muthulakshmi Reddi (1886–1968) became president in 1931, later chairing the 1933 session in Lucknow; Margaret Cousins (1878–1953) became president in 1936 and, as the prime mover behind its formation in the first place, was hailed as the 'mother' of the organisation; and Rameshwari Nehru (1886–1966) became president in 1940, also acting as chairperson during her term of office.[2] Indeed, in different ways and at different times, they all advanced the cause of 'equal rights' whether by recourse to traditional or liberal references.

104

The Liberal World-View

The liberal world-view developed in the modern West and was associated with the main themes of the Enlightenment. The Enlightenment had emphasised that knowledge could be attained through the autonomous exercise of human reason and that such knowledge was the basis of the social and political standards deemed conducive to human welfare. This insistence upon reason was accompanied by an assertion that everything was explicable in terms of the same factors. One consequence of this outlook was the characteristic rationalist antipathy towards religious belief systems because of their reliance on revealed truth. As Alisdair MacIntyre comments, 'the project of founding a form of social order in which individuals could emancipate themselves from the contingency and particularity of tradition by appealing to genuinely universal, tradition-independent norms . . . was and is the project of modern liberal, individualist society' (MacIntyre 1988: 335). Yet whereas liberalism represented itself as transferable to any context and as predicated upon an immediate apprehension of natural laws, it was by no means culturally neutral or value-free. Rather it was both produced by and typical of the modern West, though its assumption of general relevance and complete objectivity allowed this world-view to be communicated to those outwith its original constituency. This was possible on the grounds of liberalism's ostensible independence and isolability from the philosophical and intellectual tradition in which it was first formulated. Certainly, liberalism was accepted by many members of the Indian elite who, as Purushottama Bilimoria relates, 'began to revise their ideas on traditional patterns of social arrangement and practice' so that 'a shift gradually took place in the locus of authority from caste, linguistic, regional and religious bases to the ideal state' (Bilimoria 1993: 46). Notwithstanding, liberal principles were not widely shared in Indian society outside the comparatively narrow confines of the westernised elite.

The attraction of liberalism was enshrined in what Shivesh Thakur describes as 'its truly emancipating vision of the human person – the uncompromising priority it places on the autonomy, that is, the freedom and dignity of every individual human being' (Thakur 1996: 110). This vision is one in which as he also indicates emancipation is 'theoretically possible for each individual, irrespective of birth, wealth, colour of skin, religion and gender' (Thakur 1996: 111). For women, the significance of liberalism was its belief in equality which was understood to entail the equality of the sexes thereby denying the superiority of men and the inferiority of women. This idea was to make a major impact on women's expectations of their lives and the rights to which they believed themselves entitled by virtue of their common humanity. Consequently, this idea helped to shape the aims and objectives of women's movements world-wide as it came to do in India. Members of the women's movement in India belonged to that westernised elite among whom liberalism found a receptive audience. Nevertheless, even when this liberal consensus was established, the women's movement had to work in a more diverse social setting where there was no such consensus in favour of liberal principles. At least in part, this accounted for the movement's traditionalisation of 'equal rights' long after liberal tenets had become axiomatic in progressive circles.

The Traditional Justification of 'Equal Rights'

Before 'equal rights' had gained predominance as the ideology of the westernised elite, women who were introducing 'equal rights' chose to justify it in much the same way that 'women's uplift' had been justified. This was to ascribe 'equal rights' to supposedly traditional sources so that, like 'women's uplift' from which it was not always easily separable, it was attributed to ancient India.

For instance, Kamaladevi Chattopadhyaya's survey article on 'The Status of Women in India' which opened a volume entitled *Women in Modern India* (1929) stated:

> It is indeed pretty obvious that no country could have attained the height of civilisation which India attained, nor have given to the world the wealth of knowledge that she gave, if her women-folk had been kept down and denied equal opportunities and rights with her men-folk.
>
> (Chattopadhyaya 1929: 1)

In this way, she referred to the connection made between the greatness of a civilisation and the position of women to argue that the greatness of ancient India proved that ancient Indian women had benefited from 'equal rights'. Hers was, then, a revivalist message in which an interpretation of India's past was adduced as evidence to establish the legitimacy of 'equal rights' for modern Indian women.

This portrait of ancient India was important as a corrective to what was, in her opinion, a western misapprehension about the miserable condition of Indian women before imperial intervention, and its corollary, the western self-image as having brought about a change for the better. Contradicting this western perspective on the position of Indian women, she claimed that 'even a cursory glance over the history of India from the Vedic times right down to the modern day reveals a very different state of affairs from what these original historians try to make out to the world' (Chattopadhyaya 1929: 1). These preliminary remarks explained her insistence that 'the history of the women's movement in India has to be traced from its very source' on the premise that 'modern India is but the shadow of her past and in order to gauge the significance of this shadow one must know the light which cast it' (Chattopadhyaya 1929: 1). Having thus shown why it was essential to locate the Indian women's movement in an historical context, she embarked upon her chronicle of India's past in which she stressed the roles and responsibilities assumed by women in earlier eras.

Kamaladevi Chattopadhyaya's chronicle began with an idealised version of the Vedic era, an idyll 'the glory of which still surrounds the country like a faint halo' (Chattopadhyaya 1929: 1). At this time, she suggested, far from being restricted to domestic and private concerns:

> Women took part freely in the social and political life of the country, and, in the celebration of religious functions and rituals, they had a special place of importance assigned to them.
>
> (Chattopadhyaya 1929: 1–2)

Corroborating her contention that women were able to make a contribution to ancient Indian spirituality, she included women among the Vedic seer poets who 'composed and chanted hymns at the Vedic sacrifices' (Chattopadhyaya 1929: 2). She cited the names of Viśvavārā, Lopāmudrā and Vāc in this regard, the last of whom she also credited with conveying the core of Vedantic teaching. In so doing, she was drawing the most expedient and extensive conclusions from a few obscure examples. The hymn attributed to Viśvavārā invoked Agni, god of fire, entreating him to ensure the welfare of her household (*Ṛg Veda* 5.28.1–6). The two verses of a hymn attributed to Lopāmudrā, a devoted wife of many years, called for the love and affection of her husband (*Ṛg Veda* 1.179.1–2). The hymn attributed to Vāc, said to be a sage's daughter but later assimilated to Sarasvatī as Word or Speech, identified the self with the reality underlying the universe (*Ṛg Veda* 10.125.1–8).

107

This tendency towards a favourable reading of India's past was also obvious in what followed where Kamaladevi Chattopadhyaya gave priority to any positive points for women. She did this although expressing the view that the position of women had worsened over the centuries in tandem with India's fall from greatness. Accordingly, her account of remote epochs was markedly more positive in tone than her account of recent events, albeit that both were illustrated by reference to outstanding female figures. When relating the conditions under which women lived in bygone ages, she declared:

> Such social disabilities as purdah and child-marriage were entirely unknown. Women travelled about freely and had a voice in their selection of their partners in life.

> (Chattopadhyaya 1929: 2)

In support of this statement, she mentioned Sītā, Sāvitrī and Draupadī, 'all those who are held so reverentially as great ideals', as having 'enjoyed a high degree of freedom and asserted their individuality' and as being 'by no means content to be mere shadows of their husbands' (Chattopadhyaya 1929: 2). This testimonial to the conditions under which the Epic heroines lived was very different from her characterisation of the conditions prevailing during the preceding century, conditions so poor that women's successes were won in spite of adversity. She observed:

> Even within the last hundred years which have marked the rapid decline of India and consequently a deterioration in the position of women, there have still struggled to flicker a few flames here and there.

> (Chattopadhyaya 1929: 3)

She nominated Lakṣmī Bāī and Ahalyā Bāī as women of such eminence who had 'made for themselves an imperishable name in history' (Chattopadhyaya 1929: 3). Both of these women had become famous for their active participation in political affairs. Lakṣmī Bāī was the childless widow of the ruler of an Indian kingdom. On her husband's death, the kingdom was annexed by the British and she was pensioned off as its queen but, during the uprising of 1857–8, she attempted to recover Jhansi's sovereignty from Britain, eventually dying in battle (Mukherjee et al 1953: 396–8). Ahalyā Bāī's father-in-law trained her in matters of state, including the conduct of warfare, and delegated various administrative duties to her. On the death of her father-in-law, she took charge of the government, initially on behalf of her son, her husband having predeceased his father, and then in her own right before retiring to her devotions (Deshpande 1953: 358–60).

For Kamaladevi Chattopadhyaya, this history was vitally important because it was the inspiration of the Indian women's movement which she thus represented as a restoration of age-old ideals:

> It is with such a heritage as the foundation and such a past as the background that the present women's movement in India has evolved itself. It is not so much the establishment of a new order or a new convention but rather a revival and a regaining of a lost glory – though with a distinct desire and attempt to adjust it in concord with modern conditions.
>
> (Chattopadhyaya 1929: 4)

Laying the blame for India's fall from greatness on foreign powers, 'the constant shocks which she received by foreign invasions' culminating in 'the disturbed and unnatural state of things which we find in the country to-day', she declared 'intellectually and psychologically woman in India has never lost her honoured place' thereby limiting the worsening in the position of women caused by 'external influences' to the level of their 'external position' (Chattopadhyaya 1929: 4). Consistent with this, her summary of the origin and development of women's organisations, from the earliest efforts to the establishment of the All India Women's Conference, mentioned 'the gradual recollection that was stealing over them [modern Indian women] of the resplendent days their women ancestors and their beloved Motherland had known' (Chattopadhyaya 1929: 5) as one of the stimuli prompting women to form their own organisations. Clearly, therefore, in this article, she was arguing for 'equal rights' in avowedly traditional terms. She advocated 'equal rights' for modern Indian women on the model of the 'equal rights' which, she maintained, had been experienced by women in ancient India. Moreover, it was her claim that the equality of women had been an integral part of ancient India's antique grandeur.

In the course of her argument, Kamaladevi Chattopadhyaya hailed the rise of Buddhism for providing 'a fresh impetus to women's education and general progress' and commented on the situation in the south 'that the Dravidian women too enjoyed perfect equality and freedom' (Chattopadhyaya 1929: 3). These were themes taken up and elaborated upon by the Rani of Mandi and Muthulakshmi Reddi in their respective presidential addresses to the All India Women's

Conference. The Rani of Mandi endorsed 'equal rights' by appealing to the Buddha's ruling in favour of the spiritual equality of women and Muthulakshmi Reddi by appealing to the equality of women in ancient South India.[3]

The presidential address of Lalit Kumari Sahiba, the Rani of Mandi, made much of the Buddhist associations of Patna where the 1929 session of the All India Women's Conference was held, allying Buddhism with the ideology of 'equal rights' to which she gave her allegiance. She urged:

> It is time that the justice of the equality of opportunities for both sexes was enunciated in no uncertain language and its recognition enforced in all directions in this country.
>
> (Mandi 1929: 313)

Having insisted on the implementation of 'equal rights' in modern India, she continued by asserting that 'this great principle was acknowledged in no indefinite terms by our great ancestors' (Mandi 1929: 313). The example she used to corroborate this claim was 'an episode in the history of Buddhism which happened in this very neighbourhood, at Vaisali beyond the Ganges, in the very life-time of the great Buddha himself' (Mandi 1929: 313), specifically the story of the admission of women into the Buddhist *sangha* (monastic community) which, she professed, demonstrated the Buddha's acceptance of women's spiritual equality.

Notwithstanding the non-sectarian nature of the audience to whom she was speaking, that the Rani of Mandi as a Hindu woman should have concentrated on Buddhist material (and that it should be considered in the same context as references to the Hindu tradition) perhaps requires explanation. So far as the speaker was concerned, there need have been no other motivation than the selection of supportive material relevant to the locality. However, Buddhism was an attractive prospect to many: as an indigenous tradition, it seemed to raise none of the sensitive nationalist issues that Islam and Christianity did; as a religion with few, if any, adherents, it seemed to avoid stirring up communalist feelings. Certainly, the presence of common ideas had facilitated the appropriation of Buddhist beliefs and practices by Hindus such that Buddhism was often regarded as either an adjunct to, or a sub-set of, the Hindu tradition. Again, since Buddhism had enjoyed a scholarly, rather than a popular, revival, the association between Buddhism and India's ancient glory was not complicated by the existence of a religious minority and so could be welcomed as an uncontroversial reservoir of Indian values.[4] Whatever her reasons, the Rani of Mandi's reference to Buddhism occurred in a speech which concluded with an invocation from the *Upaniṣads*, maybe suggesting a holistic and integrated attitude towards the two religions and, indeed, Indian history.[5]

The basic outline of the Rani of Mandi's version of the story was the same as the account given in Buddhist scripture (*Culla Vagga* 10.1) and was as follows. Mahāpajāpatī, already denied admission into the *saṅgha*, had her hair shorn, donned monastic dress and travelled to where the Buddha was staying. Moved by her plight, Ānanda interceded on her behalf, asking the Buddha whether women who had entered the monastic life were able to attain *arhatship* (enlightenment). The Buddha agreed that women were competent to achieve enlightenment. Then, when reminded of Mahāpajāpatī, he allowed her to enter the monastic life on condition that she abide by Eight Regulations. According to the Rani of Mandi:

> Ananda asked if a woman who had gone forth from the house to a houseless life in the doctrine and discipline declared by the teacher, was capable of realising the *arhatship*. 'A woman is capable, Ananda,' said the Lord and on being informed of Mahaprajavati's appeal, he said that if she was willing to take upon herself the eight Strict Rules of the Order, 'let this be her ordination'.

> (Mandi 1929: 313)

Nevertheless, excluded from her version of the story was the section where Ānanda framed his question as Mahāpajāpatī had done on a previous occasion, directly asking the Buddha to grant his permission for women to enter the monastic life. Ānanda's request, like Mahāpajāpatī's earlier entreaty, met with repeated rejection. In the scriptural account, it was then that Ānanda decided to frame the question differently and asked whether women who had entered the monastic life were able to attain *arhatship*. Furthermore, the Rani of Mandi merely alluded to the Eight Regulations stipulated by the Buddha and omitted the Buddha's prediction of the premature demise of his teaching. The Eight Regulations institutionalised the subordinate and inferior status of the Order of Nuns, typified by the instruction that a nun, however senior, must bow before a monk, however junior. Moreover, after Ānanda had communicated these Regulations to Mahāpajāpatī and she had vowed to abide by them, the Buddha predicted that his teaching would endure for but 500, instead of 1,000, years as a consequence of admitting women into the *sangha*. Such exchanges, if included, would have proved problematic in the light of the Rani of Mandi's interpretation of the meaning and significance of this story.[6]

After narrating this story, the Rani of Mandi affirmed that the Buddha's decision to admit women to the *sangha* amounted to a decree of the spiritual equality of women. This enabled her to exhort the extension of this spiritual equality to women's ordinary lives in modern India. She pronounced the opinion:

> And thus at Vaisali there began the declaration by Buddhadeva of equality between man and woman in their fitness for the highest spiritual life. I am only asking for the application of the same principle to every aspect of our daily life.

> (Mandi 1929: 313)

What she wanted to achieve was, therefore, 'a recognition of this fundamental equality' which, together with 'the removal of our numerous social disabilities' and 'unremitting attention on our part to the cause of our educational advancement', she believed would 'lead to a new era of development in our history without which our beloved Motherland can never hope to take her rightful place among the civilized nations of the world' (Mandi 1929: 313).

Just as Kamaladevi Chattopadhyaya had cited an Indian past precedent for the equality of women, the Rani of Mandi offered what she represented as a traditional rationale for 'equal rights', in this case derived from Buddhism on the basis that the Buddha was one of the forefathers of modern Indians.[7] Presuming that the Buddha's acquiescence to the proposition that women had the same spiritual capacities as men had the most profound implications possible, her goal, like that of Kamaladevi Chattopadhyaya, was to lend legitimacy to 'equal rights' for modern Indian women, guaranteeing the authenticity of this ideology by identifying it in ancient India.

Muthulakshmi Reddi's presidential address, delivered at the 1931 session of the All India Women's Conference, reflected her own South Indian roots. Her depiction of India's past not only detected 'equal rights' in ancient South India but also included discussion of two female figures, Mīnākṣī and Auvaiyār, whose biographies were presented as proof of this. Introducing these South Indian references on the grounds that conference delegates were already 'familiar with the names of the many vedic women writers, philosophers as well as warriors and rulers', she suggested that her listeners might be interested to learn about those whom she described as 'ancient Dravidian women' (Reddi 1931: 367).

Muthulakshmi Reddi was probably correct in assuming that most members of her audience were less acquainted with South Indian tradition than the more commonly cited references which were strongly slanted towards the northern religious and cultural heritage. This bias towards the North was evident in many speeches and writings by leaders of the women's movement whose repertoire featured female figures drawn chiefly, if not exclusively, from Sanskritic scripture and the legends and history of North India. Indeed, this bias was typical of much Hindu apologetic, whether within or outwith the women's movement, when seeking to show that the position of women in India had not been one of perpetual oppression. While in some measure this bias may have been due to the backgrounds of the persons involved, it may also have had something to do with the way in which the Hindu tradition was reconstructed by western scholars whose studies, enormously influential on the westernised elite and on westerners who were interested in the subject, concentrated on northern religion and culture.

In her account of ancient South India which, at least to some extent, redressed the regional imbalance in treatments of the Hindu tradition, Muthulakshmi Reddi was further attesting to 'equal rights' since, as she contended:

From the records now available to us, we come to know that they [ancient Dravidian women] had enjoyed absolute equality with their men.

(Reddi 1931: 367)

Having made this statement about the position of women, she went on to recount the life-stories of the goddess Mīnākṣī and the poetess Auvaiyār as witness of its accuracy, Mīnākṣī as the warrior and ruler and Auvaiyār as the writer and philosopher counterpart of the famous Vedic women.

Muthulakshmi Reddi narrated:

In the famous city of Madura, once the prosperous capital of the King Pandya, the Goddess Meenakshi who is worshipped to-day, is said to have been a woman warrior sent by her father to fight his enemies. She, after subduing her father's enemies, herself chose her husband, the bravest and the wisest she ever came across.

(Reddi 1931: 367)

113

This differs in some significant respects from the official version of the Mīnākṣī myth, mainly through omission of Mīnākṣī's conduct on first catching sight of her future husband. In the official version of the myth, Mīnākṣī was the daughter of a hitherto childless king. The king had performed rituals for the birth of a son, only to receive a three-breasted daughter. The king was charged to rear her as a son and it was prophesied that her extra breast would vanish when she met her husband. On the king's death, Mīnākṣī who had been brought up as a boy succeeded him, leading her army to many victories in an attempt to achieve her ambition of subjugating the world by force of arms. She even gained the advantage over Śiva's army, but, when Śiva entered the fray and Mīnākṣī saw him, her extra breast vanished and she began to behave with maidenly modesty. A servant having identified Śiva as her husband, Mīnākṣī returned home where she became Śiva's wife and Śiva became king. Thus was Mīnākṣī transformed from a mighty general to an obedient spouse (Shulman 1980: 202 cf. Kinsley 1987: 202–3). Notwithstanding Mīnākṣī's earlier military exploits, mention of the domestication and subordination of Mīnākṣī would have contradicted Muthulakshmi Reddi's reading of the myth so perhaps she was drawing on popular beliefs about Mīnākṣī.[8] Yet, in any event, be it by emphasising elements of one version or even by electing one version over another, hers was a selective approach. It lent itself to a defence of women's participation in public life and rejection of child marriage, and as such was suited to her purpose.

Discussing Auvaiyār, Muthulakshmi Reddi observed:

> The beautiful verses of the learned "Avvai", a woman scholar, are used even to-day in our primary schools. In style, in simplicity, in sweetness of rhythm, in moral truths, nothing can equal them. . . . She came of a poor and unknown family. Though she had received a high degree of education, she never cared to marry. Her poetic genius, her purity, her high learning and her wisdom made scholars, kings and emperors pay homage to her. The life of "Avvai" shows that at that period of the South Indian history, education was made available even to the poorest in the land.
>
> (Reddi 1931: 367)

This certainly drew on popular esteem for Auvaiyār. The name Auvaiyār, meaning 'Old Woman' or 'Venerable Lady', properly designated at least two female poets, the one classical, the other medieval, who were conflated and syncretised in the popular imagination (Zvelebil 1974: 125). The type of poems which Muthulakshmi Reddi attributed to Auvaiyār were probably compositions of the 'second' Auvaiyār of the medieval era; at least some of the items Muthulakshmi Reddi included in her tale of Auvaiyār seem to derive from what little is known about the career of the 'first' Auvaiyār of the classical era (Jesudasan and Jesudasan 1961: 138, 26).[9] Whereas the ambivalence of the available historical evidence make it difficult to arrive at academically acceptable conclusions about the character of Auvaiyār, Muthulakshmi Reddi was not seeking to satisfy scholarly criteria, instead she was tapping a deep vein in popular consciousness. This enabled her to portray Auvaiyār as having an alternative lifestyle as a single woman. In addition, she saw Auvaiyār's literary excellence as an indication that women were educated. The clear implication of this was that women should be permitted to remain unmarried with no family responsibilities and that women should receive a good education.

Muthulakshmi Reddi, like both Kamaladevi Chattopadhyaya and the Rani of Mandi, offered what she represented as a traditional rationale for the ideology of 'equal rights', though in her case the Indian past precedent cited for the equality of women was taken from ancient South India, specifically the biographies of Mīnākṣī and Auvaiyār. She used these two female figures to substantiate her statement that women had been accorded equality with men in ancient South India and thereby justify 'equal rights' for modern Indian women.

Thus, in these examples, Kamaladevi Chattopadhyaya, the Rani of Mandi and Muthulakshmi Reddi all ascribed 'equal rights' to traditional sources, attributing it to ancient India. By claiming as they did that the equality of women for which they were currently campaigning had been accepted in ancient India, they were indigenising and archaising the ideology. This strategy revealed a clear line of continuity with the strategy employed to legitimise 'women's uplift', an ideology from which it was sometimes not coherently or systematically differentiated. However, as 'equal rights' came to command an ever increasing level of support within the westernised elite, appeal to the liberal beliefs and values with which this ideology was so closely associated tended to supersede the provision of professedly traditional references as a rationale of women's equality.[10]

The Liberal Justification of 'Equal Rights'

The liberal justification of 'equal rights' on the model of the modern West was evident in the speeches and writings of Margaret Cousins and Rameshwari Nehru but, even so, some traditional references still occurred in certain contexts.[11] For example, both women were influenced by Mahatma Gandhi, chiefly in respect of concern for Untouchables whom he called Harijans or Children of God and commitment to non-violence for which he believed women to be specially suited by virtue of their superior moral qualities. In addition, Margaret Cousins' involvement with Theosophy led her to include many spiritual allusions whereas, on occasion, Rameshwari Nehru disavowed any concern with equality in order to concentrate on family and domestic harmony. However, liberal beliefs and values were prominent in their advocacy of 'equal rights' for modern Indian women.

Margaret Cousins' duography with her husband, James, *We Two Together*, gave an insight into her lifelong and heartfelt belief in the equality of women. When writing about her childhood in Ireland, she commented sadly that 'it was counted a kind of curse in those days to be born a girl; and I used to wish deeply that I had been born a boy' (Cousins and Cousins 1950: 55). In contrast to this extremely negative conclusion which arose from her own experiences within her home and family, the preference shown for her brothers over her and her sisters and the subordination of her mother to her father, she urged both that the present position of women could be improved and that women could know the full dignity of common humanity. She related how 'it was a joy later to find that such inequality and injustice and limitations were the result of circumstances which could and would be changed', adding also 'that there was true love and understanding in which the inequalities of the sex relationship disappeared' (Cousins and Cousins 1950: 55). As she recalled, 'one of my missions in life, Equal rights for men and woman [*sic*], was finding me' (Cousins and Cousins 1950: 55). Yet the event which was in her words 'a turning-point in my life' (Cousins and Cousins 1950: 128) was a meeting of the National Council of Women in Manchester in 1906.

The importance of the National Council of Women for Margaret Cousins was that it was 'a large organisation already challenging the continuance of inequality of opportunity between man and woman' (Cousins and Cousins 1950: 128). Not only was it attended by a considerable number of women but, in her opinion, it demonstrated the great potential of women, 'the possibilities that were latent in womanhood', while raising her consciousness of the condition of women, making her 'aware of the injustices and grievances which were taken for granted as the natural fate of my sex' (Cousins and Cousins 1950: 128). Although she made clear that this was her first encounter with the women's movement, she emphasised that she was predisposed towards its point of view because 'even as a child I had felt that girls and women did not get fair play in life' (Cousins and Cousins 1950: 129). Portraying herself as 'a born rebel against conventions which gave women less freedom than men, fewer opportunities, smaller pay, less education, lower status' (Cousins and Cousins 1950: 129), she broached the subject of female suffrage, a cause which was to demand much of her in her subsequent career in Ireland and, eventually, India. Since in Britain the constitutional means of the Suffragists had failed 'to bring women within the expanding circle of democracy' (Cousins and Cousins 1950: 129), her sympathies lay with the more militant approach adopted by the Suffragettes. In Ireland, she became one of the leading lights of the campaign for the enfranchisement of women, enduring imprisonment for taking direct action – breaking the windows of Dublin Castle which was the seat of British government – in protest against the exclusion of women from the franchise in the legislation on Irish Home Rule.

Margaret Cousins was less optimistic about the prospects for Indian women. She recalled a conversation with her husband once the couple were settled in India. During this conversation, he had asked her about the enfranchisement of Indian women and she had answered that this issue would not emerge for a century or so. Explaining that this 'estimation . . . was based on a western notion of the age-long subjection of Indian women by their men-folk, and their consequent backwardness', she admitted that she was soon to disprove this assessment, referring in this respect to 'a great company of Indian women who, unknown then to me, were awaiting the signal of emancipation' (Cousins and Cousins 1950: 298). Thus she introduced her earliest involvement with the women's movement in India while insisting that she 'had no notion . . . of the nature of the signal and the direction from which it would come' (Cousins and Cousins 1950: 298–9). The significance of this statement was that it enabled her to deny that she was somehow influencing the developments taking place among women and hence to represent what was happening as authentically Indian, 'arising out of the inherent genius of Indian womanhood' (Cousins and Cousins 1950:

117

299). She reported how social gatherings of women led to the establishment of a women's association, the Abala Abhivardini Samaj (Weaker Sex Improvement Society). The name of this association was clearly not her choice nor congenial to her but, fortunately for her, it 'quickly became an obvious misnomer through the growth of initiative and ability in the members and influence beyond its local boundaries' (Cousins and Cousins 1950: 299). Indeed, this association was to inspire the formation of the Women's Indian Association in 1917, becoming one of the branches of this new organisation, the Women's Indian Association in turn being instrumental in the foundation of the All India Women's Conference. Both the Women's Indian Association and the All India Women's Conference took up the cause of women's suffrage to which she was to make a valuable personal contribution.

Margaret Cousins reported how her husband's query about women's enfranchisement, raised in the context of possible progress towards Indian self-government, 'was the simple beginning of the movement which, in less than a decade instead of my ignorantly anticipated century, saw women exercising the political franchise on the same terms as men . . ., saw women ultimately sitting in the Provincial Parliaments, and one of them . . . elected by the men of the Parliament of Madras to be its Vice-President' (Cousins and Cousins 1950: 308). She played a major part in this campaign, at its outset describing herself as 'the one voice publicly explaining and proclaiming the suffrage cause . . . because the womanhood of India had not yet found its authoritative voice' (Cousins and Cousins 1950: 370). Notwithstanding, according to her own account, even then Indian women were working with her and, in time, they were to take the lead though welcoming her as a colleague. Moreover, women's ambitions were not limited to winning the vote but extended to establishing women's eligibility for membership of the legislatures and for holding political office.

A measure of the esteem in which Margaret Cousins was held by her Indian co-workers was her election as president of the All India Women's Conference, the foundation of which she characterised as 'the climax' of 'work for the emancipation of women' (Cousins and Cousins 1950: 447). As the then secretary of the Women's Indian Association, it had fallen to her to organise the first meeting of the All India Women's Conference in 1927. Indeed, she had maintained a close connection with this body over the years and supported its alignment with the nationalist principles of the agitation for Indian independence, a stand for which she was incarcerated by the British authorities. For all these reasons, she was regarded as a pioneer of the organisation, her role in the inception of the women's movement in India recognised by honouring her with its presidency.

Margaret Cousins' presidential speech appealed to liberal beliefs and values, the humanistic and secular norms of the modern West, in defence of the equality of women. She did this by referring to the history of the All India Women's Conference, specifically its work for equality, and by setting out the organisation's egalitarian principles.[12] In addition, her account of the campaign for women's political rights in which the organisation had taken a lead was predicated upon liberal ideals.

Margaret Cousins reviewed the achievements of the All India Women's Conference, praising the organisation for mobilising public opinion behind its progressive agenda and behind its work for women's political rights. She summarised what had been achieved as follows:

> We have . . . created a public opinion on women's questions of a strength which did not exist previously. We have raised the prestige, dignity, influence, power and capacity of our united womanhood, and gained a new and deep appreciation from the public for women's ability and for their rights of citizenship, – a wider vision of women's sphere and responsibilities, nationally as well as domestically.

> (Cousins 1936: 329–30)

Having praised the organisation's achievements, she was by no means complacent about the position of women in India or the issues which were still to be addressed. Yet she did not merely catalogue such ills but offered an interpretation of the underlying cause of these ills, and, in the light of this, an interpretation of the women's movement.

Margaret Cousins lamented that women were judged by their sex and not on the same basis as men, discrimination which was pronounced to be present in all aspects of life. She declared:

> There has been acquiescence everywhere in the idea that there shall be one standard for men, and another different standard for women. There is a double standard in morality, in wages, in education, in citizenship, in opportunities for work and service, in religion.

> (Cousins 1936: 332)

It was this discrimination against women which she regarded as motivating them to act. Moved by the plight of their oppressed sex, she stressed that women were resolved to secure for themselves a position equal with men. As she made clear, professing the view:

> All women's struggles for reforms when analysed are our expression of revolt against a double standard. . . . Here lies the Centre of the women's movement. Having become aware of the injustices, cruelty and depreciation under which the mass of women suffer because of the double standard we are determined to establish ourselves as an order of humanity equal in spiritual degree to our brothers . . .
>
> (Cousins 1936: 332)

Certainly, her belief in equality was evident in her discussion of the franchise and related matters where she criticised the practice of discriminating against women as candidates and as voters.

Thus Margaret Cousins' commentary on political questions was one in which she noted how women candidates were to be selected and voted in by men, given the overwhelming numerical superiority of men as voters. She also observed how few women had been nominated as candidates for general seats as distinct from seats reserved for women. This meant that women were doubly under-represented politically, in terms of their dissociation from those women who were candidates and also in terms of the limited number of women candidates. As she informed her audience:

> We find to our disappointment that our elected women will be the chosen of men and of vested interests of grouping of men rather than in any way representatives of women because men voters are nearly seven times as many as women. It has been especially painful to us that the political parties have put forward only a couple of women for general seats . . .
>
> (Cousins 1936: 331)

Her remedy for this was to recommend the introduction of universal adult suffrage which would bring to an end the discrimination against women by eliminating all supplementary qualifications for the franchise, be they marital or economic, which dictated the size and shape of the electoral roll. She stated:

> The whole election subject is a muddle without principle or consistency. It can be set right only by the substitution of adult

120

franchise, and we will ccntinue [sic] to work for that with might and main, to obtain our freedom from the undesired and unnatural qualification of marriage, and the disparity of numbers, and the limitations of a monetary status instead of a human and rational status.

(Cousins 1936: 331)

These remarks reflected her commitment to women's equality in political as in other areas of life and how she went about justifying women's political equality by referring to liberal norms.

Margaret Cousins' presidential speech defended 'equal rights' by appealing to liberal beliefs and values. She located these liberal norms in the context of the organisation, what it had already done and what she saw as its fundamental convictions. On this basis, she advanced an argument for 'equal rights' for women in the roles of candidates and voters, the realisation of this equality being an aim to which she rededicated the organisation.

In a similar manner, Rameshwari Nehru's presidential speech appealed to the liberal beliefs and values of the modern West in defence of the equality of women. She too referred to the history of the organisation and its principles, in her case when offering a liberal rationale of the campaign for women's social rights as an extension of the organisation's work for equality and as an embodiment of its egalitarian principles.

Rameshwari Nehru gave particular prominence to the organisation's work for women's social rights in her resumé of the impact of the All India Women's Conference. Listing the changes for which the organisation had pressed to improve women's social position, she claimed:

In the social sphere, we have made an humble contribution towards the removal of evil customs and the obliteration of unjust laws. Amongst the many reforms that we have urged are the removal of *purdah* and of early marriage, widow remarriage, abolition of the dowry system, equal moral standard for men and women and economic independence of women.

(Nehru 1940: 334)

This list of the social objectives of the organisation, ending female seclusion, child marriage and the dowering of brides and enabling widows to remarry, together with the aspiration for gender-free morality and women's financial security, was inspired by the drive for equality.

Although Rameshwari Nehru subscribed to the liberal norm of equality, she recognised that this aroused some anxiety and so was at pains to try to relieve these concerns. Addressing herself to the organisation's detractors, she pleaded for men to have faith in women and hence the organisation:

> To those of my brothers who do not agree with the policy of the women's Conference, who see danger in our demand for freedom and sex equality, I say cast off these fears and have trust in us.
>
> (Nehru 1940: 336)

Furthermore, she presented the organisation's programme as comparatively moderate, maintaining that it was merely to regulate dealings between the sexes in the same way as those between men. Moreover, she was insistent that this was in everyone's interests, not just those of women. She declared:

> All that we want to do is to establish equity and fairplay in the relations of man and woman as well as man and man. That is the only foundation on which a stable structure of civilized society can be built.
>
> (Nehru 1940: 336)

This liberal tenet, that equality for women was in the common good, was one way in which she could endorse reform of Hindu personal law to legislate for women's social equality.

Rameshwari Nehru set out the organisation's case for reform of Hindu personal law consistent with the equality of women. She mentioned laws already on the statute book which the organisation sought to have modified. She also alluded to the additional measures which the organisation sought to have enacted. She explained:

> We have advocated radical changes in the personal laws particularly of the Hindus, and have demanded that the law with regard to inheritance, marriage, guardianship of the children and other matters should deal equitably with the rights of women. We want that polygamy should be intradicted [sic] by law and divorce on specific conditions should be introduced amongst the Hindus.
>
> (Nehru 1940: 334)

As attempts to reform Hindu personal law theretofore had generally proven unsuccessful because the proposed legislation had not received sufficient support to be enacted, she concluded that another course of action was required. In this respect, she gave her approval to the concept of a new inclusive law enshrining women's equality in marital and familial issues. Nevertheless, she allowed that there was a case for the jurisdiction of this law being limited to those who had opted for this code over the codes associated with the different religious traditions. She commented:

> I agree with the suggestion made by some of our members that an equitable comprehensive law based on the equality of the sexes should be enacted even though its adoption by individuals in place of the present divergent laws of the community may be voluntary.
>
> (Nehru 1940: 334)

For her, as for her colleagues, the present state of Hindu personal law was unsatisfactory since it stood in the way of women's social equality, this equality being justified in liberal terms.

Rameshwari Nehru's presidential speech, like that of Margaret Cousins delivered four years previously, defended 'equal rights' by appealing to liberal beliefs and values. Again, as had Margaret Cousins before her, she located these liberal norms in the context of the organisation. Accordingly, she selected equality as the criterion for reform of Hindu personal law without citing any authority for so doing other than that of liberal thought as acknowledged by the organisation. Many of the same themes, including and especially the liberal justification of 'equal rights', were evident in other of her works.

Thus Rameshwari Nehru's 'Reflection on the Women's Conference' ironically reiterated the rhetorical excesses of men who paid charming, if inconsequential and insincere, compliments to women. Caricaturing these oratorical flights of fancy, she repeated the romantic tributes conventionally made to women. Such tributes, 'women are angels, women are goddesses, they are the personification of all goodness, power, energy and strength', involved an understanding of the respective responsibilities of men and women in which women 'are the inspirers, they are the dictators' whose task 'is but to command, and it is the joy of mem [sic] to obey' (Nehru 1950: 27). She mocked this extravagant flattery, illustrated by literary and historical examples, 'where empires have been made or marred by a smile on a women's [sic] lips or a tear in her eye' (Nehru 1950: 27) because it bore little, if any, relation to the reality of women's lives.

Indeed, these platitudes about the respect shown to women served to obscure the truth. This, in her opinion, was that women, however much they were honoured with honeyed words, had never in any place or at any time enjoyed equality with men for 'in spite of all the lip homage that is paid to her, woman has never had a fair deal from the world of men' (Nehru 1950: 28). She contended that, irrespective of geographical region or historical period, 'the customs and practices of society and its laws have been unfair' but she was also clear that 'the objection raised by the modern woman to her subordinate position in society' was neither emotional nor doctrinaire, rather a perception of an ethical crisis with adverse consequences for society as a whole (Nehru 1950: 28). This thesis, that the equality of women conduced to the welfare of society whereas the inequality of women militated against it, was a major motif of her liberal justification of 'equal rights'.

Certainly, Rameshwari Nehru's consideration of 'Woman in the New Social Order' emphasised that the women's cause had wider implications for other disadvantaged and oppressed sections of the community. On the premise that 'freedom and equality are principles which are universally accepted as good for the human race' and that 'India is also a great devotee of these golden principles' (Nehru 1950: 25), she argued that women should benefit from the extension of these principles to them and to relationships between the sexes. She urged that these principles be 'applied to women as well as to men and that the mutual relationship of the sexes is regulated in strict accordance with them' (Nehru 1950: 25) instead of the prevalent discrimination against women. In her view, however, it was important to realise 'that the question of women's emancipation is only a part of the larger question of emancipation of submerged and suppressed humanity' (Nehru 1950: 24–5). She insisted that in order for women to become equal, it was necessary to transform attitudes towards women, indeed, suggesting that women's equality might require a concomitant transformation of society, saying 'for a full realization of their aspirations the whole framework of society may have to be changed' (Nehru 1950: 25). Yet, indicating that 'human freedom is inherent in women's freedom' (Nehru 1950: 25), she was concerned to stress how efforts to improve the position of women were to the benefit of men as to women.

Rameshwari Nehru also explored this link between the position of women and the condition of society in her discussion of the 'Women's Movement' where she stated 'that whenever nations have arisen and civilizations are at their best and highest, women have enjoyed comparatively more rights' (Nehru 1950: 10). Though she accepted the oft-quoted maxim that 'the fate of woman has varied with the rise and fall of nations' (Nehru 1950: 10), she was not prepared to go so far as to accept that women had ever been equal with men. Refuting the view that women's equality had existed at some time in the past, she remarked 'the fact remains that in known history women have never attained equal rights with men either in law or in practice' (Nehru 1950: 10). She contrasted this inequality with the ideals of the women's movement which she conceived as being committed to achieving equality for women. Describing the movement's aims, she asserted that 'it stands for the full equality of woman with man in all spheres of life, her complete emancipation from the legal and customary disabilities inflicted on her during the present times' (Nehru 1950: 11). There was, then, no doubt of her belief in equality, an equality which she did not attribute to ancient India nor justify with traditional references. On the contrary, she defended women's equality in liberal terms and on the subject of their social equality, 'the demand for equal rights of inheritance, equal marriage laws, equal moral standards, equal rights of work and the like', proclaimed 'that it will lead to liberty, fraternity and equality and the future constitution of such a society will be based on love, truth, beauty and wisdom' (Nehru 1950: 12). This was a liberal rationale of 'equal rights' in which she championed women's social equality.[13]

Both Margaret Cousins and Rameshwari Nehru offered liberal justifications of 'equal rights' on the model of the modern West. Appealing to liberal beliefs and values, they legitimised the equality of women in political and social matters. The approach they adopted was typical of that adopted at one time by leaders of the women's movement. Perhaps, though, this was when addressing a particular audience, comprising fellow members of the westernised elite, which was sympathetic to liberal norms. So long as spokespersons for the women's movement were speaking and writing to those who shared their expectations for the equality of women, there was no need to justify 'equal rights' except by the espousal of liberal tenets. These liberal tenets were widely endorsed within the influential and progressive social groups from which the women's movement drew its members and to which it looked for support.

Before 'equal rights' had become established as the dominant ideology, it was far more likely that it would be portrayed as having a traditional pedigree as part of India's past but, of course, whether it was traditionalised in this way also depended on other factors. Yet even after 'equal rights' had become established as the dominant ideology, though it was less likely for traditional substantiation to be claimed for it, traditional references were still employed when the women's movement was campaigning for change in highly controversial areas where opposition to change was stated on religious grounds. An example of this was the movement's campaign for change in Hindu personal law, however much the traditionalisation of 'equal rights' was greeted with derision by opponents.

CHAPTER FIVE

Legislation and Change:
Campaigning for Women's Rights

This chapter examines how the Indian women's movement sought to effect change in the position of women through legislation. The movement's conduct of two major campaigns for legislation, addressing women's political and social rights respectively, is discussed. Of these two campaigns, however, that for women's social rights, culminating in the controversy surrounding the Hindu Code Bill, is demonstrated to have given rise to greater religious debate. For this reason, arguments rehearsed by opponents and proponents of reform of Hindu personal law are treated in depth, concentrating on those arguments which centred on contrasting interpretations of the Hindu tradition. Such arguments are shown to convey very different impressions of the character of the tradition and its significance for women.

The Indian Women's Movement and Women's Rights

In 1936, the All India Women's Conference submitted a memorandum to the League of Nations on the subject of the position of women. This memorandum, composed as a rejoinder to a British document prepared without reference to the women's movement, stated:

> The All-India Women's Conference wish to stress the point that they, in common with other individuals and organisations, are doing their level best to do away with all disabilities – legal, social, and political from which women suffer. In this connection they have to combat not only Indian orthodox organisations, and conservative-minded men and women but

also a Government that has so far maintained an apathetic attitude towards their point of view.

(AIWC 1936: 337)

This memorandum indicated that in its campaigns for women's rights the movement had to overcome, or at least outmanoeuvre, a significant level of indigenous opposition, including opposition from women. In addition, this memorandum indicated that the movement's attempts to persuade influential sections of public opinion at home to support its cause had to be combined with efforts to convince the British authorities to act in accordance with its agenda for improving the position of women. Indeed, such a characterisation of its campaigns diverged markedly from many other comments which stressed the consensus behind women's rights rather than the conflict they provoked both in principle and in practice.

Some measure of the problems posed can be gauged by briefly considering the complex and convoluted history of the campaigns for women's political and social rights. The movement worked to achieve and extend the enfranchisement of women, and to establish women's eligibility for electoral office and advance their membership of representative institutions. This was a protracted campaign. It began in 1917 with the appearance before the Montagu–Chelmsford Committee of a delegation of women who demanded that future constitutional arrangements for India should incorporate women's suffrage on the same terms as men. It ended some twenty years later in 1937 when elections were called under the provisions of the Government of India Act (1935), returning fifty-six women to the legislatures through a variety of mechanisms including reserved seats and nominations. During this period, different opinions were expressed as to whether women should have the vote at all and, if so, whether they should qualify for the vote on a different basis from men; similarly, different opinions were expressed as to whether women should play a more prominent part in the political process and, if so, whether their participation should be promoted by special measures.[1]

The movement also worked for reform of personal law as it impacted on women. This was another protracted campaign. It was launched in 1934 when the All India Women's Conference called a day of action to lobby for the setting up of a commission on women's legal disabilities to recommend revision of the law. It was concluded by the passage of the Hindu Code Bill between 1954 and 1956 in the form of five separate acts which regulated marriage and divorce,

128

property and inheritance, the care and custody of children and the adoption and support of dependants. Discussion ranged over whether a common civil code should be enacted or whether personal law should continue to be determined by membership of a religious community; consequently, in the second instance, it had to be decided whether reform of the personal laws of minority religious communities should be attempted or only the reform of Hindu personal law as well as whether the interests of women or the interests of religions should take priority in the event of any clash.[2]

What was at stake in the movement's campaigns for women's political and social rights was the role of women in Indian life, be it solely domestic and subordinate or encompassing involvement in public affairs and founded on a full place within the family. Religious beliefs and values surely helped to shape the conventional assumptions about women which their political rights were perceived as challenging and as such, on occasion, the Hindu tradition did feature in contributions to debate. Yet religious tenets were intimately and inextricably caught up in the question of women's social rights, an interrelationship reflected in the content of debate. This gives a special resonance to Jana Matson Everett's portrait of the 'two different images of the ideal Hindu woman' (Everett 1981: 166) developed during the controversy surrounding the Hindu Code Bill. In this account, she likens the image associated with opponents of reform of Hindu personal law to the discourse on the duty of women in probably the most famous of Hindu scriptures while attributing the image associated with proponents of reform to the tenets of western liberalism. Contrasting these images of women, the former representing women as subject to the authority of men, the latter as individuals who were equal with men, she explains:

> The opponents' image resembled the view of women presented in the Manusmriti: she needed protection of men during all the periods of her life (thus never capable of independently looking after property), and in this position of dependence she was worshipped as a goddess. The proponents' image of the ideal Hindu woman was a competent, autonomous human being interacting with others on the basis of equal rights and individual freedom. This image clearly stemmed from Western liberal thought, however imperfectly it had been achieved in practice in the West.

> (Everett 1981: 166-7)

Despite the fact that the women's movement espoused the ideology of 'equal rights' and endorsed it by reference to liberal norms, its leaders did try to establish the traditional credentials of reform of Hindu personal law because objections to reform were frequently, if by no means exclusively, religious in nature and because reform had such significant implications for the status of women.

Hindu Personal Law and the History of the Hindu Code Bill

The debate about women's social rights was defined by the British decision to administer Hindu law to Hindus (and hence Muslim law to Muslims) where that law concerned the conduct of family life. Wittingly or unwittingly, when the British assumed responsibility for administering this law, they nevertheless changed both its nature and its scope because 'British judicial administration . . . strengthened the law's Sanskritic orthodoxy while it also partly eroded its pre-British sources, substance, localism, and sanction' (Levy 1973: 90). The British concept of law was, then, at odds with the Brahmanical legal tradition in which:

> There was a complex and subtle interweaving of general and local sources by a jurisprudence with considerable refinement in the selection of sources for application. The traditional practitioner had a wide variety of textual and customary standards from which to choose and a variety of jurisprudential criteria for choosing to apply a given standard to a group of given ritual rank, region, occupation, condition of moral-religious habituation, extent and quality of pre-existing attachment to a given standard, etc.
>
> (Levy 1973: 100)

Under British rule, British legal procedures and norms were substituted for Indian ones, whatever the claims to the contrary. Consequently, although the history of the Hindu Code Bill bridged the imperial and independent periods, it was to a very great extent determined by British administration of Hindu personal law over 175 years.

The 1772 Judicial Plan designated *Dharmaśāstra* to be the sole basis for judging cases of Hindu personal law in the courts of the East India Company. Warren Hastings, the then Governor-General of Bengal, indicated in this Judicial Plan that 'in all suits regarding inheritance, marriage, caste, and other religious usages, or institutions, the laws of the Koran with respect to Mahometans and those of the *Shaster* with respect to Gentoos shall be invariably adhered to' (Hastings 1772). In so doing, Hastings was dividing indigenous law into two types, personal law ostensibly governed by traditional religious dictates and the remainder governed by unambiguously British regulations, a division deriving from the distinction made in Britain between canon law administered in ecclesiastical courts and secular law administered in state courts (Derrett 1968: 233–5). At the same time, by specifying Hindu scripture as the only standard for Hindu personal law, Hastings was favouring orthodoxy, indeed, a rather stereotypical form thereof.

In order to be able to administer Hindu personal law, Hastings commissioned a group of *paṇḍits* to compile a digest of Hindu legal literature which was then translated into Persian and finally into English under Nathaniel Halhed's supervision. This project was an important part of Hastings' efforts to resist the process of Anglicisation in every way possible (cf. Brockington 1988: 2). Exercised by the prospect of India being subjected to British rule which was not only foreign but alien, he communicated his anxieties about the rumoured preparation of 'an unadvised system' of law to the Court of Directors of the East India Company in London when he despatched the first section of the digest; he insisted that the Indian people were entitled to be ruled in conformity with that which 'time and religion had rendered familiar to their understandings and sacred to their affections' (Hastings n.d.). The completed digest, *A Code of Gentoo Laws, or, Ordinations of the Pundits*, was subsequently published with a preface written by Halhed stating the purpose the work was intended to serve. According to Halhed, the digest was to be a source for 'the legal accomplishment of a new system of government in Bengal, wherein the British laws may, in some degree, be softened by a moderate attention to the peculiar and national prejudices of the Hindoo' (Halhed 1777: xi).

Here Halhed also commented that the means whereby to 'conciliate the affections of the natives' and to 'ensure stability to the acquisition' was 'a well-timed toleration in matters of religion, and an adoption of such original institutes of the country, as do not immediately clash with the laws or interests of the conquerors' (Halhed 1777: ix). This was the context in which the digest, described by him as containing 'the genuine principles of the Gentoo jurisprudence' and as benefiting from 'the sanction of their most respectable Pundits, (or lawyers)' (Halhed 1777: x), was commissioned. In a manner reminiscent of Hastings' views and, incidentally, re-echoed in the 'Preliminary Discourse' of the *pandits* who were engaged in the compilation of the digest, he emphasised that Hindu laws were 'interwoven with the religion of the country' and thus 'revered as of the highest authority' which, together with 'long usage', meant that for Hindus 'to be obliged to renounce their obedience would probably be esteemed among them a real hardship' (Halhed 1777: xi). This idea, that because Hindu law was religious Hindus would resent its rejection by their rulers, clearly had as its corollary that, by implementing Hindu law, the British would gain Hindu goodwill and protect their own position.

So far as the specific teaching on women was concerned, Halhed announced that the axioms in the chapter devoted to this topic were 'relics of that characteristic discipline of Asia . . . where women have ever been the subjects, not the partners of their lords, confined within the walls of a haram, or busied without doors in drudgeries little becoming their delicacy' (Halhed 1777: lxvi). What was more, he felt it necessary to comment on the age of the *pandits* who had participated in the project, referring to the fact that they were 'far advanced in years' as 'apology for the observations they have selected, and censures they have passed, upon the conduct and merits of the fair sex' (Halhed 1777: lxv). In the chapter on women were excerpts describing the roles and responsibilities of husbands and wives. While there was some sense of mutuality in its precepts, the emphasis was upon the husband's legitimate exercise of authority over his wife and the wife's duty to submit herself willingly to her husband. Exacting standards of wifely virtue, enumerating qualities such as obedience, chastity and piety, were set forth along with a critical account of women's impetuous, passionate and immoral nature.

In many respects, these early events set the tone for what followed by way of British administration of Hindu personal law which, in the case of women, at least theoretically entailed the extension to all women classed as Hindu of a law hitherto applied only to those of high caste (Liddle and Joshi 1986: 26, 30). Even so, many things did change over the years. For example, other digests of Hindu legal literature were compiled and later, after digests were abandoned as impracticable for judicial use, certain texts were translated in their entirety (Edwardes 1967: 302). Or again, while initially the courts were guided by the pronouncements of Hindu Law Officers, this was discontinued and British judges deemed capable of reaching

132

judgments without recourse to the *pandits'* expertise (Derrett 1957: 15). This produced a situation in which particular texts were represented as possessing special importance and implemented as such, and in which past precedent was taken as the criterion for making future judgments. British rule thereby rendered Hindu personal law as administered in British courts in India both selective and static.

This issue was further complicated by the disparity between a nominal British policy of non-interference in religious questions and a number of overt legislative interventions in Hindu personal law which the British themselves had designated came under the heading of religion. The British policy of religious non-interference was summed up in Queen Victoria's proclamation issued in 1858 when she decreed that the religious beliefs and practices of her Indian subjects would be respected. Notwithstanding, this pledge was at least potentially at odds with her guarantee that all her subjects would enjoy equal protection under the law. Such an assurance could in theory provide a justification for ameliorative legislation, as in fact it did during Sir Andrew Scoble's defence of the proposal to raise the age of consent to 12 years when he argued that equal protection under the law extended to wives (Hemsath 1964: 172).

Certainly, in addition to the covert changes otherwise introduced, the British enacted legislation affecting women which was both permissive and mandatory in nature. In so doing, with increasing direct Indian participation, they legalised alternative lifestyles and even criminalised specific conduct in the area of Hindu personal law, albeit the form that law had assumed under British administration. For example, the bill to legalise widow remarriage referred to the way in which 'the law as administered in the Civil Courts established in the territories in the possession and under the Government of the East India Company' regarded widows 'by reason of their having been once married, incapable of contracting a second valid marriage' when proposing that 'no such marriage shall be illegitimate, by reason of the woman having been previously married or betrothed to another person who was dead at the time of such marriage, any custom and any interpretation of Hindu law to the contrary notwithstanding' (A Bill to Remove All Legal Obstacles to the Marriage of Hindoo Widows 1855). Accordingly, the legalisation of widow remarriage was perhaps a partial restoration of conditions prevailing before the British had proscribed widow remarriage, only partial because circumstances were so different in other respects. In any event, without clearly conceding the position of religious neutrality, the British were on occasion minded to offer a rationale for reform as they were in the case of sati. Hence the act to criminalise sati acknowledged the under-taking 'that all classes of the people be secure in the observance of their religious usages' as 'one of the first and most important principles of the system of British government in India', from which undertaking this legislation declared that it did not dissent (Regulation XVII of the Bengal Code 1829). However, it legitimised change not only by disputing the religious basis of sati but also by subordinating religious neutrality to 'the paramount dictates of justice and humanity' (Regulation XVII of the Bengal Code 1829).

Of course, legislation affecting women continued to be enacted throughout British rule including the period immediately preceding the concerted campaign for women's social rights. It was the cumulative effect of such legislation which the All India Women's Conference regarded as unsatisfactory and which prompted it to hold the day of action on women's legal disabilities. This was reported to be a success at the organisation's annual meeting where the imperative to redouble its members' efforts to enlist support for law reform was also recognised (Mukherji 1934: 357). Subsequent experience of the obstacles to be overcome in securing the passage of favourable laws, confirming as it did the shortcomings of piecemeal legislation from the progressive perspective, only served to strengthen demand on the part of some women for a systematic and comprehensive approach to be adopted towards legal change. Eventually, the government was convinced and conceded the case for the appointment of a committee.

In 1941, a committee chaired by Sir B.N. Rau was established to study the effects of legislation already on the statute book, the Hindu Women's Right to Property Act (1937) as amended by another act the following year, along with proposed legislation and so to assess the state of Hindu personal law as it related to women's social rights.[3] In the course of its deliberations, the committee issued questionnaires to a wide variety of individuals, among them leading legal, political and religious figures, and organisations, including orthodox and reform associations as well as women's groups. After consideration of the responses received, the committee concluded that a code should be prepared.

This Hindu Law Committee was re-established in 1944, again with Rau in the chair, to prepare a code. Once the draft code had been published, from which the name Hindu Code Bill derived, the committee travelled throughout India consulting opinion and collating reaction. In 1947, the committee published a report of its fact-finding tour which included a revised draft of the code. This code did not become law because its passage was interrupted by Independence, and subsequently, the Ministry of Law revised it further. It was in this form that another committee, chaired by Dr B. R. Ambedkar, considered the code and more revisions were made.

A motion to examine the committee's report was debated in, and passed by, the Constituent Assembly in 1949. However, despite Ambedkar's best endeavours, opposition to the Hindu Code Bill was such that, in the legislative session ending in September 1951, only four clauses were approved. In recognition of this failure, another draft of the code was prepared in the hope that opposition might be reduced. After the Congress electoral victory, the Hindu Code Bill was enacted as: the Special Marriage Act (1954); the Hindu Marriage Act (1955); the Hindu Succession Act (1955); the Hindu Minority and Guardianship Act (1956); and the Hindu Adoptions and Maintenance Act (1956).

The Hindu Tradition and Opposition to Reform of Hindu Personal Law

Speaking on the day of action called by the All India Women's Conference in 1934, Lady Sircar had maintained:

> Indian women of the present day did not base their claim for the removal of legal disabilities on the great rights and privileges enjoyed by women in the past. It did not matter whether the Sastras sanctioned their claims or not. The women's demand for the removal of legal disabilities was based upon justice and equity. It was high time that Indian women asserted themselves for the removal of their legal disabilities.
>
> (Sircar 1934)

However, as was clear when the controversy developed, the position of women in ancient India and the teaching of Hindu scriptures, differently interpreted, were far from being irrelevant or unimportant subjects. During the history of the campaign for women's social rights, opposition was often rationalised and articulated in terms of a specific reading of the Hindu tradition. Opponents of reform of Hindu personal law claimed that Hindu law was divine in origin, hence both revealed in status and timeless in nature, and essential to the social and spiritual welfare of the Hindu community (Derrett 1957: 38; Levy 1973: 385–6). Thus, they claimed that the proposed changes in Hindu personal law substituted human for divine authorship, introduced western tenets of social justice and affirmed the necessity of changing laws in the light of changing conditions, thereby imperilling the identity and integrity of the Hindu community.

The *Madras Law Journal* (1941) published two responses to the questionnaire issued by the Hindu Law Committee, one of which was the response of H. H. the Jagatguru Sri Sankaracharya Swamigal of Kamakoti Pitham, a leader of orthodox opinion, who roundly condemned the proposed changes in Hindu personal law. From the outset, he made plain his profound opposition to the premises on which the questionnaire was issued.[4] At the close of his introductory remarks, he contended:

> On principle we need not give any answers to the Questionnaire except to state that all the innovations proposed by them are uncalled for and unnecessary. But yet we have set forth the answers to the several questions from the viewpoint of preserving the rules of Hindu law according to the Smritis.
>
> (Sankaracharya 1941: 132)

Moreover, in a response making numerous references to *Manu's Dharmaśāstra* as well as other law-books, he denied the legitimacy of any modification of that law, and decried the substitution of alien values into it, predicting that, were any revision to be attempted, it would have calamitous consequences for the Hindu community.

Sri Sankaracharya testified that Hindu law was derived from the *Vedas*, so that, unlike human law, there was no possibility of adapting it to meet different needs or expectations. He noted:

> Hindu law is founded upon the revealed Vedas. The Vedic law has regard to the welfare of all creation. Man-made laws have regard to the happiness of individuals or particular groups. They change when the people's desires, or the desires of those who rule over them, change. But the law whose source is the Veda, cannot be changed to suit man's changing standards or whims. Its applicability stands valid for all time and for all men.
>
> (Sankaracharya 1941: 132)

He interpreted the motivation behind the measures under discussion as being 'to ensure the woman's happiness as an individual, in spite of adverse circumstances' whereas it was his belief that 'individuals should accept the hardships and sufferings incidental to social life (*Samsara*) as steps in the path of moral and spiritual progress' (Sankaracharya 1941: 132). Drawing on his analysis of the individualism and hedonism underlying the cause of Hindu law reform as against the social focus and religious importance of Hindu law, he stressed that reform, resting as it did on assumptions antithetical to their tradition, should not be enacted on behalf of Hindus. He affirmed:

> It would . . . be undesirable, to frame new laws based on notions of individual liberty and individual happiness, and apply them to a society governed by principles based on the eternal revealed law and designed to attain high social and spiritual ends.
>
> (Sankaracharya 1941: 133)

Thus, while reiterating 'that there are provisions in the *Smritis* to cover all cases where relief should legitimately be given' (Sankaracharya 1941: 133), he argued that the proposed changes were to be rejected on the grounds that they were inspired by western norms and values which conflicted with the nature and purpose of Hindu law.

According to Sri Sankaracharya:

> Historians and contemporary observers agree that the Hindu ideal of marriage and the Hindu system of family life have conduced both to secure a high degree of family welfare and happiness, and the preservation of Hindu society.
>
> (Sankaracharya 1941: 133)

It was this domestic felicity and social harmony which, he maintained, reform would put at risk. Describing the position women held in the Hindu home, he emphasised that the proposed changes would weaken the institution of the family, and, consequently, caste and society in general, by allowing and encouraging women to abandon their familial responsibilities. He explained:

> By law and custom, Hindu women have always lived as inseparable units of Hindu families, exerting a unique moral and spiritual influence over the whole family atmosphere. Legislation of this kind will create and tend to multiply the occasions and temptations for women to tear themselves away

137

from family life, and live separately. Ultimately, the purity and integrity of Hindu family life, and the strength and stability which caste-life has given to Hindu society will disappear.

(Sankaracharya 1941: 134)

As an authoritative spokesperson for the orthodox view of the roles and responsibilities of women, his response could have left the committee in no doubt of the depth of his objections.

Further examples of Sri Sankaracharya's pronouncements on the issues raised by the questionnaire were when he dealt with the inheritance of property and polygynous marriage. On the subject of the inheritance of property, he showed that for Hindus the right to inherit was linked to the ability to make *piṇḍa* (balls of rice) offerings to the dead since it was the obligation of beneficiaries 'to continue the traditions and the ideals of the ancestors whose property they take' (Sankaracharya 1941: 128). The clear implication of his argument was that women were barred from inheriting family property on the basis of their ineligibility to perform the *śrāddha* (memorial) ceremony for deceased family members. On the subject of polygynous marriage, he railed against the dissolution of a husband's second simultaneous union because such marriages could be celebrated only when specific conditions, and here he gave as an instance the first wife's failure to bear children, were satisfied. He insisted that Hindu marriage was intended to produce a son 'so as to ensure spiritual benefit to the line of ancestors, and to perpetuate Vedic culture and the practices of Dharma through unbroken continuity of lineage' (Sankaracharya 1941: 135). In such fashion, Sri Sankaracharya defended the orthodox outlook on the legal position of women. This he contrasted with the western concepts of personal freedom and fulfilment which he regarded as foreign to Hindu society and which he alleged underwrote the campaign for change in Hindu personal law.

Furthermore, Sri Sankaracharya's orthodox convictions were widely shared. Certainly, the *Report of the Hindu Law Committee* (1947) included excerpts from the evidence of many witnesses who were in sympathy with his opposition to Hindu law reform. Mr R. M. Kate of the Hindu Nationalist Party stated that the draft code ran counter to Hindu legal precepts. He argued:

The draft Code was opposed to the basic principles of Hindu Law. . . . Our culture is based on the divine law and the vedas are only the expression of that law. It is an immutable law. Our

138

Sanatanism is ever fresh and suitable to all times. It is not merely an old historical relic, devoid of present significance.

(HLC 1947: 101)

The Bar Association of Ajmer was concerned that the draft code would corrupt Hindu law with incompatible elements. The Association submitted that:

Instead of codifying the tenets of the Hindu Law [the draft code] obviously aims at engrafting upon the Hindu society practices repugnant to the Hindu Dharmashastra.

(HLC 1947: 108)

Another Bar Association, the District Bar Association of Sylhet, described the draft code as 'the cumulative result of the co-ordination and combination of . . . anti-Hindus [sic] forces' and continued by speculating that the draft code would effect a total collapse in Hindu civilisation:

In our opinion the proposed code if passed into law will bring about economic ruin, social disintegration, and cultural degeneration of the Hindu Community as a whole.

(HLC 1947:104)

Nor was it only men who expressed such fundamental opposition to the proposals.

For example, Srimathi Vidyavathi Devi, Secretary of the Arya Mahila Hitakarini Mahaparishad (Noble Women's Welfare Great Circle), concurred with Sri Sankaracharya in defending the inequality of women as heirs. In order to ensure that the family's duty to the ancestors was discharged in the performance of religious ritual, she required that the man who made the *piṇḍa* offerings inherited the family property. She claimed: 'The daughter should not be a simultaneous heir with the son as she goes into another gotra and performs no ceremonies for her father or his ancestors' (HLC 1947: 129). Sri Mathi Sundari Bai, headmistress of the Arya Mahila Vidyalaya (Noble Women's College) and editor of the *Arya Mahila* magazine, also agreed with Sri Sankaracharya, in this case with his disapproval of the enforcement of monogamy in circumstances, such as the absence of sons, where polygyny was allowed by Hindu law. She claimed that the importance attached to monogamy reflected a misunderstanding of the character and constitution of Hindu marriage. She recalled: 'The Shastras permit a man to marry a second

139

wife, if he has no male issue. Marriage is not for carnal pleasure but for spiritual benefit' (HLC 1947: 168). As the evidence given by these last two witnesses demonstrated, women (and thus organisations of, and institutions for, women) were among those who viewed the prospect of changing Hindu personal law with disquiet.

This opposition attracted attention given the impetus behind reform. Indeed, the committee referred to this as the reason for considering women's attitudes towards the proposed changes in Hindu personal law, explaining:

> The primary aim of most of the alterations in the existing Hindu Law proposed in the draft Code being to effect an improvement in the status of women, it will be useful to state the reception which it has met with from them.
>
> (HLC 1947: 6)

When summarising women's thoughts on the draft code, the committee began by indicating that it was supported by 'almost all Women's Associations of standing', adding that 'women who çonfidently claimed to represent the views of the vast majority of their educated sisters heartily welcomed the proposals' (HLC 1947: 6). The committee contrasted this support from the women's movement and its educated constituency with the opposition from other women whom it identified as 'those who are deeply attached to the orthodox or *sanatani* way of life and those who belong to the aristocratic classes of society' (HLC 1947: 6). Commenting on the motivation of orthodox and aristocratic women, the committee's interpretation was that orthodox women 'were on principle opposed to all change' while aristocratic women 'seemed specially to dislike the provisions relating to succession' with both groups professing themselves content with the unreformed state of Hindu personal law (HLC 1947: 6).[5] However, the committee was not satisfied simply to document these differences of opinion. On the contrary, it went to some lengths to criticise such opposition, repeating the allegation that opposition to reform was aroused by misinformation and quoting a statement to the effect that women's anxieties could be allayed by their being better informed. On its part, the committee deprecated the exclusion of women who supported the draft code from meetings held to debate the subject and also attributed many women's opposition to the influence of their male relations. In this way, the committee contrived to condemn and trivialise the case against change.[6]

Enumerated in the conclusion of the *Report of the Hindu Law Committee* were reasons other than those that Hindu law was unchangeable and thus that any changes proposed were inimical to Hindu civilisation. However, for women as for men, the religious argument was of great significance. This, the importance of religion for opponents of reform, was recognised by the committee who discussed the subject in the section on *'Religion in danger'* under the heading 'General Objections'. The analysis of this 'religion in danger' argument was contextualised by acknowledging that 'it was . . . freely voiced by many witnesses who appeared before us as well as in numerous written memoranda submitted to us' (HLC 1947: 7). Having set forth the rationale for the comparatively detailed treatment meted out to this particular objection, the committee concentrated on the question of whether the proposed changes in Hindu personal law did in fact endanger religion as opponents so often and outspokenly insisted. Rejecting this accusation, the committee remarked that 'when they [witnesses] were confronted with *smriti* texts or other original authorities entitled to the highest credit, which supported a suggested alteration, they said that they preferred the existing law, even though it might be based only on a custom in derogation of the texts or on a decision of the Privy Council' (HLC 1947: 7). Clearly, therefore, in finding fault with the religious argument advanced by opponents of reform, the committee was advancing an argument of its own which, among other things, characterised the proposed changes in Hindu personal law as authentic and authoritative in Hindu terms.[7]

That many people were not persuaded to the committee's point of view was apparent in the passionate opposition to the Hindu Code Bill. For instance, the following year, the All-India Anti-Hindu-Code Convention resolved:

> That it [the Hindu Code Bill] cuts at the root of the Vedic and Shastric origin of the Hindu Law and will seriously and inevitably undermine the foundations of the Hindu religion, Hindu culture and Hindu Social structure.
>
> (All-India Anti-Hindu-Code Convention 1948)

Perhaps this made it seem all the more necessary for the Indian women's movement to offer a Hindu justification of the Hindu Code Bill, based on another alternative reading of the Hindu tradition, albeit an approach quite dissimilar from that adopted when the audience to be addressed was drawn from within its own ranks.[8]

The Hindu Tradition and Support for Reform
of Hindu Personal Law

Renuka Ray (b. 1904), involved with the All India Women's Conference from 1931 onwards and president of the organisation between 1952 and 1954, was one of the protagonists of the controversy surrounding the Hindu Code Bill.[9] The day of action called by the All India Women's Conference to discuss women's legal disabilities was staged under her leadership (Everett 1981: 149). During the Legislative Assembly debates in 1943–4, she was the government appointed All India Women's Conference representative (Levy 1973: 340). She continued to be a major advocate of the Hindu Code Bill during the Constituent Assembly (Provisional Parliament) debates in 1949 and 1951 (Everett 1981: 173).

The 1951 crisis aroused apprehensions among supporters of the Hindu Code Bill that their cause was lost. However, the Congress Party victory in the 1952 General Election gave renewed impetus to reform. It was in this context that Renuka Ray wrote an article entitled 'The Background of the Hindu Code Bill' where she appealed to Congress' electoral victory as a mandate for enactment of the bill. She explained:

> Since the Hindu Code Bill was not enacted by the time that Parliament was dissolved in preparation for the General Elections, it has remained one of the Congress Party's legislative objectives. That Party has now been returned to power with a sizable majority, and it is reasonable to conclude that the great majority of the people have voted in favour of enactment of this reform measure.

> (Ray 1952: 275)

In the course of the same article, she marshalled a variety of arguments in support of the Hindu Code Bill, including appeal to her version of the Hindu tradition in order to justify changes in Hindu personal law.[10]

Renuka Ray began this article by drawing attention to what she considered 'a paradox' (Ray 1952: 268) which was that women's political rights were far in advance of their social rights. She noted with approval that 'the women of India seem to be finding their rightful place [in civic and national affairs] with . . . ease and rapidity' while deploring the fact that 'there still exist laws and social customs which are inequitable and impediments to women's progress' (Ray 1952: 268). It was women's poor social position which concerned her and led her to endorse a legislative remedy in the form of the Hindu Code Bill. Declaring that the bill was 'designed to equalise the social laws of marriage and property between men and women for the vast majority of Indians who are guided by Hindu law', she nevertheless minimised the extent and profundity of the changes proposed by labelling it 'a mild reform measure' (Ray 1952: 269, 277). Consistent with this apparently modest and moderate ambition, she intimated that the bill's major function was not to revolutionise Hindu personal law and commented that, where modifications were required to take account of contemporary conditions, these modifications were justified by early Hindu scripture or by laws in force in different regions of India. She wrote:

> The Bill, which has been so long on the anvil of the legislature, seeks in the main to achieve unification and codification of the Hindu social laws of marriage, property, guardianship and adoption. Apart from this, it introduces certain provisions which are necessary to adapt the laws to the changed social outlook of the present day. These changes derive their sanction from ancient Hindu texts or from progressive laws existing in some parts of the country.
>
> (Ray 1952: 274–5)

Among the evidence adduced to corroborate her statement that there were indigenous precedents for reform, she cited an early Hindu scripture which allowed divorce in some situations and preferential property rights for women under laws in force in Bombay. Moreover, her discussion of the Hindu Code Bill contrasted early equality with later inequality between men and women.

Renuka Ray portrayed the Vedic and Epic periods in such a way as to sketch a process of degeneration in the status and image of women originating in the teaching of *Manu's Dharmaśāstra* which banned women from receiving *upanayana*, the *saṃskāra* or sacrament of initiation.[11] She stated that 'in the remote past of the Vedic and Epic ages, women enjoyed a position of social equality with men' (Ray 1952: 269), substantiating this statement by providing a favourable account of ancient India as a time when women exercised important religious roles, and excelled in various activities and occupations. According to her, the teaching of *Manu's Dharmaśāstra* on women's ineligibility for investiture with the sacred thread was to blame for subsequent developments which were to the detriment of women, both socially and legally. She observed:

It is a generally accepted fact that women once participated in public life and enjoyed a position of social equality with men. Their spiritual disfranchisement came at the time of Manu, the law-giver who placed a taboo upon the participation of women in the Upanayan (or sacred thread) ceremony. Since religion was the basis of society, this prohibition had a tremendous effect upon the status of women in other respects as well, and from that time onwards they gradually lost their position in society. . . . As women's position in society worsened, the process found reflection in the laws.

(Ray 1952: 270)

Her account of these historical developments made particular mention of the deteriorating position of women in respect of property and marriage under Hindu law, thereby classifying 'the old social laws of marriage and property which still operate and impair the position of women in India' (Ray 1952: 269) as degenerations from even older legal standards. Thus, she suggested that a polygynous marriage was afterwards allowed when no son was produced, and not only when a union was childless as had earlier been the rule. She further suggested that *strīdhana*, gifts given to a wife on or after marriage by her family or her husband which were regarded as her personal property and devolved in the female line, had been eroded, but not eradicated. Such an argument was consistent with her portrayal of the Indian women's movement as 'dedicated to the restoration, not the creation, of women's rights' (Ray 1952: 273).

Renuka Ray presented her argument in support of the Hindu Code Bill by contrasting what she represented as the Vedic and Epic norm of the equality of women with what she represented as the norm of inequality established by *Manu's Dharmaśāstra*. She interpreted the proclamation of the religious inequality of women by *Manu's Dharmaśāstra* as effecting a general and progressive decline in their position, which was only worsened by British administration of Hindu law when the 'rights of women suffered curtailment as a result of interpretations and translations offered to British judges by reactionary pandits and priests' (Ray 1952: 270). The insistence of opponents of the Hindu Code Bill that changes in Hindu personal law endangered Hinduism was challenged by reference to what she argued were authentic Hindu beliefs and practices. The Hindu Code Bill was thus regarded as a reinstatement of genuine Hindu ideals and values and recommended as such, despite conflicting claims by opponents of the Hindu Code Bill.

In common with other supporters of the Hindu Code Bill, Renuka Ray defined Hindu law in terms very different from those used by opponents of the Hindu Code Bill (Everett 1981: 177–9). Far from accepting the absolute status of Hindu law as constant in time and consistent in application, she stressed its dynamism and diversity. In her opinion, the dynamism of Hindu law gave rise to the conditions under which 'contrary texts can be cited, as they often are, by reformers on the one hand and by die-hard conservatives on the other to support their own particular arguments' (Ray 1952: 270). Her understanding of the diversity of Hindu law was illustrated in part by reference both to 'the Brahmanical Hindu law . . . which guides the so-called upper classes of society, and the . . . laws observed amongst the lower strata' (Ray 1952: 271). This view of Hindu law contradicted the case made by opponents of the Hindu Code Bill whose opposition was often predicated upon the immutability and invariability of Hindu law.

Notwithstanding, appeal to the Hindu tradition along these lines was probably not Renuka Ray's chosen mode of argument (Levy 1973: 24–6).[12] Hence, in all likelihood, more indicative of her own convictions was appeal to the constitution as 'guaranteeing a position of legally enforceable equality to women' (Ray 1952: 269). This enabled her to declare not only that opponents of the Hindu Code Bill were 'defending iniquitous social laws' but that these laws were 'in direct contravention of the provisions of the Constitution' and so susceptible to legal challenge, whether by individual judgments or by the Hindu Code Bill itself (Ray 1952: 269). There was no doubt that she opted for the legislative rather than judicial route as the more straightforward solution. In this vein, and in relation to 'a rallying of progressive elements', she wrote of the foundation of a Fundamental Rights Organisation 'to acquaint citizens with the fundamental rights accorded them by the Constitution and to prevent violation of these rights', an organisation intended to campaign for the removal of laws which conflicted with the fundamental rights enshrined in the constitution (Ray 1952: 277).

Appeal to the constitution was also more typical of the final stages of the controversy surrounding the Hindu Code Bill when appeal to the Hindu tradition, however defined and deployed, was on the wane (Levy 1973: 499).[13] This was at a time when much of the heat had gone out of the controversy with substantive concessions made to opponents and court decisions favouring the cause of reform (Everett

1981: 187–8). These were not the circumstances in which the Indian women's movement or, indeed, other supporters of the Hindu Code Bill were likely to feel compelled to offer a type of traditional justification of the proposed changes and yet, however unconvincing this case was to those who opposed the bill, the movement had offered such a justification when the debate was at its height in an attempt to meet the religious objections of opponents. Whether, for what end and with what effect to appeal to an interpretation of the Hindu tradition continues to be an issue for the contemporary movement.

CHAPTER SIX

The Contemporary Debate: Activists, Academics and the Hindu Tradition

This chapter examines the contemporary debate concerning the possibility of promoting alternative perspectives on the position of women from within the compass of the Hindu tradition itself. This debate is contextualised in terms of the failure of earlier efforts by independent India to improve the position of women, in the light of which many women were moved to reappraise their methodology. It is shown that there are now a number of activists and academics who argue that the orthodox beliefs and practices which they criticise for condemning women to a subordinate status can be countered without casting aside the Hindu tradition. Some of the suggestions made by commentators for positive, or at least potentially positive, Hindu ideals, pre-Aryan India, heroines such as Sītā and Sāvitrī and the goddess Kālī, are explored in order to establish what these writers see as the prospects for change. Thus, the reasons given for referring to Hindu concepts and characters when stating the case for change are considered.

The Position of Women in Independent India

The constitution of independent India enshrined the principle of equality for all its citizens. The preamble to the constitution included equality as one of the objects it was dedicated to achieving, while equality was also among the fundamental justiciable rights guaranteed by the constitution. Equality was represented as the means whereby both individual dignity and national unity could be fostered, and interpreted as the rejection of discrimination on the grounds of caste, colour, conviction and, indeed, sex. In this and other ways, the constitution pledged independent India to improving the position of women.

In a manner typical of the centralised and bureaucratic mechanisms of state socialism, the government founded a number of agencies and introduced a number of programmes with the express purpose of improving the position of women. Women were active participants in the political life of independent India, universal adult suffrage gave women the vote and women occupied prestigious political offices. Reform of Hindu personal law, though not a uniform civil code, was enacted to enhance women's marital and familial roles. All of this led many to believe that the equality of women, if not yet attained, would be attained in due course as the measures already taken eventually bore fruit.

There was no recognition that there might be a chasm between the constitutional principle of women's equality and the unequal condition of women. The agencies and the programmes which the government had established to ensure women's equality were assumed to be effective and expedient. Questions were not asked about the nature or scope of women's political participation nor about the viability and applicability of legislative measures to enhance women's marital and familial roles. There was no sense that further action was necessary to make certain that women did enjoy the equality which had been promised to them. However, these comfortable and complacent notions of the inevitability of progress and the redundancy of activism were challenged by a report commissioned by the government in response to a request from the United Nations for International Women's Year which was to be held in 1975.

This report, entitled *Towards Equality*, highlighted by the interest and publicity surrounding the United Nations' International Women's Year and the Decade for Women which it inaugurated, was issued in May 1975 immediately before the State of Emergency was proclaimed. *Towards Equality* demonstrated that change, commensurate with the constitutional commitment to equality and in conformity with the stated aim of government agencies and programmes, had not taken place. It also indicated that the political and social rights theoretically enjoyed by women were in practice the preserve of a few; so far as the vast majority of women were concerned, these provisions made little, if any, impression on their lives. What was more, the report recognised the importance, though not paramount importance, of religion in determining the position of women.

The Committee on the Status of Women in India which produced *Towards Equality* was constituted by the Ministry of Education and Social Welfare in 1971. Members of the committee defined their terms of reference as designating three main areas of investigation, these being:

(a) To assess the impact of the constitutional, legal and administrative provisions on the social status of women, their education and employment particularly in the rural sector during the last two decades;

(b) to examine the status of women in the changing social pattern; and

(c) to suggest remedial and other measures in the fields of law, education, employment, population policy etc., "which would enable women to play their full and proper role in building up the nation."

(CSWI 1974: 1)

In so doing, the committee wrote a report which was a damning indictment of the present position of women, pointing not only to a lack of progress towards equality but even to a worsening of conditions in certain respects.

In the chapter on 'The Socio-Cultural Setting of Women's Status', the report gave an account of the part played by religion in influencing the position of women. The report identified religion as providing a philosophical and ethical rationale of women's place, showing how society's attitudes to women were informed by religious understandings of women's qualities and attributes. It explained:

Religion provides ideological amd [*sic*] moral bases for the accorded status and institutionalised roles of women in a society. The social restrictions on women and also the people's notions about their proper roles in the domestic and extra-domestic spheres, are largely derived from the religious conceptions of a woman's basic characteristics, her assumed "virtues" and "vices", her proverbial strengths and weaknesses, and the stereotypes regarding her nature and capacities.

(CSWI 1974: 38)

The report's treatment of the Hindu tradition contrasted two different images of women, the one of purity and power, the other of dependence and debility. The report related the story of a holy woman who dedicated herself to the practice of austerities, only to be told that as an unmarried woman she could not go to heaven. The woman's solution was to promise to give half of the merit she had earned by her asceticism to the man who consented to marry her and so she was able to find a husband and hence go to heaven. This story was told to illustrate the insistence on being married. However, the report also referred to the Bhakti movement which it cited as a devotional discipline offering comfort and consolation to women, an alternative lifestyle in which they could be considered as saints. Despite this ambivalent reading of the Hindu tradition which recognised something of the complexity and diversity of its teaching about women, the report regarded religion as a factor which, together with familial responsibilities and cultural ideals, excluded women from involvement in the public arena and prevented them from making the most of their talents. It claimed:

Religion, family and kinship roles, and cultural norms delimiting the spheres of women's activities obstruct their full and equal participation in the life of the society and achievement of their full potential.

(CSWI 1974: 37)

Consequently, in summarising its findings on the social and cultural context of the position of women, the report represented religion and other related influences as militating against the achievement of equality.

The report was critical of the disparity between constitutional pledges on women's equality and their actual inequality which it documented in some detail. It was also critical of the failure to create a new consensus in favour of women's equality and set up a new organisational structure to put this equality into effect. Its conclusion was:

The reviews of the disabilities and constraints on women which stem from socio-cultural institutions, indicates that the majority of women are still very far from enjoying the rights and opportunities guaranteed to them by the Constitution. Society has not yet succeeeded in framing the required norms or institutions to enable women to fulfil the multiple roles that they are expected to play in India today.

(CSWI 1974: 101)

Moreover, the report declared that there was greater inequality between men and women as measured by specific indices, in which respect it mentioned dowry, while it lamented the reversal of the standards of the nationalist struggle, maintaining that there had been a loss of interest in and sympathy for women's issues.

On the subject of the political position of women, the report accepted that women were playing a bigger part in politics but did not detect any significant change accompanying women's inclusion in politics. It attributed this to the lack of effort put into raising women's political awareness. It characterised political parties as chauvinistic since their predominantly male membership subscribed to prevailing views about women. Accordingly, it made clear that the political parties considered women to be electors who would cast their votes as their male relations commanded. As it related:

> The structures of the parties make them male dominated in spite of outstanding exception, most party men are not free from the general prejudices and attitudes of the society. They have tended to see the women voters and citizens as appendages of the males and have depended on the heads of families to provide block-votes and support for their parties and candidates.
>
> (CSWI 1974: 301)

This situation was one in which, as the report stressed, some women had the opportunity to hold high office but most women were left without advocates for their advancement who could influence public policy. The same analysis of the manner in which most women had not in fact benefited from independent India's egalitarianism was evident in the report's discussion of legal measures to ameliorate the social position of women. In this respect, the report emphasised that most women had no knowledge of their entitlements in law, noting:

> The social laws that sought to mitigate the problems of women in their family life have remained unknown to a large mass of women in this country, who are as ignorant of their legal rights as they were before independence.
>
> (CSWI 1974: 250)

Lacking even this knowledge, they were unequipped and unprepared to seek redress for any violation or infringement of their legal entitlements.

Indeed, the report evaluated dependence on the law as an engine of change. It noted that dependence on the law to eradicate inequality was typical of ex-imperial possessions, and that independent India's leaders had espoused women's equality. Referring to the idea that a nation's laws were an expression of its principles and quoting a statement that the treatment of women was an indicator of a nation's progress, the report reiterated the imperative to ensure both the enactment and the enforcement of legislation, commenting:

> If legislation reflects the social values of a country "the degree of women's emancipation is the natural measure of the general emancipation in any given society". It is, therefore, necessary not only to legislate but to see that it is implemented.
>
> (CSWI 1974: 103–4)

It was in posing this problem, how to translate legal equality into real equality, that the report envisaged a role for other groups in working towards equality.

Certainly, the report envisaged women's organisations making a valuable contribution. It acknowledged that it would take time to change the social climate although arguing that change could be expedited by adopting a planned approach. It saw the need for a partnership between the state and the wider community, chiefly those citizens who supported the cause of women's equality. Thus it appealed to community organisations, including and especially women's organisations, to help bring about a consciousness of women's concerns within wider society. In addition, it appealed to community organisations to reinforce the agitation against practices such as plural marriage, dowry, lavish marriage ceremonies and child marriage and also to publicise what rights women already had in law. Hence the committee members' exhortation:

> We . . . urge that community organisations, particularly women's organisations, should mobilise public opinion and strengthen social efforts against oppressive institutions like polygamy, dowry, ostentatious expenditure on weddings and child marriage and mount a campaign for the dissemination of information about the legal rights of women to increase their awareness.
>
> (CSWI 1974: 101)

In this way, it represented these attempts to achieve women's equality as the common duty of community organisations and government, the legislative and the executive branches.

It would be difficult to overestimate the impact of *Towards Equality*. It was greeted with great dismay and disillusionment because it demonstrated that women's equality was as far off as, or even farther off than, ever. Yet as well as exposing the inequality of women, notwithstanding a rhetoric of equality, *Towards Equality* was also a clarion call to action and inspired new endeavours to achieve this end. Indeed, *Towards Equality* has been described as a cause of the resurgence of the women's movement.[1] Another cause of the resurgence was primarily economic. It was popular protest against poverty and exploitation in which both urban working class and rural peasant women were involved. This occurred at a time when the Indian economy was weak, inflation was high and other issues relating to subsistence, such as the adulteration of food and the concentration of land ownership, were pressing. These conditions prompted a rise in agitation (Desai n.d.: 13–16).

However, this resurgence was interrupted by Indira Gandhi's proclamation of a State of Emergency in 1975. The early 1970s were troubled and turbulent years for India. Disaffection with Indira Gandhi's regime was growing, charges of corruption and incompetence were levelled against her administration while her style of government was denounced as autocratic and dictatorial. Her decision to proclaim a State of Emergency was, though, precipitated by a High Court ruling against her for electoral malpractice. The Emergency involved the systematic violation of human rights and infringement of civil liberties. Under its provisions, unrest was controlled and contained. When the Emergency was lifted, discontent which had been so brutally repressed finally erupted and overflowed. For women, as for other groups with grievances about their position in independent India, the Emergency imposed restrictions on their activities so that the reappearance of these activities was even more marked once those restrictions no longer applied and the political situation returned to normal.

Of course, women's organisations of longer-standing were still in existence in independent India but, for various reasons, by the last quarter of the twentieth century they were no longer able to offer leadership for the women's cause.[2] What was clear was that these older women's organisations were not in fact challenging the position of women in independent India, irrespective of the ameliorative impact of their work. Moreover, in so far as these organisations set about catering to traditional interests and concerns, notably feminine beauty and family life, they confirmed stereotypical roles and responsibilities. For example, in the case of the All India Women's Conference which was the most important and influential of these organisations, although it continued to function it had largely relinquished its radical credentials. Its espousal of a moderate rather than a militant agenda was explicable in terms of both internal developments and external links. Internally, the All India Women's Conference had become institutionalised and bureaucratised with an orientation towards the welfare of women and children for whom it provided social, educational and medical services. Externally, the All India Women's Conference was part of the new establishment and was not sufficiently independent to make constructive criticism of the government with which it was so closely associated. Given that the All India Women's Conference had previously been the premier women's organisation, its changed role revealed the extent to which it had ceded the initiative. Thus, even if it was capable of responding to the new spirit of radicalism which characterised the post-Emergency period, this once pioneering women's organisation was not proactive but reactive in approach. None of the older women's organisations were now in the forefront of the women's movement or on the leading edge of feminist thought and action. Despite making a valuable contribution in some areas and despite lending their support to campaigns on certain issues, leadership passed from these older organisations to the newer organisations which proliferated from the mid-1970s onwards.

The Contemporary Debate and the Hindu Tradition

One of the major features of the resurgent women's movement is debate about the nature and impact of the Hindu tradition. Many women have been scathing in their censure of the conventional code of conduct for women which they connect, implicitly or explicitly, with the Hindu tradition. Hence Saroj Vasaria, a correspondent to the feminist journal, *Manushi*, emphasises the way in which women are subjugated by the standards applied to them and contrasts the positive epithets with the negative reality which they so misrepresent. She writes:

> The ideals, ethics and morality heaped on women since time immemorial are suffocating and killing. They [sic] adjectives used to praise us have become oppressive. Calling us loving, they have locked us in the closed room of culture, calling us gentle, they have reflected us in a mirror of helplessness, calling us kind, they have tied us in cowardice, they have handcuffed us with modesty and chained our feet with loyalty, so that far from running, we have not been able even to walk . . .

> (Vasaria 1984: 298–9)

154

Renouncing the oft-accepted foci of identification for women, she states that 'our exclusion from the scriptures, from temples, from *smritis*, is also our strength' and that 'we can be fearless since we have no models', she suggests that women are 'Saritas, flowing, free' and 'Manushis, singers of liberation' (Vasaria 1984: 299). Yet women's rejection of the Hindu tradition is frequently informed and inspired by different ideologies both secular such as Marxism and religious such as Buddhism.[3]

For instance, in its draft manifesto the Progressive Organization of Women gives a classic Marxist analysis of the origin of women's inequality. This inequality is attributed to economic causes though is then justified in other terms, with the explanation that 'the centuries-old economic dependence on man is the base for all sexual, cultural and political domination' (POW 1974). In turn, economic dependence is traced to the division of labour between the sexes which means that 'women have been, for centuries, isolated in the home, forced to carry out work that is considered unskilled' (POW 1974). In order to justify this inequality, 'an impressive number of theories have been designed and implemented to keep women "in their place"' (POW 1974). The remedy for this was, therefore, for women to become financially independent of their spouses and for household tasks to be shared by husbands and wives. Further, 'along with the base of economic dependence and private work at home, the superstructure of male dominance should also be destroyed', in which respect socialism is recommended because it 'will also create the necessary and genuine climate for the equality of women' (POW 1974). From the perspective of the Progressive Organization of Women, the Hindu tradition can only be part of the 'feudal culture' which justifies the 'age-old oppression' of women (POW 1974).

Unlike the Progressive Organization of Women which relegates religion to a secondary status derivative of and determined by the means of production, the Mahila Samta Sainik Dal (League of Women Soldiers for Equality) regards religion as primary. Arguing in its manifesto that 'the social structure of India has been based from the beginning on inequality' and that 'it is the custom here to nourish this slavery under the name of religion', the Mahila Samta Sainik Dal states that 'it is this religion which has enslaved women' (MSSD 1976). The religion in question is clearly the Hindu tradition as evinced by the exhortation 'to fight against the thoughts of Manu which treat women . . . as inferior, against the caste system which sticks the label of *karma* on everything, against god who puts woman among the untouchables' (MSSD 1976). For this group, however, another religion, Buddhism, is espoused as the means of opposing the inequality which is believed to be essential to the Hindu tradition. The claim is made that 'Buddha, the great one, was the first to free women from slavery', declaring that 'Lord Buddha is the commander of this fight' for women's equality (MSSD 1976).

For very different reasons, neither the Progressive Organization of Women nor the Mahila Samta Sainik Dal consider restating the Hindu tradition to be a viable option for improving the position of women. The adoption of this critical stance towards the Hindu tradition, rejecting it entirely and unreservedly, is typical of the tenor of many of the newer women's organisations which emerged from the mid-1970s within 'a new atmosphere of cultural radicalism that had been absent for most of the preindependence movement women's leaders, who had tended to insist on their own "Hindu" roots' (Omvedt 1993: 83). Yet while this continues to be a significant strand of thought, there is also another strand, gaining ground during the 1980s, which sees some value in the Hindu tradition once restated. This alternative approach makes 'the attempt to re-appropriate traditionally accepted women's spaces . . . through attempts to re-interpret myths, epics and folktales' (Kumar 1993: 145). Some insight into the nature and implications of such a process of reinterpretation can be gained by scrutinising contemporary examples of, and arguments for, referring to Hindu concepts and characters, viz. pre-Aryan India, heroines such as Sītā and Sāvitrī and the goddess Kālī.

Pre-Aryan India

In *India's Woman Power*, Tara Ali Baig, a writer on women's issues, biographer of eminent women and social worker with a special interest in child welfare, appeals to pre-Aryan India as a model for improving the position of women. She condemns patriarchal Aryan India as the source of male domination and commends matriarchal pre-Aryan India as the springboard for change in contemporary conditions. In her version of events in ancient India, she presents a picture of Aryan tribes sweeping into the sub-continent where the pre-Aryans had already established a civilisation. She characterises the invading Aryans as nomadic and pastoral, the indigenous pre-Aryans as settled and agricultural, explaining that their distinctive lifestyles derived from the different heritages of hunting, in the case of the Aryans, and husbandry, in the case of the pre-Aryans. Eventually, according to her, the interaction of the invading Aryans with the indigenous pre-Aryan people gave rise to a hierarchical social system, 'the lower elements being the darker, vanquished races and the upper elements the Aryans with their layered arrogance of patriarchal superiority' (Baig 1976: 8). Her evidence for this reconstruction in what she acknowledges to be the absence of 'writers or writing stemming from pre-Vedic times' is 'the discovery of the Indus Valley Civilisation in the 20th century' (Baig 1976: 4).

Tara Ali Baig's theory of religious and social developments compares 'the earth cultures', with which she aligns the pre-Aryans, and 'the northerly hunter cultures', with which she aligns the Aryans, in terms of the deities worshipped and the position of women (Baig 1976: 4). Describing the religion of 'the earth cultures', she asserts 'tilling the soil was the beginning of the Earth Goddess cult', whereas describing the religion of 'the . . . hunter cultures', she asserts 'Gods must have grown out of perennial terror which may account for the fearsome, vindictive nature of those early gods' (Baig 1976: 4, 6). Describing the society of 'the earth cultures', she asserts 'men and women worked the soil together to reap her blessings and bounty', whereas describing the society of 'the . . . hunter cultures', she asserts woman 'was . . . not only his [man's] dependent, but his "helper"; an automatic subordinate' (Baig 1976: 4, 6). Furthermore, she correlates the worship of the Goddess with a favourable position of women in 'the earth cultures' and correlates the worship of gods with an unfavourable position of women in 'the . . . hunter cultures'. Of 'the earth cultures', she declares:

> It is only in the Mother Goddess belt or that of the Earth Mother, that maleness has not been glorified above femaleness. In these geographical regions there is really no such thing as the *dominant* male, but rather a reasonable biological acceptance of the difference which gives man and woman clear-cut earthly functions.
>
> (Baig 1976: 5)

Of 'the . . . hunter cultures', she declares:

> Women or Goddesses did not feature in such a world. Women were the helpers, the gentle ones, frail and needing protection. They gave their bodies and their humble services to pay for the food man provided.
>
> (Baig 1976: 6)

Accordingly, she relates that 'the transition from the earth-mother, matriarchal to patriarchal societies probably took place over a long period of time under the Aryan impact' (Baig 1976: 61).

Thus, Tara Ali Baig's portrait of the pre-Aryans stresses a Goddess-oriented religion and a woman-centred society. In the pantheon of this Goddess-oriented religion she nevertheless includes a God, Śiva, whose cult she detects 'in an elementary form in the Indus Valley culture' (Baig 1976: 5). Calling Śiva 'the oldest known deity in India' and sketching his subsequent career in which he was identified with the Aryan god, Rudra, and ultimately linked with Brahmā and Viṣṇu as a member of the *trimūrti*, she locates him in the context of pre-Aryan spirituality when commenting 'Siva's earliest consort was probably, the Mother Goddess' (Baig 1976: 5). Referring to this Goddess-oriented religion, she maintains:

> Fertility was the perennial miracle. Life came from food. Food came from soil, man came from woman, woman gave life. It is not astonishing that god was a woman. She was the earth, strong and sustaining; she was worshipped. In turn, earthly woman, basking in the relevance of her existence, helped with the reaping, bore children, served and stored, preserving food and tradition alike.
>
> (Baig 1976: 7–8)

Moreover, when she considers how to improve the position of women, she appeals to this woman-centred society which, in different places, she labels 'probably matriarchal' and 'possibly matriarchal' (Baig 1976: 4, 6), affirming:

> The answer to justice for the women of India must, it seems, comes [*sic*] out of our ancient partnership of the soil, a return to the values of the Earth Mother and an end of the Aryan glorification of the male.
>
> (Baig 1976: 29)

In this way, she resists the tendency to portray 'the Vedic past [as] a period of feminine glory and, inevitably, also of masculine sagacity and liberalism' (Baig 1976: 3). On the contrary, she blames 'Aryan paternalism' for causing the position of women to deteriorate until 'the patriarchal pattern was completely entrenched' (Baig 1976: 4, 9).

Narrating how, 'once the Aryans were in full possession of India', their pre-eminence produced 'a patriarchal society and a layered social system, the law and the castes, with men in safe control of divinity and the mysteries through the Brahmins' (Baig 1976: 61), Tara Ali Baig's depiction of Indian society and religion under Aryan hegemony is diametrically opposed to her depiction of pre-Aryan society and religion. However, in the course of her account of Aryan influence on the position of women, she expresses the opinion that 'women quietly retreated to an apparently secondary and inferior position' (Baig 1976: 61). This statement, suggesting as it does that – in spite of the oppresssive power exerted by the Aryans – women were still in some sense neither secondary nor inferior, enables her to identify religious concepts in which pre-Aryan ideas later resurfaced. In this regard, she mentions Tantra 'dominated by the concept of the Mother of the Universe and the principle of Primal Energy' as an instance of how women 'in their matriarchal guise began to re-assert their power' (Baig 1976: 9). Whatever the subversive possibilities of Tantra, she does admit that 'the Tantric cult served only to transform and not alter' the patriarchal religion of the Aryans which 'laid down in unequivocal terms the duties and scope of life for women' (Baig 1976: 9). Yet notwithstanding, she attaches great significance to the pre-Aryan influence over India, especially in relation to the women's movement. This is evident in her explanation of what she interprets as the contrasting nature of the women's movement in the West and in India. In her view, the difficulties faced by women in the West are a legacy of the Aryan exclusion of women from the hunt whereas the pre-Aryan belief in the divine feminine gives Indian women a considerable advantage over their western counterparts. She remarks on the likelihood 'that the struggle of women against men that has characterised western society . . . stemmed from the simple fact that centuries ago women did not share in the hunt' (Baig 1976: 6). In India, though, where women have 'knowledge of . . . the power of the female principle' which she traces back to pre-Aryan times, she claims women 'did not have to fight suffragette and militant battles as women have done in other parts of the world' (Baig 1976: 65). Clearly, for her, pre-Aryan India retains its relevance.

Tara Ali Baig's picture of pre-Aryan India is predicated upon archaeological excavations during the 1920s which revealed the existence of an advanced literate urban culture named the Indus Valley Civilisation after the location of the earliest sites to be unearthed. A number of theories were advanced to interpret these finds, including the relation with the Aryans and the character of its religion.[4] Sir Mortimer Wheeler advanced the theory that the Indus Valley Civilisation had been destroyed by the incoming Aryans on the basis of skeletons found in Mohenjodaro, interpreted as victims of Aryan aggression, and Vedic references to the god, Indra, as the destroyer of forts, interpreted as records of the conquest of the fortified cities of the pre-Aryans. Sir John Marshall advanced the theory that the citizens of the Indus Valley Civilisation had worshipped a Goddess on the basis of terracotta figurines of the female form, naked or but scantily-clad, sometimes wearing jewellery and often a fan-shaped headdress, interpreted as statues of the Great Mother. Though these theories came to be influential, even by the time that Tara Ali Baig authored the book wherein she makes her appeal to pre-Aryan India, they had been the subjects of scholarly debate which has, if anything, intensified since then.[5] It is now widely accepted that the Aryans were not responsible for bringing the Indus Valley Civilisation to a violent end because the civilisation continued to flourish in more southerly regions with its eventual demise blamed on ecological and/or economic factors rather than military defeat. There is still a wide measure of agreement on the idea of Goddess worship, indeed, arguably wider agreement than previously as the earlier identification of Śiva in his manifestation as *Paśupati*, Lord of Animals, on a seal has been questioned and instead variously associated with a Goddess. Yet, as with all material remains where no other sources of information are available, any reconstruction is necessarily tentative and, in these circumstances, can be criticised for reading back into the Indus Valley Civilisation the more familiar features of the later Hindu tradition. So far as a Goddess is concerned, then, questions have been asked about whether the figurines have any religious importance and, if so, whether they were merely fertility symbols of a household or domestic cult.

Furthermore, even if it is conceded that the religion of the Indus Valley Civilisation was Goddess-oriented, the connection between this and a woman-centred society is unclear, albeit often asserted.[6] Hence, irrespective of the frequent insistence that where a Goddess is worshipped, women enjoy a favourable position, the conclusion that the Indus Valley Civilisation had a matriarchal society on the grounds of conjecture that its religion was focused on a Goddess is highly speculative to say the least.

Tara Ali Baig's appeal to the concept of pre-Aryan India demonstrates one way in which the Hindu tradition can be restated, in this case both extending the scope of that tradition by positing some continuity between the pre-Aryan and Aryan periods and explaining its character by attributing ambivalent attitudes towards women to the different norms of the pre-Aryans and Aryans. This dichotomy allows her to offer an ancient and indigenous model for change with considerable latitude for reinterpreting the past. However, given her emphasis on motherhood on the human level as on the divine and her over-riding concern with family life, perhaps her approach is far from radical.

Heroines such as Sītā and Sāvitrī

Suma Chitnis and Madhu Kishwar both advocate appeal to heroines such as Sītā and Sāvitrī. Neither accept the conventional feminine values and virtues, constancy and loyalty, chastity and faithfulness, with which these heroines, commonly characterised as perfect wives, are associated. However, neither recommend rejection of these heroines who occupy a special position in the Hindu imagination and consciousness but rather recommend reimaging these heroines in the light of their meaning and importance for women. This strategy seeks to recast these heroines through coming to a new appreciation of them and the esteem which they enjoy, thereby redefining the role models for women.

In 'Feminism: Indian Ethos and Indian Convictions', Suma Chitnis, Head of the Unit for Women's Studies at the Tata Institute of Social Services, rehearses some of the reasons why the position of women is so adverse. She differentiates between those causes which 'are visibly responsible for the poor status of women in India', social, political and economic, and 'the value system by which women abide', describing the latter as 'the greatest obstacle to change in the directions [*sic*] of equality' (Chitnis 1988: 90). Explaining what she means by this value system, she comments on the way in which honour for their male relations, especially their husbands, is instilled in women:

> Women are conditioned to revere the father, and to serve the husband as a devotee serves God. Devotion to the husband is cultivated among girls of all religions, but it is particularly idealized and firmly institutionalised in the Hindu concept of *pativrata*.
>
> (Chitnis 1988: 90)

The *pativratā* ideal thus constitutes the proper conduct of a wife towards her husband which she defines as the conduct of 'a wife who has accepted service and devotion to the husband, and his family, as her ultimate religion and duty' (Chitnis 1988: 90). She illustrates the *pativratā* ideal, 'romanticized through legend, folklore and folksong, and reaffirmed through ceremonies of different kinds' (Chitnis 1988: 90), by relating the stories of Sītā and Sāvitrī as exemplary wives. She points out that they 'exhibit sharp wit, intelligence, resourcefulness, tenacity and affection' though as she makes clear 'these qualities have never been held up for emulation' (Chitnis 1988: 91). Summarising the conventional teaching on women derived from and developed in relation to the stories of Sītā and Sāvitrī, she concludes 'tradition has only emphasized women's self-immolation' (Chitnis 1988: 91).

The significance of this for Suma Chitnis is that it is the value system, demanding of women their submission and subjugation, which prevents women from taking advantage of their entitlements under the law and constitution. Since, according to her, the priority is not to achieve new rights but to ensure that women's existing rights are translated into reality, she concentrates on the issue of how to raise consciousness about the position of women. Here she suggests that Sītā and Sāvitrī can play a part. She allows that the dominant message of tradition has been oppressive towards women but asserts that some aspects can be constructively appropriated and applied in the cause of women's equality. Among such aspects, she singles out those traits of Sītā and Sāvitrī, heretofore neglected, to which she has already drawn attention, arguing:

> Although Indian tradition has for the major part encouraged the subservience of women, applauded their self-effacement, and thus promoted their subjection, it contains several elements that can be developed towards establishing equality for women and towards a new assertion of the full dignity of their personhood. It is important that Indian feminism grasps firmly at these elements as features to build upon. For instance, feminists could work towards building new attitudes among women by highlighting the spiritedness, the intelligence and the resourcefulness of figures like Sita and Savitri.
>
> (Chitnis 1988: 91)

The stories of Sītā and Sāvitrī are cited simply as examples of how tradition can be restated. Elaborating on this, the way in which a new value system supportive of women's equality can be popularised, she warns of the consequences of feminists cutting themselves off from the means whereby they can convince people of the legitimacy of their cause:

They [feminists] must give conscious and careful thought to how folklore, folksongs, epics and age-old models of virtuous womanhood can be bent to speak for the new value system. Feminists tend to turn away from traditional images, and in the process snap vital links of communication with the masses . . .

(Chitnis 1988: 92)

Suma Chitnis, therefore, approves the approach of reimaging Sītā and Sāvitrī and hence redefining the role models for women.

Similarly, Madhu Kishwar makes a persuasive case for this approach in her introduction to an anthology of contributions to the journal she edits entitled *In Search of Answers: Indian Women's Voices from Manushi*. She does so when urging that 'there has to be a total and consistent struggle against the ideology of subservience, and the varied ways in which it has been woven into the very fabric of our life' (Kishwar 1984: 45–6). The importance she attaches to this is clear in her statement that 'the struggle against oppressive cultural values' is a vital component of the 'struggle to challenge the current power relations between men and women' (Kishwar 1984: 46). In order to confront what she calls 'the culture of women's subservience in India', she indicates that it is necessary to find the fundamental basis of this culture, the 'common underlying . . . sources of discrimination against women' which give rise to many different forms of misogyny (Kishwar 1984: 46). Discussing the fundamental basis of this culture, she describes the conventional concept of self-sacrificing femininity upheld by invoking heroines such as Sītā and Sāvitrī which, she stresses, exerts a profound hold over women:

The pervasive popular cultural ideal of womanhood has become a death trap for too many of us. It is woman as a selfless giver, someone who gives and gives endlessly, gracefully, smilingly, whatever the demand, however unreasonable and however harmful to herself. She gives not just love, affection and ungrudging service but also, if need be, her health and ultimately her life at the altar of her duty to her husband, children and the rest of her family. Sita, Savitri, . . . and various other mythological heroines are used as the archetypes of such a woman and women themselves are deeply influenced by this cultural ideal.

(Kishwar 1984: 46)

Yet she contends that efforts to overcome the conventional concept of femininity have failed because they are expressed in terms of an alien outlook which estranges the audience that it must address in order to be successful. This leads her to advise that consideration be given to the ways in which women are inspired by traditional icons, hence she claims:

> Those of us who wish to combat or reject these ideals have, however, been largely ineffective because we tend to do so from a totally "Western, modernist" standpoint. The tendency is to make people feel that they are backward and stupid to hold values that need to be rejected outright. We must learn to begin with more respect for traditions which people hold dear. We have to make the effort to develop an understanding of why these images of Indian women have such power over the minds and hearts of women themselves.
>
> (Kishwar 1984: 46)

In these circumstances, she declares that it is vital 'to begin to separate the devastating aspects from the points of strength within the cultural traditions, and start using the strengths to transform the traditions' (Kishwar 1984: 46).

Madhu Kishwar examines 'the ideal of the self-effacing woman', explaining that this ideal 'is attractive to women not because most women are masochists but because most human beings do aspire to live lives which go beyond individual self-seeking and narrow calculations about returning favour for favour' (Kishwar 1984: 46). She allows that this attitude is not inevitably damaging to women as long as there is a spirit of mutuality between the sexes whereas, according to her, it is damaging where women alone are expected always to put the welfare of others before their own. Such unconditional concern for others can, in her view, all too easily lead to the exploitation of women, especially since 'a woman's supreme virtue is supposed to reside in total and unquestioning obedience, even to the most outrageous of her husband's whims, however she may be harmed as a consequence' (Kishwar 1984: 46). Thus it is that she blames cultural norms rather than physical abuses for women's ills, declaring that 'this ideology of slavery and contempt for women in the family plays a more important part than even beatings or bullets in keeping women oppressed' (Kishwar 1984: 46–7). For this reason, she regards it as imperative to reinterpret inherited tradition as, indeed, Mahatma Gandhi had done.

164

Madhu Kishwar praises Gandhi as 'one of the few people able to make a creative use of our powerful cultural traditions' (Kishwar 1984: 47). She admires Gandhi for his capacity 'to inspire people to perform difficult contemporary tasks, using age-old symbols' (Kishwar 1984: 47). One of these symbols was Sītā and she shows how Gandhi's characterisation of Sītā differs from other characterisations of her. In this respect, she contrasts a modern westernised perspective on Sītā as 'the hallmark of women's subservience' with Gandhi's perspective on Sītā for whom she 'is not the self-effacing, fire-ordeal facing Sita' but one whose chastity has an autonomous and forceful quality which compels men to respect her modesty and whose plain and unadorned dress in exile is a prototype of swadeshī (Kishwar 1984: 47).[7] She continues by maintaining that tradition does have features favourable to women. These, she states, must be exploited in order to counter the adverse aspects of tradition as, in her opinion, this selective and sympathetic reworking of such tradition diminishes the difficulty of dealing with the problems posed by conservative and chauvinist teaching:

> Our cultural traditions have tremendous potential within them to combat reactionary and anti-women ideas, if we can identify their points of strength and use them creatively. The rejection of the harmful is then made much easier than attempts to overthrow traditions totally or to attack them arrogantly from outside, as most of us Westernized modernists tend to do, since we have been completely alienated from our own culture and the people who hold it dear.
>
> (Kishwar 1984: 47)

She concludes her account by reiterating the importance of reinterpreting tradition for improving the position of women, insisting that 'if we fail to acknowledge and help reinvigorate the deeply humane portions of our heritage, none of our other efforts are likely to succeed' (Kishwar 1984: 47). Madhu Kishwar thus also approves of the approach of reimaging heroines and hence redefining the role models for women.

In a later article published in *Manushi*, 'Yes to Sita, No to Ram! The Continuing Popularity of Sita in India', Madhu Kishwar takes up the challenge she herself set by exploring the esteem for Sītā and, in so doing, gives an example of how her story has already been used to improve the position of women. She indicates that 'self-effacing devotion and loyalty . . . have become the hallmark of the modern day stereotype of Sita' (Kishwar 1997: 20). Acknowledging that 'the Sita image . . . lends itself to diverse appeals', she attributes to this its 'sway over the minds of the people of India over the centuries' (Kishwar 1997: 20), referring to research on who is seen to be the ideal woman where the vast majority of respondents nominated Sītā. Reflecting on her own beliefs about Sītā, she relates that she 'grew up thinking of Sita as a much wronged woman – a slavish wife without a mind of her own', explaining that 'for that reason she was not for me a symbol of inspiration, but a warning' (Kishwar 1997: 20). Her involvement with *Manushi*, however, brought home to her that her own experience in which Sītā 'did not seem an important reference point – positive or negative – in my life' (Kishwar 1997: 20) was not representative of the experience of many other women. For many other women, she then discovered, 'Sita was the point of reference – an ideal they emulated or rejected' (Kishwar 1997: 21), prompting her to further investigate Sītā's significance. What emerges from her investigations is, as she stresses, a view of Sītā which recognises her moral excellence so 'that Indian women are not endorsing female slavery when they mention Sita as their ideal' (Kishwar 1997: 22). Rather, she reports that Sītā 'is seen as a person whose sense of *dharma* is superior to and more awe inspiring than that of Ram – someone who puts even *maryada purushottam* Ram – the most perfect of men – to shame' (Kishwar 1997: 22).

It was Sītā's moral excellence together with Rāma's mistreatment of her that in Madhu Kishwar's account underwrote Shetkari Sangathana's Lakshmi Mukti programme for women to be given a share in the ownership of family land. She noted that Sharad Joshi, a leader of this organisation, retold Sītā's story, introducing it by reminding his audience of the contribution a farmer's wife makes to her family and remarking that farmers frequently behave towards their wives as badly as Rāma behaved towards Sītā. Thus she demonstrates how this man represented men's transference of land to their wives as the means of ensuring that women would no longer share Sītā's sorry plight. Her judgment on this programme is that Sītā's story had much to do with its impact when implemented. In this programme, Madhu Kishwar clearly sees some proof of the potential of tradition to which she referred in her earlier discussion.

The stories of Sītā and Sāvitrī are communicated through a variety of media, both old and new, including, for instance, song, dance and drama, film and television as well as scripture and religious discourse. While their stories are closely connected with a concept of femininity in which a wife is to defer to her husband's wishes in all things, this does not mean that no other interpretations were offered previously or that no other interpretations are presently possible. In the case of Sītā, though 'her unique standing in the minds of most Hindus, regardless of region, caste, social class, age, sex, education or modernization, testifies to the power and pervasiveness of the traditional ideal of womanhood' (Kakar 1988: 63), alternative representations are extant. For example, the Sītā of the *Adbhuta Rāmāyaṇa* is shown as superior to Rāma and, far from being his submissive and subservient wife, is herself the victor over Rāvaṇa's yet more terrible brother when Rāma lies dead in defeat and subsequently the recipient of her revived husband's praises as the Great Goddess (Grierson 1926). This is an example of an ongoing process of reinterpretation, other examples being Kumaran Asan's 1919 poem 'Chintavishtayya Sita' where Sītā shows the maturity to forgive her husband's faint-heartedness (Chaitanya 1971: 222–5) and, more recently still, Mallika Sarabhai's dance drama called *Sita's Daughters* devised in celebration of Sītā's spirited defiance of her husband's iniquitous behaviour (Lynton 1995: 113–14). These examples of alternative representations of Sītā indicate that, in the past as in the present, the character of Sītā has been restated.

Suma Chitnis' and Madhu Kishwar's advocacy of appeal to heroines such as Sītā and Sāvitrī thus proposes a way in which the Hindu tradition can be restated. They agree about the conventional feminine values and virtues with which heroines such as Sītā and Sāvitrī are associated. They also agree on the ambivalence of the Hindu tradition at least in so far as they attribute to it dimensions other than the dominant one which oppresses women, arguing that these sub-dominant dimensions can be developed to support improvements in the position of women. Clearly, however, this does not exclude there being subtle, if significant, differences between them. Suma Chitnis sees potential in the stories of Sītā and Sāvitrī which has not been exploited in the past; Madhu Kishwar looks to Gandhi for inspiration in reworking the story of Sītā, while her study of Sītā raises interesting issues about how Sītā is understood and by whom as well as illustrating the ability of her story to move not just women but men too.

The Goddess Kālī

In 'Kali, the Savior', Lina Gupta, a lecturer in the Department of Asian Studies at California State University, appeals to the goddess

Kālī as a figure who challenges patriarchy. She seeks to remove what she regards as patriarchal accretions which obscure the figure of Kālī and describes patriarchy as an aberration of the Hindu standard of equality. Accordingly, she compares the status of goddesses with the status of women, deploring the patriarchal annexation and arrogation of goddesses which authorises the inequality of women. Moreover, she detects in Kālī the potential to promote a post-patriarchal Hindu vision. Reflecting on her own upbringing and recalling her realisation of the inequality of women, she regards Kālī as an image and role model of liberation.

Lina Gupta stresses 'that the systematic subjugation of women has often been sanctioned by mythological stories, symbols, and images in world religions' and states that 'feminists have realized the over-whelming need for women to identify personally with positive images and role models' (Gupta 1991: 15, 16). Turning to the Hindu tradition, she identifies Kālī as just such a positive image and role model for women, insisting that the figure of Kālī has to be freed from its patriarchal overlay while drawing upon its insights. She declares:

> I believe that Hinduism does indeed contain a model and image that could be used to fit the needs of today's women, and that this model lies at the very heart of Hinduism itself. This image centers on the goddess Kali and her many manifestations. I also believe this image must be extricated from patriarchal inter-pretations and understandings that have clouded its essential meaning even while tapping into – and using – the many layers of meaning that surround it.
>
> (Gupta 1991: 16)

Fundamental to her argument is the assumption that at heart the Hindu tradition upholds the equality of women and, consequently, that once this truth is reclaimed, the tradition can contribute towards improving the position of women.

Lina Gupta allows that 'though portrayals of female characters in the Hindu epics and the Hindu scriptures . . . appear to depict traditional roles of mothers and wives, deeper egalitarian connotations and religious interpretations of these images and stories have been accepted by many traditional Hindus' (Gupta 1991: 16). This, the distinction she draws between a superficial social reading of the Hindu tradition and a substantial spiritual reading, the former representing women's inequality and the latter recognising their equality, enables her to express the view that 'Hinduism is not inherently patriarchal' even though she admits that 'traditional Hindu life by and large has remained patriarchal' (Gupta 1991: 16). In this vein, she contrasts 'the equality and importance of the goddesses' with 'the lives of women as subservient daughters and wives' (Gupta 1991: 16), neither of which, the prestige of goddesses nor the poor position of women, she believes is in any doubt. Further, on the subject of the relationship between goddesses and women, she contends that the goddesses have been pressed into the service of patriarchal ideology in order to justify the subordination of women. She comments:

> It seems to me that patriarchal understanding has appropriated the goddesses and the feminine aspects of the Ultimate Reality at the heart of Hinduism in ways that sanction the unequal treatment of women.
>
> (Gupta 1991:16)

So it is that 'in the absence of a clearly or totally patriarchal tradition', she is prepared to consider 'the question of a post-patriarchal version of Hinduism', in which connection she cites Kālī (Gupta 1991: 16). She emphasises that she is not referring to the goddess 'as she has been understood through patriarchy', rather she is referring to the goddess 'in her deepest and most essential meaning', observing that 'in getting to the deepest meaning of the goddess, we approach more completely the central meanings of scriptural Hinduism itself' (Gupta 1991: 16).

It is to her upbringing as a Hindu that Lina Gupta ascribes her argument concerning Kālī. She recounts worship of Kālī, daily at home and weekly at Dakshineswar temple, and recollects that there arose from this upbringing a recognition of the low social position of women despite the high religious status of the goddess, remarking:

> Soon my daily experiences made me aware of discrepancies between a religious view of the goddess and the everyday lives of women. The scriptures and religious tradition proclaim that the beloved Devi resides in women. But these same women are not simply revered and protected; they are also dominated and excluded from the decision-making process that gives male members of Hindu society significant power and authority.
>
> (Gupta 1991: 17)

Speaking for herself, while she denies having had 'direct experience of oppression', she concedes having felt 'a subtle pressure to conform to an ideal form of womanhood' (Gupta 1991: 17). This autobiographical information sets the scene for her discussion of Kālī who, as the Great Goddess, she extols as 'an alternative vision to the limitations of patriarchal consciousness' (Gupta 1991: 17).

Lina Gupta announces her intention to 'focus on the goddess as a dramatic embodiment of conflicts found in the struggle of women to assert their social rights through spiritual freedom from within the limiting structure of a patriarchal society' (Gupta 1991: 17). She maintains that 'male domination violates the basic principle of equality integral to Hinduism' and analyses the Hindu tradition so as to expose its 'egalitarian core', central to which is Kālī whom she welcomes as 'offering a way of liberating tradition itself from its patriarchal bias' (Gupta 1991: 17). Her account of Kālī 'from a post-patriarchal point of view as a resource for liberation and empowerment' is based on an examination of 'the goddess's femininity and femininity in general both in light of patriarchal interpretations . . . and in the religious and more liberating interpretations' contained within the Hindu tradition (Gupta 1991: 17–18). In this context, she counters the attitude towards women exemplified in legal literature with the awareness of the goddess expressed in Tantric and other texts.

Blaming the codification of Hindu law for bringing about the situation in which 'the role of women was relegated to wife and mother' (Gupta 1991: 18), Lina Gupta gives priority to Manu as the earliest lawgiver who inaugurated this process. She pays particular attention to Manu's teaching on the ambivalent nature of women, lustful and capricious hence demanding restraint on the one hand, and blessed and auspicious hence deserving respect on the other. She explains this in terms of the power of women, a power, inspiring men's anxiety and their acclaim, leading them either to dominate or to dignify women. Introducing Kālī at this point in her argument, she indicates that 'it is in the goddess Kali that . . . the inherent power of women [is] made explicit' (Gupta 1991: 20). Although she acknowledges that 'the patriarchal perspective often depicts the goddess as nothing more than a great but biologically dependent mother and wife', she asserts that from a Tantric point of view 'Kali can be taken to symbolize the Ultimate Principle that transcends any form of duality' (Gupta 1991: 20–1). The significance of this for her is that Kālī is the Great Goddess herself who 'can be taken as a fruitful post-patriarchal model of the feminine in whom the beauty, power, and independence of the female can be understood and appreciated' (Gupta 1991: 21). She develops this argument in more detail in her review of iconographic, philosophical and mythological representations of Kālī in Tantric scripture, throughout determined to demonstrate that her Tantric approach reveals Kālī as she truly is and her relevance to women.

For instance, when assessing the implications of Kālī's relationship with her husband, Śiva, Lina Gupta paints a very different picture of marriage from the patriarchal model. She professes the opinion that the subordination of women to men 'can neither be verified nor established in Vedic or Upanishadic terms' and so that 'both the husband and the wife are considered to be reflections of the divine nature' (Gupta 1991: 35). This, she continues, has been perverted by the patriarchal model of marriage 'in which women's understanding and experience of their own power have been severely restrained' (Gupta 1991: 35). In contrast, she affirms that Kālī, 'as the fountain of creative energy' in whom the belief that 'union transcends sexual differences and the individual ego' is made manifest, 'symbolizes a form of marriage that necessitates equality and individuality' (Gupta 1991: 36). This is but one example of how she portrays Kālī's power, and thereby the power of women, in a positive way as part of a post-patriarchal agenda which redeems feminine power, divine and human, from the negative stereotypes of patriarchy.

Coming to her conclusion, Lina Gupta comments that 'behind the diverse characters of Sati, Sita, Durga, and Parvati, lies the single, unchanging face of the true hero, the wrathful goddess Kali, the savior' (Gupta 1991: 36). This is not merely of theological importance, however, because she theorises that women associate themselves with the Great Goddess in her various roles and thus that in Kālī women can relate to a liberating figure. She declares:

> I think there is an interaction between a contemporary woman's psyche and the mythic behavior patterns of the goddess, patterns that inform and are played out in a woman's life. . . . By identifying ourselves with the ways Kali acts on the mythic level, with the actual and potential embodiments of Kali, we begin to find a transpersonal source of liberation within her character and nature.
>
> (Gupta 1991: 36)

This interpretation of Kālī, she acknowledges, arises from an exegetical process in which the criterion employed is whether the material conduces to what she styles 'our over-all welfare' (Gupta 1991: 37): if it does, she deems it to be valid; if it does not, she denounces it as illegitimate. Reiterating that 'the images and stories of Kali can be liberating and empowering to all', she urges that in order to break the bounds of the patriarchal concept of feminine power as wild and dangerous, requiring to be checked or curbed, it is imperative to 'understand Kali at various levels, at more essential levels than . . . patriarchal readings reveal' (Gupta 1991: 37). This theme, whereby she links the power of Kālī and the power of women, means that for her one of the facets of Kālī is that which 'reflects the behavioral reality of a subjugated woman in search of her identity' (Gupta 1991: 37). Elaborating on the theme of the senses in which Kālī stands for women, she sets forth Kālī's significance as follows:

> The dark goddess is perpetually present in the inner and outer struggles faced by women at all times. Her darkness represents those rejected and suppressed parts of female creativity, energy, and power that have not been given a chance to be actualized.
>
> (Gupta 1991: 37)

Defining equality as a primary property of the Hindu tradition and hence portraying patriarchy as a perversion of the truths of the tradition, she commends Kālī as one who promises much for a post-patriarchal Hindu tradition and, therefore, by extension, for a post-patriarchal society in which the position of women is improved.

Lina Gupta's casting of the goddess Kālī in this part is, perhaps, appropriate; certainly, it is not unprecedented or unparalleled in contemporary feminist discourse. For example, Sunera Thobani's poem, 'Indian Woman', has as its climax the interplay of Kālī with the Indian woman, so that it is as Kālī that the Indian woman expresses her anger and vows her revenge, as Kālī that she warns all those who oppress and tyrannise her that they invite their own destruction (Thobani 1989: 11). Important and influential as Kālī has been religiously, she is a liminal character who challenges the conventional and conservative with her terrible appearance and outrageous behaviour. So it is that 'to meditate on the dark goddess, or to devote oneself to her, is to step out of the everyday world of predictable dharmic order and enter a world of reversals, opposites, and contrasts and in doing so to wake up to new possibilities and new frames of reference' (Kinsley 1987: 130). Clearly, as Lina Gupta suggests, Kālī's character lends itself comparatively easily to a concomitant challenge to the position of women. Notwithstanding, even if in the past women whose religious path centred on Kālī did enjoy considerable freedom from social constraints, Lina Gupta's claim is far wider in its scope and more profound in its implications. She is, then, engaged in a theological enterprise, offering a prescriptive rather than a descriptive account of the Hindu tradition in which her interpretation of Kālī is cited as a critique of the tradition's patriarchal content. She asserts that many Hindus have always appreciated what she believes to be the tradition's egalitarian message. It is this message which she prescribes as the real meaning and import of the tradition, despite allowing that this message has been obscured and corrupted by patriarchy which she deems neither true nor valid. Thus she is not simply describing what the tradition is and has been because her account is programmatic.

Lina Gupta's appeal to the goddess Kālī demonstrates yet another way in which the Hindu tradition can be restated. By adopting a normative stance towards the Hindu tradition, she is able to differentiate egalitarian from hierarchical tendencies; the egalitarian she approves as authentic whereas the hierarchical are disapproved as deviations from the tradition's true standards and principles incorporated in the figure of Kālī. This restatement of the Hindu tradition in terms of equality is conducive to an improvement in the position of women since she recognises that the position of women is informed by religious beliefs and practices.

These are, then, some of the suggestions made for positive, or at least potentially positive, Hindu ideals. Pre-Aryan India, heroines such as Sītā and Sāvitrī and the goddess Kālī are championed as ways in which the Hindu tradition can be restated to improve the position of women in contemporary circumstances. This reference to Hindu concepts and characters may be inspired by awareness of the vital importance of changing attitudes which is present in both the 'rights' and 'empowerment' wings of the contemporary women's movement in India. So far as the future is concerned, it is not clear if women will choose to appeal to Hindu ideals in meeting new challenges.

Tradition and Liberation

The 'People of India' project, an anthropological study sponsored by the government and conducted over a period from the mid-1980s to the mid-1990s, has shown that women still do not enjoy equality with men (Patel 1996). 75 per cent of the over 4,500 communities identified and investigated in this project are classified as Hindu, and in 71 per cent of the communities surveyed women are reported to have a low status (Patel 1996: 40, 42). Whatever the shortcomings of this project both theoretically and methodologically, especially in respect of gender, it pointed, for example, to a decreasing incidence of child marriage and to a widespread acceptance of widow remarriage, although it also determined that in 99 per cent of communities dowries are provided (Patel 1996: 41–2). Clearly, therefore, the Indian women's movement is still confronted with many obstacles to the empowerment of women in contemporary India. It is by examining the circumstances of contemporary India in more detail, both in terms of specific issues and wider trends, that tentative conclusions can be arrived at concerning the continuing debate about tradition and liberation in the Indian women's movement. In so doing, it is possible to identify some aspects of continuity and change in the ideology and methodology of the Indian women's movement over 150 years or so of campaigning.

Sati, Dowry Death and Female Foeticide

Among the most well-known and best publicised issues now facing the Indian women's movement are sati, dowry death and female foeticide, all of which have given rise to, or are intimately associated

175

with, past controversies about the position of women. That these issues are among the most well-known and best publicised does not necessarily imply that they are either paramount or representative. It may be argued that other issues are of equal or greater importance (such as survival issues surrounding the conditions of subsistence) and that these issues primarily concern particular groups (whether defined by culture, class and/or caste). However, in that sati, dowry death and female foeticide can be seen as different forms of violence against women, they relate to a central theme of present-day feminist activity. Moreover, because sati is accorded a religious rationale, and because the norms and values which, directly or indirectly, inform and inspire dowry death and female foeticide are also sanctified by religious ideals, an examination of these issues contextualises the continuing debate about tradition and liberation.

Sati

The controversy about sati predates the modern period, extending back to ancient and medieval India when contrasting opinions were expressed about the acceptability or otherwise of the act, a controversy in which protagonists of very different persuasions played an active part (Sharma 1988). With the advent of British rule, the controversy about sati took on a new form and, although it is frequently suggested that sati was brought to an end by the criminalisation of the act in 1829, this is by no means true as recent incidents have shown.

The contemporary controversy about sati revolves around the death of Roop Kanwar, an 18 year old woman who died on the funeral pyre of her 24 year old husband on 4 September 1987 in Deorala, Rajasthan. The course of events which culminated in her death, far from unique in being labelled a sati, has been bitterly contested. According to one version, the loving bride of but eight months declared her intention to join her husband in death and would not be dissuaded from this action by the admonitions of her distraught in-laws. According to another version, the unhappily married wife of an inadequate husband was murdered by her venal in-laws when she was burned alive with her husband's corpse. Thus Roop Kanwar is honoured by some as a *mahāsatī* (Great *Satī*), and consequently her death has become the centre of a devotional cult and Deorala a place of pilgrimage. Yet for others she is a particularly pitiable example of the cruelty and brutality to which women are subjected in Indian society.

As public opinion has polarised, one group pays homage to Roop Kanwar as a goddess while the other views her as a tragic victim. These groups are diametrically opposed in their assessment of sati:

> Should the practice of *sati* be regarded as a highly meritorious religious act, in which divine reality expresses itself in a female form, or is it only a social evil and a crime, characteristic of a culture which is dominated by blameworthy "macho-values" presenting themselves disguised in a religious lustre of holiness?
>
> (van den Bosch 1990: 185)

The arguments of the two groups may be summarised as follows. The pro-sati group, led by the specially formed Dharma Raksha Samiti (Council for the Defence of Religion) which was originally known as Sati Dharma Raksha Samiti, insists that sati is a religious practice, still more that it is a splendid and glorious affirmation of the virtuous wife's enduring love for her husband. This group cites the constitutional guarantee of freedom of religion in defence of a woman's decision to accompany her husband in death as in life. The anti-sati group, led by various women's organisations including the Jamadi Mahila Samiti (Women's Popular Council), maintains that sati is politically motivated and manipulated, asserting that it is one of the many violent acts perpetrated against women. This group rejects the claim that a woman has the means and opportunity to exercise choice, on the grounds that a woman is routinely deprived of the power to choose, not least in respect of whether and whom to marry. In due course, the campaigning of this group led to the promulgation of new state and national legislation, the Rajasthani Anti-Sati Ordinance (1987) and the Commission of Sati (Prevention) Act (1988) (Dhagamwar 1988: 37), but there remain serious misgivings about the nature and implementation of these laws. There is also uncertainty about the necessity of enacting additional legislation, instead of the rigorous enforcement of existing laws.

Pro-sati activists relate a narrative replete with religious references which is associated with a characterisation of Roop Kanwar as a good wife and a concept of sati as a heroic act of self-sacrifice. Their hagiography of Roop Kanwar portrays her as deeply devout since childhood and a regular worshipper at a sati temple who revered the ideal of a wife's total dedication to her husband, even to the extent of determination to share her husband's destiny to the end. Their eulogisation of sati portrays sati as the means whereby a wife who is totally dedicated to her husband dies with him in order to discharge her duty of protecting him from harm. That Roop Kanwar did indeed perform sati is established by numerous mythological and iconographic embellishments of the account of her death. Thus they are clear that Roop Kanwar was indwelt by the divine power of *sat* (reality), burning from within, which enabled her to transcend fear and pain and invested her with the status of a goddess. They contend that her conduct during the procession to the cremation site amply testified to the sincerity and seriousness of her intent when, calm and composed, they related that she chanted *mantras* and blessed bystanders. In addition, they also include in their testimony much miraculous material. For example, the funeral pyre is said to have been ignited by supernatural means, a ray of the sun, rather than her husband's younger brother, while Roop Kanwar's hand is said to have been stamped with the shape of a *pan*, the symbol of the *satī*. Subsequently, they commemorated Roop Kanwar's death in the triumphant terms of what they called a *chunari mahotsav* (veil festival). Photomontages of the couple have been produced purporting to show the sati itself with a smiling Roop Kanwar embracing her husband's body in the midst of the flames and the place where she died has been designated as a *satī sthal* (sati shrine) acquiring various ritual and other trappings. Pro-sati activists, therefore, see sati as religious and are able to rally religious leaders to their cause, both by such leaders issuing statements that sati is sanctioned in Hindu scripture and by their participating in ritual performance at the site. In this way, they argue that any attempt by the government, state or national, to interfere with what they conceive as a spiritual concern is a gross violation of their rights since, in their opinion, to do so would be to impugn Rajput traditions and/or imperil the Hindu religion (Dalrymple 1997; Kishwar and Vanita 1987; Kumar 1993; Oldenburg 1994; van den Bosch 1990).

Anti-sati activists have pointed to innovative elements in the modern sati cult, emphasising its political tone and content. For instance, Madhu Kishwar and Ruth Vanita declare:

> The sati cult in its presentday [sic] form is primarily the product of a phoney religiosity that is the accompaniment of newfound [sic] prosperity, harnessed by political leaders for their own vested interests.

(Kishwar and Vanita 1987: 18)

In their account of the Deorala sati, politicians are alleged to have exploited Roop Kanwar's death for their own purposes. Among the evidence adduced to authenticate this analysis is a profile of the leaders of the modern sati cult. In contrast to the pious stereotype asserted by supporters of sati, these leaders are described as men rather than women, young rather than old, educated rather than illiterate and town- rather than village-dwelling. Their aims and activities, promoting a particular perspective on the status and image of women, are categorised as political, whether to rally Rajput electoral strength or to unite the Hindu community as a whole. Thus they conclude:

> It is important that we demystify it [the Deorala sati] and see it as a case of a woman being hounded to death under a specious religious cover, and of her death being made a symbol by certain power groups to demonstrate their clout.
>
> (Kishwar and Vanita 1987: 24)

This interpretation of the modern sati cult in which it is represented as a political phenomenon contrasts with the religious legitimation offered for sati by pro-sati activists.

Many anti-sati activists are reluctant to consider the question of sati's religious status, if any, because for them this is beside the point when what is really at stake are women's lives. Yet in the process of suggesting that the modern sati cult is political instead of religious, they nevertheless draw attention to the question of sati's religious status, if only by explicitly rejecting it. In this connection, it may be pointed out that Hindu religious leaders are far from unanimous in claiming that sati is sanctioned in Hindu scripture or in preparedness to participate in ritual performance at the site of Roop Kanwar's death. Certainly, this controversy has led to a wealth of writing of various types which denies sati's religious status and tends to evince a strong bias towards textual sources. However, this strategy has been much criticised for perpetuating essentialist and normative definitions of the Hindu tradition (e.g. Kishwar and Vanita 1987). In this writing, a range of scriptural references are given to qualify the precedents for the performance of sati identified in the Epics and *Purāṇas* and to question didactic passages praising a woman who joins her husband in death and promising her heavenly happiness and continued marital felicity. Such scriptural references include, for example: the silence of *Manu's Dharmaśāstra* on the subject; the unambiguous condemnation of sati in Medhātithi's commentary on this law-book where sati is

179

classified as irreligious and unscriptural; and the denunciation of sati in the *Mahānirvāṇa Tantra* which describes women as forms of the goddess and warns that hell will be the reward of any woman who immolates herself (e.g. Thapar 1988). While it is understandable that many anti-sati activists resent the religious status of sati becoming a major focus of debate and regard it as imperative to change the conduct of debate so that it ceases to turn on a religious axis, they have to face the fact that sati is legitimised in religious terms despite their treating this as disingenuous or counterfeit.

Sati is, then, accorded a religious rationale and in a manner which dowry death and female foeticide are not. In these instances, religious ideals sanctify the norms and values which, directly or indirectly, inform and inspire them by setting forth a religious basis for the practice of dowry and the preference for sons respectively.

Dowry Death

Dowry achieved great notoriety with the suicide of Snehalata Mukhopadhyay on 30 January 1914. This 15 year old girl committed suicide by setting herself alight to prevent her father from being reduced to poverty in the attempt to satisfy the dowry demands of her future husband's family. Her decision to kill herself was, therefore, a reaction to her father's inability to endow her with the money and jewellery required by her prospective father-in-law without mortgaging the family home. News of her death provoked a storm of protest and prompted many attacks on the dowry system although there was some ambivalence as to whether dowry should be abolished completely (Bandhopadhyay 1987). Interestingly, the debate about dowry, while ranging widely over the possible causes and correctives of the practice, also contained discussion of the religious status of dowry – another example of how debate about the position of women has a religious character even if, from one point of view, this is dismissed as a displacement of the real issue into a remote and irrelevant pursuit.

In the absence of a consensus on its elimination, legislation against dowry did not reach the statute book until 1961. The Dowry Prohibition Act (1961) made providing or profiting from dowry punishable in law, invalidated agreements on dowry and reallocated any such monies or goods as the woman's property. Growing concern about dowry deaths, that is the deaths of brides through both murder and suicide in relation to demands for dowry, led to other legislation. For example, the Dowry Prohibition (Amendment) Act (1984) which redefined dowry as being 'in connection with marriage' prohibited dowry but permitted the exchange of voluntary gifts, stipulating only that they should be of a 'customary nature' and not of an 'excessive value'. Obviously, then, this legislation had large loopholes, not least in its description of dowry which took insufficient account of the timescale of dowry demands and its permitting the exchange of voluntary gifts without determining what they were or their worth. Such criticisms of the formulation of this act led to calls for further amendment of the legislation against dowry which has followed. Notwithstanding, despite the law now regarding dowry as an abuse to be brought to an end, anxieties about the application and, indeed applicability, of this law have not been allayed (Ghadially and Kumar 1988).

Dowry demands take a number of forms, the most popular of which are money, consumer durables and jewellery, mirroring contemporary social and economic conditions and aspirations. Moreover, it is clear that dowry now lays an even heavier burden on the bride's parents than it did in the past and, the harder it has become to provide an acceptable dowry, the more dangerous it has become to default on these demands. The perverse logic behind dowry death, irrespective of statute, is that, when his wife dies, a widower can retain whatever dowry she brought with her and at the same time seek to remarry making new dowry demands in the process. In these circumstances, should the groom or his family take the view that a bride is inadequately endowed and no additional funds are forthcoming from the bride's family, there is little disincentive to them taking their revenge on the young woman by making her life so miserable that she ends it or by taking it themselves. Many of these dowry deaths, suicides and murders, take the form of death by fire as women burn in the kerosene fuel used for cooking.

Thus, as Rehana Ghadially and Pramod Kumar make clear, 'many a young woman has died for not fulfilling the expectations of the groom's family' (Ghadially and Kumar 1988: 167). They explain that these dowry deaths are mainly associated with demands for dowry made after marriage, these demands interpreted as the groom and his family exerting their rights as the superior partners in this alliance or their emphasising the inadequacy of the original marriage settlement either in its own or relative terms. They demonstrate that the failure of the bride's family to fulfil these demands sparks a rising spiral of domestic violence, culminating in the bride's suicide or murder. A common pattern emerges from their examination of these events and typically unfolds as follows. A wife experiences domestic violence, be it physical, emotional or both, which worsens until she meets her death, at her own hands in despair at her plight or at the hands of her husband or another member of his family, especially her mother-in-law, in a final fatal act of spite. They point out that part of this victimisation is the way in which the wife is portrayed by her husband's family as a disturbed young woman, unprincipled and promiscuous, on whom, implictly or explicitly, is placed all the blame for any marital or domestic discord. Perhaps this, they suggest, coupled with a belief in privacy, contributes towards a disinclination to intervene in what are regarded as private domestic disputes which are fundamentally the fault of the wife.

Such disinclination to intervene by those who are in a position to help a victim of violence in the home, Rehana Ghadially and Pramod Kumar suggest, means that, where action is taken, it is usually taken after a death has occurred rather than at an earlier stage of dowry demand or domestic violence. Furthermore, in their opinion, neither the conduct of the police nor the judiciary is effective with very few cases of dowry death registered and investigated, fewer still coming to court where fewer yet result in convictions. This they attribute to the indifference of the police and the chauvinism of the judiciary, leading the police to make basic mistakes in preparing cases and the judiciary to dismiss even strong cases. Thence they determine that dowry death can not simply be viewed in terms of irreconcilable differences over a bride's dowry between her natal and marital kin but as 'a question of the inter-relatedness of psychological, social and economic factors' (Ghadially and Kumar 1988: 177). Commenting on the superficiality of the coverage of the issue in which its cause is not considered nor its remedy recommended, they observe that such coverage 'seldom sees them [brides who die in relation to dowry] as victims of a particular form of oppression or of socially prevalent sex biases', indicating 'an internalization of prevailing patriarchal values which view women as inferior' (Ghadially and Kumar 1988: 177). The consequence of this complex of factors, including 'the burden of tradition, a prevailing ideology of male superiority, . . . and a society that condones violence', is, they conclude, 'a chamber of horrors where even angels fear to tread' (Ghadially and Kumar 1988: 177). Clearly, then, dowry death can not be divorced from dowry demands and from the practice of dowry more generally.

Certainly, there is no sense in which religion sanctifies dowry death but the practice of dowry does have a religious dimension. This religious dimension is evident in a concept of marriage whereby marriage is believed to involve the gift of a girl (*kanyādāna*) by her guardian for the acquisition of righteousness (*dharma*), wealth (*artha*) and pleasure (*kāma*). This gift of a girl is regarded as a meritorious ritual gift (*dāna*) and as such requires to be sealed by a suitable offering (*dakṣiṇā*) from donor to donee. This means that dowry (*varadakṣiṇā*) is the offering made by the bride's guardian to the groom which seals the former's gift to the latter (Pandey 1969: 165–6, 189, 214–5). Even though this is far removed from dowry death as a contemporary issue, this religious ideal does sanctify the practice of dowry, a norm which stands in some sort of relationship with dowry death. A similar relationship between a religious ideal and a contemporary issue is evident in respect of female foeticide.

Female Foeticide

Female infanticide, using a variety of methods including drugging, poisoning, smothering and choking the child, was widely practised throughout India at the advent of British rule. Often associated with hypergamous marriages in which a woman could not marry a man who was her social inferior and so had to have a generous dowry to make a suitable match with a man of high social position, a practice which made it expedient to end the lives of daughters, female infanticide was also associated with ideas that the death of a baby girl ensured the birth of a baby boy and that girls brought bad luck to the families in which they were born. The British legislated against this practice in Regulations XXI (1795) and III (1804) as well as the Act for Suppression of Female Infanticide (1870) but they also tried to change attitudes towards female infanticide, in particular by seeking to regulate dowry as a significant contributory factor to female infanticide (Krishnaswamy 1988).

While female infanticide continues to be practised and, according to some, as widely as in the past, recent advances in obstetrics have allowed parents to establish the sex of the foetus during pregnancy and thereby to abort unwanted female foetuses. Chief among the advances is amniocentesis, a medical procedure by which a sample of amniotic fluid is withdrawn from the womb and analysed. This sample can be used to detect foetal abnormality but also reveals the sex of the foetus which can, of course, be relevant in the case of certain genetic disorders. In India, however, the primary role of amniocentesis has not been to detect foetal abnormality but to discover whether the foetus is female and, if so, to terminate the pregnancy forthwith. This takes place in a country where amniocentesis is comparatively affordable and widely available and where it is administered and even advertised for the sole and specific purpose of avoiding the birth of daughters. In response to sustained campaigns against female foeticide, legislation has been enacted on a state and national level to ban the use of sex-determination tests for the selective abortion of female foetuses. Notwithstanding, such legislation is adjudged to be seriously flawed in that it is frequently flouted, mainly because offences under such legislation are extremely difficult to prove.

Vibhuti Patel denounces the tendency 'to make Indian women "male-child-producing" machines' (Patel 1989: 3) which she finds in the use of amniocentesis. She relates how amniocentesis is used by slum-dwellers of modest means on the grounds 'that it is better to spend Rs200 or even Rs800 now than give birth to a female baby and spend thousands of rupees on her marriage when she grows up' (Patel 1989: 3–4). She recounts how amniocentesis has become popular in India, from the outset recognised as a means of finding out the sex of the foetus and regarded as a valuable procedure. She reports the findings of a study conducted by Dr Sanjeev Kulkarni of the Foundation of Research in Community Health into the performance of amniocentesis in Bombay. This study revealed that 84 per cent of gynaecologists were performing the procedure as a method of sex-determination with an average of 270 procedures per medical practitioner every month performed on women from all backgrounds, some of whom already had a male child or male children. She then refers to the findings of other studies which show that about 78,000 female foetuses were aborted after sex-determination tests in India between 1978 and 1983 and that of the nearly 16,000 abortions performed during 1984 and 1985 at an abortion centre in Bombay almost all were performed after sex-determination tests. She draws attention to the way in which, whereas female infanticide tends to be practised in certain communities, female foeticide is far more common in society at large. Linking foeticide with infanticide and other mistreatment of girls by acts of commission and omission alike, she indicates how the imbalance of the sex ratios has worsened over the century and with the use of sex-determination tests is likely to continue to worsen.

Another aspect of the issue which Vibhuti Patel discusses is the use of sex-preselection methods which claim to procure the conception of a child of the desired sex which is, of course, in the majority of cases, male. She also examines the arguments advanced in favour of sex-determination and/or sex-preselection. These arguments include those that it is preferable to prevent a girl being born if her lot in life is so poor, that if fewer girls are born it will lead to women having a higher status and that it is better for parents to achieve a balanced family by having a son without producing any number of unwanted daughters in the process. However, she stresses that sex-determination and sex-preselection techniques are neither benign nor neutral: to argue that it is preferable to prevent a girl being born is to concede that the position of women can not be changed; to argue that if fewer girls are born it will lead to women having a higher status is to underestimate the misogyny of Indian society; and to argue that it is better for parents to achieve a balanced family is to ignore the fact that corrective action would not be taken where parents have sons but no daughters. In rebutting the allegation that women support these techniques, she insists that women have had instilled in them that their worth rests on them giving their husbands sons and rejects any claim that it is a question of women having the access to family planning services with which they can exercise control over their fertility.

Accordingly, Vibhuti Patel contends that 'we must situate this problem in the context of commercialism in medicine and health care systems, racist bias of the population control policy, and the manifestation of patriarchal power' (Patel 1989: 7). For these reasons, she is loathe to rely on legislative measures alone to combat these practices, looking to a campaigning strategy to 'raise public awareness of the implications and repercussions of the use of sex-determination and sex-preselection techniques to eliminate female offspring' (Patel 1989: 10). She concludes by expressing her hope 'that an increased public awareness will not only bring an end to these abuses of modern technology, but will also lead to changes in the societal values and attitudes towards women underlying these abuses' (Patel 1989: 10). Thus female foeticide can not be understood in isolation from prevailing views about the preference for sons.

Again, there is no sense in which religion sanctifies female foeticide but the preference for sons does have a religious dimension. This religious dimension of the preference for sons is evident in a concept of family ritual whereby family ritual, specifically the *śrāddha*

185

(memorial) ceremony in which sacrifices of water and rice are made to deceased relatives, is absolutely dependent on sons. Through this ceremony, deceased relatives are provided with sustenance for the after-life and joined with the family ancestors in *pitṛloka* (the world of the Fathers). Indeed, the word for son, *putra*, is claimed to be a compound of *put* and *tra*, meaning 'saviour from the hell of Put'. This preference for sons is articulated in the conduct of marriages which feature vows, prayers and blessings that the couple may have sons and enacted in the *puṃsavana* (male production) sacrament celebrated in the third month of gestation to secure a male child (Pandey 1969: 60–3, 218–24). Again, though this is far removed from female foeticide as a contemporary issue, this religious ideal does sanctify the preference for sons, a value which stands in some sort of relationship with female foeticide.

This is not to represent sati, dowry death and female foeticide as essentially religious but religion is complicit, if only in an arguably secondary or derivative capacity, such that it accords sati a rationale and its ideals sanctify the norms and values which, directly or indirectly, inform and inspire dowry death and female foeticide. These issues contextualise the continuing debate about tradition and liberation in the Indian women's movement which also occurs when the Hindu radical right is on the rise.

Women and the Hindu Radical Right

The rise of the Hindu radical right has a direct bearing upon the continuing debate about tradition and liberation. The roots of the Hindu radical right can be traced back into the modern period from the nineteenth century onwards, with groups seeking to define the relationship between Hindu culture and religion and Indian national life, and especially from the early to mid-twentieth century, with groups developing the ideology of *hindutva* (Hinduness). However, recent years have witnessed much greater militancy, most dramatically manifested in the destruction of a mosque in 1992 which it was claimed had been built on the site of the birthplace of Prince Rāma, the righteous ruler of Ayodhya, and on the ruins of a commemorative temple. This event was itself the culmination of a protracted, always bitter and sometimes violent, dispute about ownership of this sacred site but the shocking scenes attending the destruction of this mosque, in many ways typical of the tenor of the times, demonstrated the power and impact of the Hindu radical right. The Hindu radical right, notably the Bharatiya Janata Party (Indian People's Party) – Rashtriya Swayamsevak Sangh (Nationalist Volunteer Organisation) – Vishwa Hindu Parishad (World Hindu Council) alliance, asserts that Hindus are under attack in India where the modern state, in a pretence at neutrality, privileges other groups at their expense. It looks towards the establishment of a Hindu nation on the model of its view of an idealised ancient India before any alien incursion arrived bringing decline in its wake. In so doing, it appeals to a rich religious symbology and sense of national destiny in which the religious and the national are fused together as patriotic faith.

The Hindu radical right is the term Ainslie Embree prefers to alternatives such as Hindu communalists, Hindu reactionaries and, presumably, also Hindu fundamentalists. He explains:

> The thrust of the Hindu radical right can be seen most significantly in its attitudes toward the four major goals of the dominant political culture. These goals – national unity, social justice, democracy, and secularism – are not rejected by the Hindu radical right but transformed through redefinition. Its adherents allege that it is the dominant political groups who, through a false interpretation of the goals, are destroying India.
>
> (Embree 1990: 46)

Thus he argues that the Hindu radical right's concept of national unity is that of a harmonious whole, the harmony of which is believed to reside in the identity between the Indian and the Hindu. Consistent with this, social justice is given an explicitly Hindu gloss, referring to *dharma* especially as expounded in relation to the duties of the four classes of priests, warriors, merchants and peasants. In similar fashion, democracy is presented as a process by which the Hindu community, conceived as a majority of the population, permit the Muslim community, conceived as a minority, to live if only on sufferance. Moreover, secularism is claimed to consist in non-Hindus honouring Hindu culture and religion as the basis of Indian life. This analysis can be extended beyond the scope of Ainslie Embree's discussion to apply also to the Hindu radical right's agenda on women's equality with men.

As Ratna Kapur and Brenda Cossman's study shows, the notion of women's equality with men is indeed transformed through redefinition. Taking examples from various groups on the Hindu radical right, they show that, though 'the discourse on women is often characterised by its strikingly religious overtones defining women in the images of Hindu goddesses and consorts – as mothers and wives dutiful and sacrificing', this can be combined with 'the discourse of equality' (Kapur and Cossman 1995: 96–7). Yet they emphasise that in the hands of the Hindu radical right equality takes on a very different meaning. They argue that 'the discourse on equality is fused with the more fundamentalist discourse that seeks to reclaim a glorious and ancient past' in which 'the objective of equality . . . becomes the restoration of women to the position that they once enjoyed in this "Golden Age"' (Kapur and Cossman 1995: 97). Even so, in their opinion, this does not imply that the picture of women portrayed by the Hindu radical right is predicated upon feminine weakness nor that the Hindu radical right opposes women entering work or having education. Instead, they conclude that the Hindu radical right upholds feminine strength on an overtly religious prototype and justifies opportunities for employment and education by reference to the primary marital and domestic responsibilities allotted to women. Thus their description 'of the new Hindu woman of Hindutva' is as follows:

> The constitution of the new Hindu woman – a woman who may be educated, and who may work outside of the home, a woman who is strong and powerful, inside her family, and her community – is still a woman constituted through traditional discourses of *matri shakti*, as mother and wife; and of Sita, as chaste, pure and loyal. The new Hindu woman is strong, but she is strong in restoring the glories of an ancient past, a past which, as reconstructed through communal discourses, accords a particular role for women in the family, and in society: dutiful wives, and self-sacrificing mothers. Any additional roles that women may perform are ancillary to these. Indeed, women's work and education are seen as a means of strengthening their roles in the family.
>
> (Kapur and Cossman 1995: 105–6)

Accordingly, their account indicates that the Hindu radical right accepts both that there are essential differences between men and women and that, because the sexes are different, women have a vital contribution to make.

What has been particularly noteworthy about the Hindu radical right from the perspective of the Indian women's movement is the active participation of women within it. Women were among those who were involved in the Babri Masjid – Ramjanmabhumi (Babur's mosque – Rāma's birthplace temple) agitation in Ayodhya and elsewhere. In this agitation, they were by no means advocates of moderation but militants in their own right, condoning the violent prosecution of their ends. Women's active participation in protests of this sort is significant for a number of reasons. For instance, it demonstrates that there are many women who do not share the Indian women's movement's vision of women having a common cause with the same interests and concerns. Or again, it also demonstrates that there are many women who do not subscribe to the Indian women's movement's progressive agenda for women. Rather, women in the Hindu radical right identify themselves with the Hindu community over and against women of other communities, especially Muslims, even to the extent of endorsing their assault and rape, while supporting a neo-traditionalist programme for women, including some welfare elements. Women's active participation in the Hindu radical right is problematic too because it provides women with opportunities to attain public prominence as leaders on a platform which paradoxically upholds women's place in the private sphere of home and family. An integral part of this is, therefore, criticism of the Indian women's movement which is condemned for introducing modern western norms and encouraging an attitude of selfishness in women. Certainly, the Indian women's movement has come into direct conflict with women of the Hindu radical right on a range of issues.

An impression of the opinions held by women on the Hindu radical right can be gained by considering some statements which have been made by major figures of the women's auxiliaries of radical right organisations, frequently themselves organisations of long-standing. These statements are, of course, considered with the proviso that such statements are made by specific individuals and fall within a sometimes broad spectrum of opinion. Krishna Sharma of the Vishwa Hindu Parishad's Women's Wing insists on the necessity for women to be selfless, saying:

> Ram's greatness was because of Sita, Kaushalya and Kaikei. Ram took Kaikei into confidence and requested her to ask for the two boons so that he could go in to exile to destroy Ravan. It was Kaikei's sacrifice that enabled Ram to accomplish his mission. A happy life is not possible unless women compromise and are willing to sacrifice.
>
> (Sharma, K. 1995: 332)

Elaborating on this theme, she advises a wife to defer to her husband so that, in commenting on the subject of wife-beating, she uses the analogy of a parent disciplining a child, urging a woman to comply with her husband's wishes in order to preserve family unity and, if all efforts to please her husband fail, urging a woman to smother her cries in order to preserve this as a domestic matter.

Asha Sharma of the Rashtra Sevika Samiti (National Service Society), the women's section of the RSS, lends her support to women's education and employment. Her support for women's education is couched in terms of passing on patriotic principles to the next generation. Hence:

> We encourage women's education; as an educated mother she will be better equipped to inculcate the right values in her children – the values of nationalism and pride in Indian culture.
>
> (Sharma, A. 1995: 331)

Her support for women's employment is qualified by being dependent on family circumstance and consent and subordinated to maternal duties. Thus:

> We teach women to give first priority to the family – a career should be taken up only in case of financial need and should be subject to the approval of the family. There is a natural division of labour – women, being more sensitive, should take care of children. Everything else is secondary.
>
> (Sharma, A. 1995: 331)

Moreover, her comments on sati show how she understands feminine strength. She declares:

> Sati is derived from the word *satitva* which means "purity of mind and of the body" and the willingness of a woman to give supreme sacrifice to save this purity.
>
> (Sharma, A. 1995: 331)

She illustrates this by citing women who chose to die at the time of Partition and by appealing to Sītā who stayed true throughout many trials and tribulations, but she rejects the sati of Roop Kanwar on the grounds that it was not her decision and so recommends physical training for women. The sub-text of such statements often seems to consist in the contention that the establishment of a Hindu nation will benefit women who, in consequence, will once again enjoy the privilege and prestige enjoyed by women in ancient India before

Muslim rule brought about a worsening in their position. Thus the rise of the Hindu radical right has a direct bearing upon the continuing debate about tradition and liberation.

Debate in the Indian Women's Movement

Religious references run through the rhetoric of the Hindu radical right's spokespersons, not least in respect of women. Such references, together with the role of religion in justifying various practices, raise the question of whether this requires that the Indian women's movement reject appeal to Hindu beliefs and values. Flavia Agnes, for example, relates how the Indian women's movement has appealed to Hindu beliefs and values, a course of action which she criticises for sustaining the claims of the Hindu radical right. She explains that, in an effort to communicate its message to women of other backgrounds and affiliations, members of the movement have tried to win a wider base of support for its activities by using Hindu imagery. Describing this policy, she observes:

> In order to reach out to women from a different class, caste and culture and to propagate the new ideology of the strong and assertive woman, the movement adopted a populist approach and relied upon mythical symbols of Shakti and Kali to convey the newly constructed feminist ideology.
>
> (Agnes 1995: 139)

In her view, this has involved the movement having recourse to 'myths and fictions' (Agnes 1995: 139), a strategy which it is clear she does not condone. Her preferred strategy for the movement would seem to be recourse to what she calls 'the history of a pluralistic society that encompassed within its framework the cultural idioms of minority communities' (Agnes 1995: 139). Though she acknowledges that the movement has not been trying to promote Hindu culture and religion by its use of Hindu imagery, she argues that the movement has not accorded priority to a secular ideal and so has not developed its own secular imagery. Thus she insists:

> The intention of using the symbols from the dominant religious culture was not to propagate Hindu ideology. But since the movement did not have "secularism" as one of its prime objectives, no conscious efforts were made to evolve alternate symbols.
>
> (Agnes 1995: 139)

The movement's failure to develop its own secular imagery, she concludes, has led to 'the cultural expressions with which women who were in the forefront were familiar' (Agnes 1995: 139), namely Hindu imagery, entering into the Indian women's movement in what she characterises as a clandestine manner.

Flavia Agnes' account of this policy is located in the context of accusations which have been levelled against the Indian women's movement that it is western-influenced. In her opinion, this has prompted the movement to present itself as authentically Indian through the use of Hindu imagery, an adverse by-product of which has been to consolidate the position of the Hindu radical right in the equation of what is Hindu with what is Indian. She comments:

> The feminist movement also had to constantly counter the allegation that it was "Western". So in order to establish its "Indianness" it relied on Hindu iconography and Sanskrit idioms denoting woman power, thus inadvertently strengthening the communal ideology that Indian, Hindu and Sanskrit are synonymous.
>
> (Agnes 1995: 139)

In 'this social milieu of a high caste Hindu culture', she claims not only that the movement's non-Hindu membership has 'internalised the dominant trend' but also that such individuals have 'willingly divorced themselves from their own traditions and cultural symbols of women's strength and power' (Agnes 1995: 139). The implication of this is that in this respect too the movement has been playing into the hands of the Hindu radical right by reducing India's cultural and religious diversity into a Hindu-based unity, even uniformity.

After a brief discussion of Shiv Sena (Army of Śiva), a party of the Hindu radical right, Flavia Agnes points to the similarity between the Hindu radical right's 'construction of the modern Hindu woman' and 'the new "feminist" woman' of the Indian women's movement (Agnes 1995: 140). She substantiates this by examining the imagery of the 'new modern Durga, the destroyer of evil, an angry and rebellious woman' (Agnes 1995: 140) which she attributes to the Hindu radical right. She recognises that 'the modern Hindu woman' of the Hindu radical right 'could come out on the streets with as much ease as the men from the community to avenge their wrongs' and that in so doing 'she had the blessings of the party and community leaders' (Agnes 1995: 140). This contrasts with the experience of a woman who takes part in the public protests organised by the Indian women's movement who benefits from no such social approval. Yet more than adopting the tactics of direct action previously pioneered by the Indian women's movement, tactics which mean that women are campaigning openly in the world at large, she stresses that the Hindu radical right with its very different philosophy has proven more effective in winning women to its cause than the Indian women's movement. As she puts it:

> Through a process of selection, Hindu communal forces usurped the external usages popularised by the feminist movement such as protest marches and road blocks (which are contrary to the conservative domestic role of the traditional Hindu woman) while at the same time rejecting the movement's ideological stance. The irony lay in the fact that the communal parties were able to mobilise women far more easily using the image of the modern Durga than the movement which had popularised these forms in the first place.
>
> (Agnes 1995: 140–1)

Summing up the sad realisation of the Indian women's movement that 'the shakti of the modern Durga was not directed against violence within the home and community but was directed externally' (Agnes 1995: 141), she further remarks on the challenging of the movement's convictions and the reworking of its rallying cries by women of the Hindu radical right.

For Flavia Agnes, therefore, the appeal to Hindu beliefs and values on the part of the Indian women's movement is counterproductive because, although unwittingly, it reinforces the tenets and teachings of the Hindu radical right. Madhu Kishwar, however, is an advocate of appeal to Hindu beliefs and values on the part of the Indian women's movement while her response to the rise of the Hindu radical right, in some measure blamed upon lack of sympathy with and knowledge of the Hindu tradition, is to recover the tradition from its contemporary corruption for political purposes.

Madhu Kishwar compares the views of India's westernised elite with those of India's imperial rulers. Stating that 'the liberal, secular intelligentsia is rooted more in the western liberal tradition and is often unable to comprehend, leave alone appreciate, the sentiments and cherished beliefs of India's diverse peoples', she likens their views with those of the British 'who contemptuously dismissed the social, religious and cultural beliefs of the Indian people as superstitious mumbo-jumbo' (Kishwar 1990a: 2). She also sees some similarity in the imperial and modern education systems in that she denounces the imperial education system as seeking 'to destroy the self respect of Indians' and insists that the modern education system continues to convey 'the same self contempt' (Kishwar 1990a: 2). Consequently, she insists that the education system 'has produced generations of people alienated from and ignorant of India's traditions of culture and learning' (Kishwar 1990a: 2–3). This is significant because she claims that such alienation and ignorance makes people 'vulnerable targets for unscrupulous politicians', the politicians of the Hindu radical right who, she professes, 'themselves are assiduously cultivating ignorance of India's cultural and religious traditions with their deliberate distortions' (Kishwar 1990a: 3). She is forthright in her denial of any religious status to the Hindu radical right whose members she maintains 'are not even remotely concerned with the religious and spiritual well-being of the Hindus' (Kishwar 1990a: 5) but are instead propagandists for a fascist-style nationalism. It is on this basis that she deplores the way in which the Hindu radical right is 'destroying all that is morally and spiritually elevating in Hinduism and forging from it a hate filled ideology of nationalism' (Kishwar 1990a: 7).

Madhu Kishwar contrasts the interpretation of the Hindu tradition she associates with the Hindu radical right with her own interpretation of the tradition. She deprecates the violent and intolerant version of the tradition which she regards as typical of the Hindu radical right for whom Rāma has become 'a national warrior hero' and whose 'Hinduism . . . resembles the many brutal periods in the history of Christianity and Islam when they wreaked destruction and massacred many peoples in proselytising and conquering all over the world' (Kishwar 1990a: 7, 9). Her version of the tradition is very different in that it is both non-violent and tolerant. She sees Rāma 'as a religious figure, religious in the sense of representing a revered moral, ethical code and as an embodiment of rare spiritual ideals which have inspired generations and generations of people to upright lives in this land' (Kishwar 1990a: 7). Consistent with this, she emphasises that the Hindu tradition inculcates respect for all life as arising from the immanence of the divine in creation and has an open and inclusive outlook towards outside influences. This leads her to comment on the Hindu tradition's capacity for internal critique:

> All this and more has provided a good deal of space for dissent and diversity within the Hindu religious and cultural traditions which counter-acts [sic] some of its oppressive aspects.
>
> (Kishwar 1990a: 10)

This normative neo-Gandhian reading of the tradition informs her action-plan. Accordingly, in this action-plan, she exhorts that true knowledge of the Hindu tradition be dissseminated. That this is necessary, she argues, is because one section of the population's neglect of the tradition enabled its abuse by the Hindu radical right. In her words:

> The Hindu community can be mobilised to save its culture and religion from being distorted beyond recognition only if they are aware of it.
>
> (Kishwar 1990a: 15)

This favourable evaluation of the Hindu tradition underwrites her advocacy of appeal to Hindu beliefs and values as a creative and constructive approach to improving the position of women.

Yet to allow that the Hindu tradition has any part to play means Madhu Kishwar is setting herself up in opposition to many other women. On one occasion, she recalls, she was censured by a feminist group at a women's college in Delhi University 'for presenting in a positive light the protest poetry of women like Mahadeviakka or Mirabai' (Kishwar 1990b: 4). She explains that this group was unable to accept the worth of women devotional saints because such saints did not measure up to contemporary feminist standards. Thus:

> Their argument was that these women did not talk of women's independence and equality as they ought to have; that they merely chose to substitute slavery to a husband for slavery to a god.
>
> (Kishwar 1990b: 4)

She is scathing in her comments on this argument which she sums up as the thesis that such saints 'were inadequate as historical sources of inspiration for women because they could not be called feminist' (Kishwar 1990b: 4). Clearly treating this as an absurdly anachronistic attitude, she contends that women's ideas should be considered in the light of the time in which they live and that the integrity of the past should be respected as shared heritage. She declares:

> We need to understand the aspirations and nature of women's stirrings and protest in different epochs in the context of the dilemmas of their age, rather than impose our own aspirations on the past. The past ought not to be studied either to seek justifications for, nor faulted for not having lived up to our

present day political inclinations, but viewed on its own terms, while acknowledging it as our inherited legacy.

(Kishwar 1990b: 4–5)

In this way, she is again deprecating the views of India's westernised elite, in this instance feminists, who reject tradition, views which as she expounds elsewhere have created the conditions under which the Hindu radical right has been able to gain ground.

The debate about tradition and liberation is, then, continuing, perhaps given greater force by the existence of issues such as sati, dowry death and female foeticide and especially by the rise of the Hindu radical right. Certainly, there is now no clear consensus on this question in the Indian women's movement for, just as Flavia Agnes renounces appeal to Hindu beliefs and values because she regards this as propping up the Hindu radical right, Madhu Kishwar recommends this appeal on the basis that the tradition does have advantageous aspects and records its rejection as one of the factors which have contributed to the rise of the Hindu radical right. Moreover, this debate in which appeal to Hindu beliefs and values is both rejected and accepted, albeit an acceptance predicated on a partial portrait of the Hindu tradition, has distinct echoes of the events of earlier eras.

The specific issues and the wider trends with which the Indian women's movement has to cope in contemporary India do shape the continuing debate about tradition and liberation. However, just as these issues and trends relate to past issues and trends, so too the continuing debate harks back to the ideology and methodology of the Indian women's movement in previous years. In the light of the varied historical experience of the Indian women's movement during which it has both appealed to Hindu beliefs and values in justifying 'women's uplift' and 'equal rights' and abstained from such appeal in respect of the latter, and given that the resurgent movement with its goals of equality and empowerment has both advocated and attacked such appeal, it is hardly surprising that the debate about tradition and liberation continues and that there is no clear consensus on this question. Perhaps appeal to Hindu beliefs and values, though never totally absent, does tend to fall in and out of favour in the Indian women's movement as ideologies and as conditions vary. This pattern can be detected in its 'First Wave' when appeal to Hindu beliefs and values was initially popular and latterly less so. Arguably, this pattern can also be detected in its 'Second Wave' when once appeal to Hindu beliefs and values was comparatively rare but grew to be far more frequent. So possibly, while different opinions are expressed, the Indian women's movement is once again due to react against appeal to Hindu beliefs and values, although the complexity of the arguments involved make it probable that this reaction, if it occurs, will only be another phase and by no means a final or decisive break with the Hindu tradition.

These arguments turn on whether appeal to Hindu beliefs and values is a concession to misogynistic norms, a futile exercise which delimits the potential for change by retaining references to a sexist tradition, or whether it is a means to mobilise mass support, a constructive strategy which maximises the potential for change by preventing the sexist monopolisation of tradition. Underlying these different opinions about appeal to Hindu beliefs and values are thus different attitudes towards the Hindu tradition. According to some, the Hindu tradition has no positive ideals for women and can not be reinterpreted in their interests whereas, according to others, the Hindu tradition does have beneficial qualities and so with care can be restated to the advantage of women. In these contrasting assessments of the Hindu tradition can be seen a major division of opinion within the Indian women's movement as its members dispute how the movement should respond to religion when religion is used to legitimise the oppression of women and when many women are religious.

Does this imply that religion is inevitably and irredeemably associated with the oppression of women and hence that it is imperative to raise women's consciousness about the evils of religion? Or does this imply that religion has been abused by being implicated in the oppression of women and hence that it is imperative to draw to women's attention the true meaning of religion? That these arguments are so complex strongly suggests that the Indian women's movement will struggle with them for the foreseeable future, first tending to one perspective then the other. Notwithstanding, a persuasive case can still be made for the Indian women's movement turning to religion in order to liberate Indian women and, even if this requires a critical and selective reappropriation of the Hindu tradition by the movement, it is no more partial than other versions of the Hindu tradition which the movement opposes.

Some Closing Remarks

This study deals with some very sensitive areas and as such invites criticism both from feminists, who are concerned that the mistreatment of women is not sanitised in relativistic refusal to impose one set of moral standards on another society, and from Hindus, who are concerned that the Hindu tradition is not represented in a wholly negative way by the concentration on practices which have an adverse effect on women. However, this study has tried neither to overlook the sufferings of women in an effort to avoid offending cultural sensibilities nor to sensationalise their suffering and in so doing give a hostile account of the Hindu tradition. Moreover, many of the same points could be made in relation to other women's movements in ex-colonial countries where conditions similar to those in India have obtained and other religious traditions which have also featured prominently in debate about the position of women and how that position could be improved. That is, other women's movements in ex-colonial countries have had to solve the dilemma of balancing their ambitions for women with their own cultural and religious environments and likewise other religious traditions have been the focus of controversy in terms of their actual and potential impact on women. This does not, of course, detract from the distinctiveness of the Indian women's movement in the imperial and independent periods or that of the teachings of the Hindu tradition about women with which this study deals.

This study has shown how the Indian women's movement has variously represented and used the Hindu tradition in the course of its campaigns. In the process, this study has shown that Indian women have not merely been the passive objects of philanthropic endeavour but agents in their own right and that they have frequently found support for their aims and activities in aspects of the Hindu tradition. Thus this study has pointed to the emergence of a considerable number of Indian women as respected public figures whose opinions on diverse subjects, not just the position of women, are taken seriously by society at large. Thus too this study has pointed to the selection of a certain range of material from the Hindu tradition in order to legitimise women playing their full part in Indian life. Therefore, this study has shown why it is worthwhile to analyse how the Indian women's movement has evaluated and interpreted the Hindu tradition since to do so contributes to understanding of the principles and policy of the Indian women's movement as well as discourse about the position of women in the Hindu tradition.

The Indian women's movement has achieved much as is evident from an examination of significant changes in society and, for all the problems of the present though these should not be underestimated, there is reason for optimism that, in the future as in the past, the Indian women's movement will rise to the challenge of its time and seek to secure advances for women. What is more, appeal to Hindu beliefs and values has been an important, albeit far from incontrovertible, characteristic of the work of the Indian women's movement and there is every chance that it will be so in the years to come. This is because, despite the attendant dangers, such appeal promises to reach a wide constituency and, by expressing this appeal in the terms with which that constituency is accustomed, convince them of the authenticity of the claims of the Indian women's movement.

Obviously, this leaves great scope for further research, especially to determine future developments in the relationship between the Indian women's movement and the Hindu tradition, but it is already apparent that simplistic notions of this relationship as always an antagonistic one are to be abandoned as inadequate.

Chapter One

1 For an excellent historical account of this period, see Heimsath 1964 from which background information for this chapter has been drawn unless indicated otherwise.

2 Consequently, western writers often concluded that any improvement in the position of women was directly attributable to the influence of the West, the progressive and enlightened canons of its thought and the individuals and organisations which disseminated them to the Indian people. J. N. Farquhar, for example, noted that 'child-marriage, compulsory widowhood, widow-burning, widow-drudgery, female infanticide and the thousand inhuman cruelties of caste were in the past regarded as inviolably sacred, even by the thinking Hindu' (Farquhar 1912: 192–3). Further, he traced to western influence 'a new attitude to women' (Farquhar 1912: 152), among other changed attitudes, on the part of the educated man of India. Of course, one Indian reaction was to paint a lurid picture of the condition of women in Britain. For instance, asserting that 'as a social entity, both at home and in the business world, the woman of England still is nothing more than a helot' (Singh 1910: 265), Saint Nihal Singh emphasised the difficulties faced by those women who campaigned for female suffrage. He declared: 'Gradually the English woman is coming to realize that she has been man's tool and plaything. She is plainly disgusted with her theoretical role of demi-divinity and her actual status as a sort of demi-monde. She chafes against her helpless, hapless position of enforced, man-ordained servility. She craves no pedestal, no stool on which to be set up as an ornamental statue. She wants to be man's equal half, with an effective voice in the government of a nation of which she constitutes an integral unit' (Singh 1910: 268).

3 How this happened is discussed in more depth in chapter five during an analysis of British administration of Hindu personal law which was in many ways weighted towards orthodoxy although involving some significant variations on the theme.

4 However, for an alternative view see Pollock 1993. Sheldon Pollock addresses Lata Mani's article in detail, arguing that 'critique, rejection and reform do not begin in 1800 in India, and their epistemological building blocks, "authentic tradition" and the like, are not ideas that

spring forth for the first time from the fevered brains of Colebrook, Bentinck, and Rammohun Roy' (Pollock 1993: 100). He also argues that 'if there was a British "Brahmanizing tendency," then, it may largely have recapitulated a precolonial Brahmanizing tendency' while asserting that 'indigenous discourses of power intersected with the colonial variety' (Pollock 1993: 101).

5 Within the hypergamous system of marriage which allows men to marry women of lower status but which does not allow women to marry men of lower status, the permissible marital partners for women of high status are restricted to men of high status. Therefore, Kulin women, who belonged to the highest group of Brahmins, were compelled to marry only Kulin men. In order to secure husbands for their daughters where the supply was limited and the demand great, fathers and guardians went to considerable lengths, often accepting a bridegroom who was already married.

6 Sati denotes both concremation where a widow is burnt with her husband's corpse (*sahamarana* 'dying with', *sahagamana* 'going with') and postcremation where a widow is burnt after her husband's cremation (*anumarana* 'dying after', *anugamana* 'going after').

7 Despite later endorsing Bentinck's decision, initially Roy does seem to have been troubled by the prospect of direct legislative action against sati, preferring a quiet and gradual approach which would have made the performance of sati more difficult and which would have relied on the powers of the police (Ray 1988: 45).

8 Roy did refer to *Ṛg Veda* 10.18.7, a version of which was used to justify sati. He expressed his view in this way: 'Whatever may be the real purport of this passage, no one ever ventured to give it an interpretation as *commanding* widows to burn themselves on the pile and with the corpse of their husbands' (Roy 1906: 369).

9 Bhandarkar concluded: 'That no text has been brought forward by Vijnânesvara, Kamalâkara, Nanda Pandita, Anantadeva, Mahesabhatta, Chandrachúda, and Kâsìnatha Upâdhyâya enjoining the Garbhâdhâna or consummation ceremony on the occasion of the first or any specific course, and that the Asvalâyana Grihaparisishta allows the liberty of performing it at any time' (Bhandarkar 1891: 22).

10 Writers have diverged markedly in their interpretations of Tilak's personal beliefs about social reform, as these passages show. Compare, for example: 'It should be noted that Tilak, who frankly admitted his firm belief in the superiority of the Hindu religion and culture over all others, was not a bigot by temperament. The proof of this is seen in his fearless criticism of religious practices which were repugnant to his conscience or which he regarded as anti-social and harmful to Hindu society. In point of fact he was no less revolutionary in social matters than he was in politics. It is true that Tilak's whole life was devoted to the cause of Indian independence and that it was his uncompromising opposition to the British Raj that made the masses worship him. Nevertheless his claim to be regarded as a social revolutionary is unchallengeable' (Tahmankar 1956: 49) with: 'A thorough examination of Tilak's private papers, however, as well as the totality of his editorial writing in the months

immediately preceding and following the introduction of Scoble's bill proves that Hindu orthodoxy was not deceived as to the viewpoint of its leader by Tilak's occasional genuflection toward the altar of social reform' (Wolpert 1961: 52). In common with Wolpert, the author is inclined to the view that Tilak's infrequent gestures in favour of reform were insincere and hypocritical. Tilak's rationale was that the nationalist cause would suffer by an association with social reform, although his acrimonious exchanges suggest that his motivation was not merely political expediency but abhorrence of such reforms. In any case, and for whatever reason, during the age of consent debate, Tilak acted as the champion of Hindu orthodoxy.

11 The revivalists explicitly rejected the West as the standard to which India should aspire but at the same time were often influenced by it, irrespective of whether they were prepared to acknowledge this.

12 Dayananda Saraswati permitted the marriage of those widows whose marriages had not been consummated. For those widows whose marriages had been consummated, he set forth three options, viz., chastity, adoption of a male heir and *niyoga*, defining *niyoga* as the temporary union of a widow and widower with the purpose of raising children for the woman's late husband. He advocated that women marry between the ages of 16 and 24 when they had completed their education. He also insisted upon monogamy and, in line with his belief that the sexes were to be treated in the same way by the rules regulating marriage, resisted the seclusion of women within their homes while men were free to work in the world. It should be noted, however, that he did differentiate between the ages at which men and women should marry and accepted a certain complementarity of roles for husbands and wives.

13 For Swami Vivekananda, education was always the first step and it was an integral part of his critique of the reformers that they had not concentrated on education for all but had confined themselves to the insular concerns of already privileged social groups.

Chapter Two

1 For example, Jana Matson Everett descibes a shift from 'women's associations started by men active in Hindu reform associations' to 'local women's associations' formed by 'women relatives of reformist - oriented leaders' to 'national and provincial women's associations . . . started by women who had acquired experience in local women's associations' (Everett 1981: 51, 60, 68). Or again, Geraldine Forbes describes how 'the first organizations for women were begun by men who belonged to the new religious reform associations' while 'women's associations . . . [formed by women] sprang up all over India in the late nineteenth and early twentieth centuries' although it was not until 'after World War I [that] national women's organizations were created' (Forbes 1996: 65, 70, 72). Similar accounts of the process by which the women's movement developed may also be found elsewhere.

2 Biographical information on Ramabai Ranade has been taken from her autobiography and from Sorabji 1929 and Engineer and Choksi 1929 supplemented by Everett 1981 and Forbes 1996.

3 There is a wide measure of agreement that the support of male reformers was a vital factor in the foundation of the Arya Mahila Samaj although there is no scholarly consensus on whether the initiative was taken by the reformers or whether Pandita Ramabai was the motive force.

4 Biographical information on Sarala Devi Choudurani has been taken from Everett 1981, Forbes 1996 and Kumar 1993.

5 As Jana Matson Everett relates when discussing the addresses given to the annual conferences of the Bharat Stree Mahamandal 'in 1912 Sarala Devi spoke on the honored position of women during the Aryan period' (Everett 1981: 71).

6 Biographical information on Pandita Ramabai Sarasvati has been taken from Rachel Bodley's introduction to *The High-Caste Hindu Woman*, Forbes 1996 and Kumar 1993. A penetrating analysis of her ideas is given by Gail Omvedt who emphasises that 'it was Pandita Ramabai who was the first to proclaim, with great clarity, backed by her personal refusal to remain a Hindu, that the Sanskritic core of Hinduism was irrevocably and essentially anti-woman' (Omvedt 1995: 26). Consequently, Gail Omvedt insists that Pandita Ramabai excluded the possibility of reinterpreting the tradition in favour of women, a possibility which, in their different ways, be they scriptural or historical, others endorsed.

7 Biographical information on Chimna-Bai, the Maharani of Baroda, has been taken from Basu and Ray 1990.

8 For the legendary biographies of Sītā and Draupadī, see the next chapter.

9 Biographical information on Saroj Nalini Dutt has been taken from Dutt 1929, Everett 1981 and Forbes 1996.

10 For the legendary biographies of Maitreyī and Gārgī, see the next chapter. Līlāvatī was traditionally regarded as the author of a mathematical treatise (Sircar 1953: 296–7) while, according to legend, Maṇḍana Miśra's wife, Bhāratī, presided over a philosophical contest between her husband and Śaṅkara, after which she challenged Śaṅkara as the victor and eventually, along with her husband, became his student (Potter 1981: 117–18; Sircar 1953: 297).

Chapter Three

1 Biographical information on Annie Besant has been taken from Aiyar 1968 and Nethercot 1963.

2 Biographical information on Sarojini Naidu has been taken from Baig 1974 and Sengupta 1966.

3 Jana Matson Everett classifies their speeches and writings as conceiving 'the goals of the women's movement in women's uplift terms' (Everett 1981: 85). Though she examines their speeches and writings in the period 1901–18 'during the heyday of revivalist ideology' (Everett 1981: 84), what is noticeable is that far earlier, in the case of Annie Besant, and far later, in the case of Sarojini Naidu, their approach was revivalist.

In the case of Annie Besant, her lecture on 'India, Her Past and Her Future' on board the Kaiser-i-Hind in 1893 criticised contemporary Hindu social practices on the basis of early Aryan society. After a glowing description of early Aryan marriage, she declared: 'In such households [of the early Aryan people] grew up the heroic women who stand out for all time from Sanskrit literature – women great not only in the home but also in spiritual knowledge; such as Maitreyi, who "was fond of discussing the nature of Brahma". Again, in an assembly of Brahmans you may read how Gargi, a woman, got up and put questions to Yajnavalkya which that learned teacher answered with full care and respect. What Hindu can there be who does not feel his heart swell with pride when he thinks of those women, or of women like Sita, Savitri and Sakuntala? And what Hindu does not feel his heart shrink with pain when he contrasts those heroic figures with the women of to-day, sweet and pure and devoted as they are by the million, but still half children, encaged in the prison of the zenana and the still worse prison of the ignorance in which they dwell?' (Besant 1917: 42–3). This lecture evinced the characteristic revivalist juxtaposition of ancient and modern norms, and hence a plea for change in present conditions on a past model, even if conservative in sentiment and limited in scope.

In the case of Sarojini Naidu, her presidential address to the Women's Indian Association in 1934 appealed to Lakṣmī, Sarasvatī and Pārvatī, the consorts of Viṣṇu, Brahmā and Śiva respectively, to inspire women to assume social and political responsibilities. She urged: 'So Indian womanhood, if it were to be perfect, must fulfil the qualities of this Triune of Godhead, each woman being in herself - not only in her own home and for her own community but for the world - Lakshmi, the giver of happiness and prosperity; Saraswati, the embodiment of wisdom, and Parvati, the eternal Mother, who uplifts the fallen, purifies the sinner, gives hopes [sic] to the despairing, strength to the weak, and courage to the coward, and recreates in man the divine energy' (Naidu 1934). This address made a call for women's participation in public life in typical revivalist fashion.

Implicit in the above analysis is an interpretation of Annie Besant's initial attitude towards Indian social issues and of Gandhi's impact upon Sarojini Naidu's ideas but these themes fall outside the scope of this study.

4 In the case of Sarojini Naidu, see also Forbes 1975 and Ratté 1985. As Geraldine Forbes explains: 'Sarojini Naidu had been active in the social and political organisations of her time and had encouraged many women to enter public life. She and the women who followed her were accepted by their society as good Indian women. Sarojini had succeeded, she had convinced her society, through speeches and personal behavior, that these activities were consistent with the activities of Indian women in a glorious "golden age"' (Forbes 1975: 63). Or again, as Lou Ratté argues: 'Sarojini Naidu provided nationalist society with a new view of gender which sanctioned non-traditional behavior through traditional references' (Ratté 1985: 368).

5 For example, Maria Mies observes: 'The social reformers of the 19th century and the freedom fighters of the 20th tried to reconstruct from the

classical Hindu texts an image of woman that could withstand the criticism of Victorian Englishmen. What they then preached as the traditional virtues of the Indian women [sic] were individual traits seen through Victorian glasses and had the goal of putting up an image of woman that could morally compete with the Western bourgeois concept of womanhood' (Mies 1980: 122).

6 Notwithstanding, the emphasis on ancient India and ancient Indian scripture must be qualified. Although the past was regarded as normative, it was not always India's ancient past which acted as the justifying past referent. Thus, on at least some occasions, Annie Besant dated the change she detected in the position of women to comparatively recent times, attributing this change to the introduction of western-style education for men under British rule which, she argued, had alienated men from women and excluded women from public life (Besant 1921: 334–5; Besant 1939: 113–15). From such statements, it would seem that Annie Besant believed that the ancient pattern had prevailed in India until the nineteenth century. Or again, Sarojini Naidu made mention of Padminī of Chitor, a Rajput heroine who ended her life by entering a communal funeral pyre when her husband and his army faced inevitable defeat in battle (Naidu 1918: 113, 122). In this way, Sarojini Naidu pointed to a great woman of Indian history just as she cited female characters in scripture. In these instances, however, what was stressed was the persistence of ancient Indian norms.

7 The following discussion has been informed by Jana Matson Everett's account of the writings and speeches of Annie Besant and Sarojini Naidu. Among the points she makes are that earlier in their careers Annie Besant and Sarojini Naidu 'communicated the idea that women could make a special contribution to development by dedication and by inspiring family members for the task of development' whereas later they 'claimed that women's roles and values within the family particularly suited them for a direct role in national development activities' (Everett 1981: 87). She also emphasises the way in which Annie Besant and Sarojini Naidu 'appealed to ancient Indian ideals' which, they insisted, 'had inspired the women's movement' whereby they associated 'the revival of Indian glory with the restoration of the ideals of Indian womanhood' based on an analysis of India's past greatness and the reason for its fall from greatness (Everett 1981: 87). However, she does not focus on the reference to scriptural figures which here is treated as an aspect of the appeal to ancient India by Annie Besant and Sarojini Naidu.

8 Both these points can be illustrated with reference to Śakuntalā. Her story is told in the Mahābhārata and also in the Abhijñānaśakuntalā (The Recognition of Śakuntalā) of the classical dramatist Kālidāsa. Kālidāsa's play was inspired by the Mahābhārata narrative but it reworked the Epic version. Kālidāsa changed the characterisation of Śakuntalā, rendering her passive and submissive by ceding the initiative to her husband. She neither stated her terms for the marriage nor confronted her husband insisting that he acknowledge her and their son; instead, she was so much in love that she accepted her husband's proposal without conditions and it was her husband, sorely troubled by his repudiation of Śakuntalā and the

loss of his heir, who yearned to find both wife and son (Thapar 1987: 3). Kālidāsa's play was translated into European languages, indeed, Goethe's response to one translation became famous in its own right. This is important because western sources favoured Kālidāsa's play over the account in the Epic and, indeed, Annie Besant made explicit mention of Goethe's high opinion of Śakuntalā.

9 There are two recensions of the tale of Yājñavalkya's decision to abandon the household life. The scholarly consensus is that 2.4.1–14 is the earlier or primary version and 4.5.1–15 is the later or secondary version. Apart from comparatively minor differences, the dialogue between Maitreyī and Yājñavalkya is the same in both recensions. The major difference is the addition of a verse (4.5.1) which designates Maitreyī as a discourser on sacred knowledge *(brahmāvadinī)* and describes Kātyāyanī, Maitreyī's co-wife, as having a woman's understanding *(strīprajñā)*. This verse thus makes explicit claims about the status of Maitreyī.

10 As Prabhati Mukherjee explains: 'The eternal triumvirate – Sita, Savitri and Parvati – demonstrates that the only goal in a woman's life was to be an ideal wife. What was being upheld was ideal wifehood not ideal womanhood' (Mukherjee 1983: 380). In a discussion which includes most, but not all, of the female characters mentioned by Annie Besant and Sarojini Naidu as well as other characters whom they did not mention, Prabhati Mukherjee suggests: 'Draupadi's polyandrous marriage, . . . Kunti's method of obtaining sons before and after marriage, . . . Damayanti's plan for remarriage, Sakuntala's parentage and her secret marriage – all these "faults" tarnished their image. Maitreyi violated the norm of an ideal by preferring knowledge to serving her husband as a god. Gargi and other women are wellknown [*sic*] for their learning – a quality not desirable in women. Therefore, by the touchstone of strict standards for ideals demanded by Hindu tradition, none of them could acquit herself as creditably as did Sita, Savitri and Parvati' (Mukherjee 1983: 379–80). However, even where characters were regarded as good women, their characterisation was stereotyped to conform with the traditional view of the perfect wife. For example, though Sītā displayed traits of wilfulness and selfishness and Sāvitrī chose her own husband, the tradition ignored these facts in favour of idealised portraits of the perfect wife (cf. Cormack 1961: 87).

11 It does seem from this survey of their speeches and writings that Annie Besant appealed to a larger number of scriptural figures and in more detail than Sarojini Naidu. If this proves to be accurate when a wider selection of their speeches and writings are reviewed, a reason for it may be found in the ways the two women were introduced to the Hindu tradition, the former experiencing it as an adult and favouring literary sources, the latter, however westernised in some respects, growing up within it and familiar with many of its manifestations, although this explanation is speculative. The different manner in which they appealed to scriptural figures, at least in the material under discussion here, also means that some of the above analysis applies more explicitly to Annie Besant, however, the import and implications of Sarojini Naidu's appeal to scriptural figures was much the same.

12 Some indication of how Annie Besant went about appealing to scriptural figures can be seen in a study of these descriptions of epic characters. What she probably had in mind in Kausalyā's case was Kausalyā's participation in the *Aśvamedha* (horse sacrifice) which was performed in order to secure the succession. In the cases of Sītā and Draupadī, where she referred to occasions when they advised their husbands on a course of action, she was possibly thinking of Sītā's recommendation that Rāma live as a hermit in the forest espousing non-violence and Draupadī's urging that the Pāṇḍavas seize the initiative against the Kauravas (though in neither instance was their advice taken). Certainly, in the case of Gāndhārī, she had in mind Gāndhārī's unsuccessful attempt to dissuade Duryodhana from further defiance when he refused to abide by the terms of the settlement made with the Pāṇḍavas. Similar points could be made in respect of other lists of scriptural figures.

13 Indentured labour was the system whereby an Indian would emigrate to another part of the British Empire, according to the terms of a contract which specified the conditions of service, such as the wages to be received, the duration of the agreement, and the arrangements on its expiry (renewal, settlement, or repatriation). However, there was growing concern about this system among Indians, who were troubled by the exploitation it involved and resentful of the principle of subordination it represented. Consequently, there were demands for its abolition. One of the most flagrant of the abuses of this system was the manner in which Indian women were compelled to submit to the sexual attentions of male emigrants and employers.

14 Although omitted from the foregoing discussion, Annie Besant and Sarojini Naidu also referred to other religions in India. For example, in the case of Islam, Annie Besant directly addressed and countered western criticisms of the status of Muslim women: rejecting the accusation that, according to Islam, women did not have souls; admitting the charge of polygyny, although representing it as an improvement on the sexual mores prevailing at the time of Muhammed and comparing it favourably with western practice where a man might take only one wife but might have extra-marital sexual relationships; indeed, while excluding polygyny, Annie Besant declared 'Musalman women have been far better treated than Western women by the law' (Besant 1917: 344), citing property rights as a case in point. Or again, Sarojini Naidu praised Islam as having 'once more asserted the abiding verity that gave woman her responsibility and her place in the National life' (Naidu 1918a: 167), noting women's property rights under Islamic law. Certainly, one of the major themes of her speeches and writings was Hindu-Muslim unity. Even so, both women drew most heavily on the Hindu tradition.

Chapter Four

1 Historical information on the founding of the All India Women's Conference has been taken from Basu and Ray 1990 supplemented by Asthana 1974 and Desai 1977.

2 Biographical information on these women has been taken from Basu and Ray 1990.

3 Jana Matson Everett analyses these two speeches, isolating 'women's uplift' from 'equal rights' elements. She assigns to the former category the Rani of Mandi's recollection of Patna's past and Muthulakshmi Reddi's reference to the lesson of India's history. She assigns to the latter category the two instances concerning the teaching of the Buddha and the position of women in ancient South India which are the foci of the following discussion (Everett 1981: 91–2). Although she did not develop her analysis in any detail, this discussion of the speeches of the Rani of Mandi and Muthulakshmi Reddi is informed by her account as is the discussion of the speeches of Margaret Cousins and Rameshwari Nehru later in this chapter, however, in their cases, a wider range of material is included.

4 This is not to ignore the way in which Dr Ambedkar politicised Buddhism and pioneered the movement to convert Untouchables to this religion. Ambedkar advocated conversion to Buddhism on the grounds that its fundamental principle was equality and as a means of securing an enhanced social status for his community. He also defended the Buddhist record on women, rejecting the authenticity of the passage on the admission of women into the *saṅgha* which, according to him, gave a negative impression of the Buddha's attitude to women. He also represented the Order of Nuns, despite the seniority of the Order of Monks, as an improvement upon ancient Hindu ideas which, he claimed, were preferable to modern Hindu beliefs. See, for example, Wilkinson and Thomas 1972.

5 This was an approach which chimed in with an Indian-style secular nationalism but Islam in particular was sometimes left in an anomalous position given the tendency to blame foreign influences for all of India's ills.

6 Evidently, the Rani of Mandi's version was selective (cf. *Culla Vagga* 10.1). Yet was this story suitable for the Rani of Mandi's purpose, given the Buddha's apparently reluctant concession to Mahāpajāpatī, his aunt and foster-mother? Uma Chakravarti refers to this story in the course of her discussion of *samaṇa* culture and social attitudes, the former accepting 'everyone had the potential for salvation', the latter being 'generally against women' (Chakravarti 1987: 31). She states: 'The Buddha did not want *bhikkunīs* in the *saṅgha*. If permission was finally (and grudgingly) granted it was entirely because Ānanda made the Buddha concede that women were as capable of salvation as men, which in itself was a recognized principle of the *samaṇa* culture. In fact, in the entire early Buddhist literature only Ānanda seems to have genuinely believed in the principles of equality between men and women, and he systematically championed their cause' (Chakravarti 1987: 31–2). However, as Nancy Schuster Barnes relates, the provenance and import of this story have been questioned, doubts about its genuineness based on its supposed unrepresentativeness of early Buddhist scriptural statements about women (Barnes 1987: 107).

7 A considerable body of literature has developed which discusses the status and image of women in Buddhism. Without rehearsing such arguments in

detail, it is possible to contrast the Buddha's pronouncements on women's spiritual capacities; according to Buddhist scriptures, the Buddha both affirmed and denied that women could achieve enlightenment. Thus *Majjhima Nikāya* 1.466 recorded the Buddha as accepting that a woman could destroy the five fetters and be released from the round of birth, death and rebirth while *Aṅguttara Nikāya* 1.27.1.15 recorded the Buddha as rejecting the possibility that a woman could attain to the spiritual ideal which he taught.

8 There are often competing traditions concerning goddesses, some portraying the goddess as an independent figure and some portraying her in a marital relationship. It is possible that there are other versions of the Mīnākṣī myth in which she retains her autonomy and sovereignty, unlike the 'official' version in which she is domesticated and subordinated. Alternatively, it is possible that those aspects of the Mīnākṣī myth in which she is free and powerful are those which are normally stressed. This would be analogous with the mythology of Kālī who is recorded as being married to Śiva and ultimately submitting to his authority although she is remembered for her fierce and dangerous unpredictability and frequently shown as dominant over her husband.

9 These statements are tentative given scholarly disagreement on the matter. There is, though, a consensus that the popular image of Auvaiyār confuses two or more Tamil poetesses.

10 Jana Matson Everett makes this point in relation to the history of the All India Women's Conference. As she explains, 'the first few AIWC presidents sought to give legitimacy to a new idea by claiming inspiration from traditional ideals' whereas 'in the second period, AIWC presidents generally appealed to liberal and scientific values to justify their advocacy of equal rights' (Everett 1981: 93, 96). Among the earlier presidents she includes the Rani of Mandi and Muthulakshmi Reddi whose traditional justification for 'equal rights' has been examined in the foregoing section. Margaret Cousins and Rameshwari Nehru whose writings and speeches are considered in the following section she includes among the later presidents who offered a liberal justification for 'equal rights'. Commenting on the advocacy of 'equal rights' by later presidents, she notes: 'There was no attempt made to convince their audience of the value of equal rights for women outside the terms of the liberal framework of individual liberty, equality, and justice' (Everett 1981: 95).

11 Jana Matson Everett's account of the liberal justification of 'equal rights' is illustrated by references to and quotations from Margaret Cousins' and Rameshwari Nehru's presidential addresses to the All India Women's Conference along with those delivered by other colleagues. Thus she shows how 'the focus on equal rights had a broadening influence on the view of women's movement tasks' (Everett 1981: 93) as well as pointing to Margaret Cousins' rejection of double standards and Rameshwari Nehru's support for reform of Hindu personal law by way of demonstrating the hold of liberal ideals and commitment to equality. However, she does not identify the manner in which their speeches diverged from this liberal and egalitarian line, especially when deferring to Gandhi's importance as a national leader (though she does acknowledge Gandhian influence on the

210

organisation in general terms and make the astute observation that acceptance of Gandhi's teaching was not unconditional so that, when Gandhian orthodoxy clashed with the organisation's objectives, the organisation was prepared to pursue an independent policy, see Everett 1981: 97–8).

12 It should be noted, however, that speeches by earlier presidents of the All India Women's Conference also mentioned the organisation's achievements along with many traditional references. Jana Matson Everett includes 'the accomplishments of the women's movement' with 'Indian tradition' as 'Indian sources of inspiration' for 'equal rights' (Everett 1981: 92). While clearly the organisation's achievements can be seen to constitute an Indian source of inspiration, this does not seem to make a sufficiently clear distinction between the example of India's past and present activities. Moreover, notwithstanding Jana Matson Everett's contention that speeches by later presidents justified 'women's uplift' by reference to 'women's movement accomplishments' (Everett 1981: 96), when the organisation's achievements are mentioned in speeches where traditional references, if any, are few, this seems to show increased confidence in 'equal rights' and in the authority of the organisation as a liberal source of authentication for this ideology.

13 She took a rather different tone in 'The Hindu Code' where she made the case that ancient Indian law 'represented a society which was much more equitable and just' while 'the Hindu law in vogue to-day is not the unadulterated gift of our Rishis but is a concoction prepared by the degenerate society of a decadent period' (Nehru 1950: 39, 41). On this basis, she portrayed the proposed reform of Hindu personal law as the means by which that law could be restored 'into conformity with the original ideas of our lawgivers' so that 'there is nothing in it which goes against the Spirit of the Hindu Shastras or of the Hindu Dharma in any material sense' (Nehru 1950: 41). This showed that she was prepared to provide traditional references in support of a measure of which she approved, presumably because it was at least a step towards equality.

Chapter Five

1 For more detailed accounts of the campaign for women's political rights on which this summary is based, see Everett 1981 and Forbes 1979, 1996. Jana Matson Everett asserts that 'in India the principle of female suffrage was quickly accepted' and that an 'easy victory' was won to which 'the Indian women's movement contribution lay in raising the issue in a manner that appealed to the values held by both Indian elites and the British authorities' (Everett 1981: 194). However, Geraldine Forbes criticises this view because 'there was considerable debate over the questions of who should have the vote, and . . . the right to vote was not "granted" without pressure from organized women' (Forbes 1979: 3). The notion that women's political rights were recognised as readily as Everett's

description 'easy victory' suggests is, as Forbes contends, rather dubious, although perhaps such a view can be justified in comparative perspective, given the hostility that the championing of women's social rights aroused in India and the acrimony the issue of votes for women engendered in Britain.

2 For more detailed accounts of the campaign for women's social rights on which this summary is based, see Everett 1981 and Forbes 1996. Jana Matson Everett stresses 'the religious significance of personal law in India', arguing that 'although Hindu men supported women's movement campaigns on secular issues, many Hindus would not accept the application of equal rights principles in the religious sphere, traditionally governed by hierarchical principles' (Everett 1981: 195). In contrast, Geraldine Forbes comments that 'franchise and civil rights [a category in which she includes reform of personal law] were ideal issues for women to pursue since discussions of them could take place without reference to sensitive social or cultural matters' (Forbes 1996: 93). A review of the controversy surrounding the Hindu Code Bill lends credence to Everett's account rather than Forbes' because a major component of this controversy was religious in nature.

3 Detailed accounts of Hindu personal law and the history of the Hindu Code Bill are given in Derrett 1957, 1968 and Levy 1973. The following outline is heavily reliant on these works but also draws on Everett 1981 and Forbes 1996.

4 A brief but useful analysis of this response is given in Everett 1981.

5 Certainly, the committee cited some statements of this sort. For example, the Hindu Women's Association announced: 'We are against the codification of Hindu Law. It is not possible nor desirable and nobody wants it. We are quite happy as we are' (HLC 1947: 87). Furthermore, the Maharani of Natore and other Purdanashin women declared: 'We object to the Code in every respect. We are quite happy as we are. For the sake of a few, such radical alterations should not be made' (HLC 1947: 86).

6 As Geraldine Forbes points out, 'unlike previous committees that dismissed women's testimony as representative of the educated elite, this committee tended to dismiss the views of orthodox Hindus' and, overall, gave 'the impression that Indian women were well informed about legal changes and supportive of them' (Forbes 1996: 118).

7 For an insightful account of the way in which reform was 'Sanskritised' during the controversy surrounding the Hindu Code Bill, see Levy 1973. An example of this is where Harold Levy explains that '"Sanskritization" of the debate occurred in the sense that rationales for and against the Code were understood, or at least presented, from an avowedly Sanskritic perspective' (Levy 1973: 463).

8 As Jana Matson Everett points out, 'none of the AIWC speeches of the 1940s justified Hindu Law reform on this basis [shastric arguments], while Renuka Ray and Durgabai used shastric arguments in Parliament' (Everett 1981: 182).

9 Biographical information on Renuka Ray has been taken from Basu and Ray 1990.

10 These arguments at least partially reprised those she had used in assembly debates as well as being typical of those often used by many supporters of the Hindu Code Bill (Levy 1973).

11 *Manu's Dharmaśāstra* 2.67. This negative reference in common with the positive references to the Hindu tradition elsewhere in the article could be challenged for accuracy, although that it is not to suggest that the arguments of opponents of the Hindu Code Bill were in any way incontrovertible. In this specific instance, the importance she gave to this one text, especially as the cause of a general, not just spiritual, loss of status, was extremely questionable but, of course, such scholarly criticism did not detract from the supposed utility of this strategy for supporters of the Hindu Code Bill.

12 Thus, in his discussion of the 1943–4 debates, Harold Levy explains: 'Her [Renuka Ray's] Sanskritic Code rationale was given with a sincere sense of satisfaction that Sanskritic Hindu tradition did provide support for the Code. But for her to give this rationale such emphasis, or even to give it at all, was a definite compromise as she would have preferred to discuss the Code on entirely secular grounds' (Levy 1973: 471–2).

13 In accounting for this change, Harold Levy further argues that Nehru made a significant contribution to the rise of the secular mode of argument: 'Nehru, especially in 1952–6, implicitly disclaimed Sanskritic authority and explicitly sought to establish a secular modern idiom of legislative discourse. Code-supporters directly relied on constitutional provisions of equality before the law, against sexual and caste discrimination, and for Hindu law reform as an exception to the religious liberty guarantee' (Levy 1973: 497).

Chapter Six

1 See, for example, comments made by Vina Mazumdar, a member of the Committee on the Status of Women in India, when asked about *Towards Equality* some years after its publication. She told her interviewer: 'Until 1980, whenever anyone asked me about the women's movement, I'd say, "There isn't one". I don't think either of us could say that today. There is something going on. A lot of interest was there earlier too, but it did not have a chance to be articulated. Whether all these people are even aware of the *Report*, I don't know, but I have been told by many women who had earlier been active that they drew fresh energy from it, realised anew that there were a lot of issues that had to be fought' (Mazumdar 1983: 270).

2 Historical information on the women's movement generally has been taken from Desai n.d. and for the All India Women's Conference from Basu and Ray 1990.

3 The two examples discussed below are also discussed in Kumar 1993 where many of the same points are made.

4 This summary is based on Allchin 1982, Chengappa 1998, Hiltebeitel 1978, Srinivasan 1984 and Sullivan 1964.

5 There are, of course, cross-cultural parallels for her argument as many feminists have argued for a patriarchal Aryan invasion which destroyed matriarchal Goddess-worshipping societies. Moreover, events in ancient India are commonly cited as proof of this. See, for example, Stone 1976.

6 For general discussion of the matriarchal hypothesis, see, for example, Binford 1982. Sally Binford refers to the problems posed for feminist anthropologists by 'the flip side of the myth-as-history coin currently in vogue in some feminist circles' which is 'the myth of Former Matriarchal Greatness and the Overthrow of the Mother Goddess' (Binford 1982: 542).

7 Mahatma Gandhi is among those who referred to Sītā, although reactions to his views differ markedly. Gandhi accepted the notion of sex role complementarity but he condemned man's arrogation of a superior status on this basis. Accordingly he insisted that Sītā precede Rāma. He attached great importance to chastity, which he combined with opposition to female segregation since he asserted that chastity could not be secured by confining women but only by personal moral choice. In support of his case, he recalled Sītā's preservation of her chastity during her captivity. He was worried not only about India's political, but also economic, independence, and actively promoted swadeshī (self-reliance) by encouraging the wearing of khadi (homespun). He countered the allure of foreign luxuries by citing Sītā's dress during exile (Tendulkar 1960–3). Clearly, Madhu Kishwar approves of Gandhi's ideas both in respect of Sītā and Mīrābāī, the latter, as she explains, becoming 'a symbol of Satyagraha' (Kishwar 1984: 47). However, for an opposing view see, for example, Mies 1975: 58.

Where the component parts of collected works or equivalents are short in length and two or more in number, parenthetical references are given to the collected works only, while full bibliographical details are confined to the bibliography (although some details about individual extracts may be included in the main text).

Agnes, F. (1995) Redefining the Agenda of the Women's Movement within a Secular Framework, in *Women and Right-Wing Movements: Indian Experiences*, ed. T. Sarkar and U. Butalia, 136–57, London: Zed Books.

AIWC, see under All India Women's Conference.

Aiyar, C. P. R. (1968) *Biographical Vistas: Sketches of some Eminent Indians*, Bombay: Asia Publishing House.

Allchin, B. and R. (1982) *The Rise of Civilization in India and Pakistan*, Cambridge: Cambridge University Press.

All-India Anti-Hindu-Code Convention. (1948) in *The History of Doing: An Illustrated Account of Movements for Women's Rights and Feminism in India, 1800–1990*, R. Kumar, 98–9, London: Verso 1993.

All India Women's Conference (AIWC). (1936) Memorandum to the League of Nations, *The Indian Annual Register* vol. II (July–December): 332–7.

Asthana, P. (1974) *Women's Movement in India*, New Delhi: Vikas.

Baig, T. A. (1974) *Sarojini Naidu*, New Delhi: Publications Division, Ministry of Information and Broadcasting, Government of India.

—— (1976) *India's Woman Power*, New Delhi: S. Chand.

Bandhopadhyay, S. (1987) Seven Decades Ago . . ., *Manushi* no. 42–3: 35–6.

Baroda, Maharani of (Chimna-Bai) and S. M. Mitra. (1912) *The Position of Women in Indian Life*, Second Edition, London: Longmans, Green & Company.

Barnes, N. S. (1987) Buddhism, in *Women in World Religions*, ed. A. Sharma, 105–33, New York: State University of New York Press.

Basu, A. and B. Ray. (1990) *Women's Struggle: A History of the All India Women's Conference 1927–1990*, New Delhi: Manohar.

Besant, A. (1901) Lecture IV Womanhood, in *Ancient Ideals in Modern Life: Four Lectures Delivered at the Twenty-fifth Anniversary Meeting at the Theosophical Society at Benares, December 1900*, 107–43, London: The Theosophical Publishing Society.

—— (1917) India, her Past and her Future [1893/4] 37–60, The Education of

Hindu Youth [1897] 107–15, The Education of Indian Girls [1904] 149–56, Girls' Education [1915] 157–62, The Necessity for Social Reform [1914] 217–36, Indian Women [1896] 303–10, Islam in the Light of Theosophy [n.d.] 329–47, in *The Birth of New India: A Collection of Writings and Speeches on Indian Affairs*, Madras: Theosophical Publishing House.

—— (1921) The Value of Theosophy in the Raising of India [1904] 154–80 [also in Besant 1917, 368–9], Congress Presidential Address, Calcutta Congress [1917] 289–99, The Government of India Bill, 1919 (submitted to Joint Commitee of Parliament on the Government of India Bill 1919 on behalf of the National Home Rule League). 3. The Statement [1919] 425–33, Presidential Address to the Reform Conference [1921] 446–79, in *Speeches and Writings of Annie Besant*, Third Edition, Madras: G. A. Natesan & Co.

—— (1939) Hinduism and Nationality [1915] 102–7, The Part of Women in the Uplift of India [1915] 113–8, in *The Besant Spirit*, vol 3, *Indian Problems*, Madras: Theosophical Publishing House.

Bhandarkar, R. G. (1891) A Note on the Age of Marriage and its Consummation according to Hindu Religious Law, Poona: Arya Vijaya Press.

A Bill to Remove All Legal Obstacles to the Marriage of Hindu Widows. (1855) in *The History of Doing: An Illustrated Account of Movements for Women's Rights and Feminism in India, 1800–1990*, R. Kumar, 18–19, London: Verso 1993.

Bilimoria, P. (1993) Rights and Duties: The (Modern) Indian Dilemma, in *Ethical and Political Dilemmas of Modern India*, ed. N. Smart and S. Thakur, 30–59, Basingstoke: Macmillan.

Binford, S. R. (1982) Myths and Matriarchy, in *The Politics of Women's Spirituality: Essays on the Rise of Spiritual Power Within the Feminist Movement*, ed. C. Spretnak, 541–9, New York: Anchor Press.

Brockington, J. L. (1988) Warren Hastings and the beginnings of British Indology, paper read at Sanskrit Tradition in the Modern World Conference, University of Newcastle.

Calman, L. J. (1989) Women and Movement Politics in India, *Asian Survey* vol. 29 no. 10: 940–58.

Carroll, L. (1983) Law, Custom and Statutory Social Reform: The Hindu Widow's Remarriage Act of 1856, *Indian Economic and Social History Review* vol. 20: 363–88.

Chaitanya, K. (1971) *A History of Malayalam Literature*, Poona: Orient Longman.

Chakravarti, U. (1987) *The Social Dimensions of Early Buddhism*, Delhi: Oxford University Press.

Chandralekha. (1983) Interviews with Vina Mazumdar and Chandralekha, interview by M. Dubey, *The Book Review* vol. 7 pt 6: 267–74.

Chattopadhyaya, K. (1929) The Status of Women in India, in *Women in Modern India: Fifteen Papers by Indian Women*, ed. E. Gedge and M. Choksi, 1–13, Bombay: D. B. Taraporewala Sons & Co.

Chengappa, R. (1998) The Indus Riddle, *India Today International* (26 January): 44–51.

Chitnis, S. (1988) Feminism: Indian Ethos and Indian Convictions, in *Women in Indian Society: A Reader*, ed. R. Ghadially, 81–95, New Delhi: Sage Publications. (Article adapted from: Feminism in India, *Canadian Women Studies*, vol. 6 pt 1 1985).

Choudurani, S. D. (1911) A Women's Movement, *The Modern Review* (October): 344–50.

Cohen, A. P. (1985) *The Symbolic Construction of Community*, Chichester: Ellis Horwood.

Commitee on the Status of Women in India (CSWI). (1974) *Towards Equality: Report of the Committee on the Status of Women in India*, New Delhi: Government of India, Ministry of Education and Social Welfare, Department of Social Welfare.

Cormack, M. (1961) *The Hindu Woman*, London: Asia Publishing House.

Coulson, M. (transl.). (1981) Śakuntalā (Introduction and Translation), in *Three Sanskrit Plays*: Śakuntalā *by* Kālidāsa; Rākshasa's Ring *by* Viśākhadatta; Mālatī and Mādhava *by* Bhavabhūti, Harmondsworth: Penguin Books.

Cousins, M. E. (1936) The All India Women's Conference Presidential Address, *The Indian Annual Register* vol. II (July–December): 356–9.

Cousins, J. H. and M. E. (1950) *We Two Together*, Madras: Ganesh & Co.

CSWI, see under Committee on the Status of Women in India.

Dalrymple, W. (1997) Flames of Passion, *The Sunday Telegraph Magazine* (9 March): 8–11.

Derrett, J. D. M. (1957) *Hindu Law Past and Present: Being an Account of the Controversy which Preceded the Enactment of the Hindu Code, the Text of the Code as Enacted, and some Comments thereon*, Calcutta: A Mukherjee & Co.

—— (1968) *Religion, Law and the State in India*, London: Faber & Faber.

Desai, N. (n.d.) Emergence and Development of Women's Organisations in India, Bombay: Vithaldas Vidya Vihar SNDT Women's University Research Unit on Women's Studies.

—— (1977) *Woman in Modern India*, Second Edition, Bombay: Vora & Co.

Deshpande, K. (1953) Great Hindu Women in Maharashtra, in *Great Women of India: The Holy Mother Birth Centenary Memorial*, ed. Swami Madhavananda and R. C. Majumdar, 343–61, Mayavati: Advaita Ashrama.

Dhagamwar, V. (1988) Saint, victim or criminal, *Seminar* no. 342: 34–9.

Doniger, W. with B. K. Smith (transl.). (1991) *The Laws of Manu*, Harmondsworth: Penguin.

Dutt, G.S. (1929) *A Woman of India: Being the Life of Saroj Nalini*, London: Hogarth Press.

Eck, D.L. and D. Jain. (1986) [Introduction to] *Speaking of Faith: Cross-cultural Perspectives on Women, Religion and Social Change*, ed. D. L. Eck and D. Jain, 1–14, London: the Women's Press.

Edwardes, M. (1967) *British India 1772–1947: A Survey of the Nature and Effects of Alien Rule*, London: Sidgwick & Jackson.

Embree, A.T. (1990) *Utopias in Conflict: Religion and Nationalism in Modern India*, Berkeley: University of California Press.

Engineer, and M. Choksi. (1929) Seva Sadan and other Social Work in Bombay, in *Women in Modern India: Fifteen Papers by Indian Women*, ed. E. Gedge and M. Choksi, 43–50, Bombay: D. B. Taraporewala Sons & Co.

Everett, J. M. (1981) *Women and Social Change in India*, New Delhi: Heritage.

Farquhar, J. N. (1912) *A Primer of Hinduism*, Second (Revised and Enlarged) Edition, London: Oxford University Press.

Flood, G. (1996) *An Introduction to Hinduism*, Cambridge: Cambridge University Press.

Forbes, G. (1975) The Ideals of Indian Womanhood: Six Bengali Women during the Independence Movement, in *Bengal in the Nineteenth and Twentieth Centuries*, ed. J. R. McLane, South Asia Series Occasional Paper no.25, 59–74, East Lansing: Asian Studies Center, Michigan State University.

—— (1979) Votes for Women: The Demand for Women's Franchise in India 1917–1937, in *Symbols of Power: Studies on the Political Status of Women in India*, ed. V. Mazumdar, 3–23, Bombay: Allied Publishers.

—— (1996) *Women in Modern India*, The New Cambridge History of India IV. 2, Cambridge: Cambridge University Press.

Frykenberg, R. E. (1991) The Emergence of Modern 'Hinduism' as a Concept and as an Institution: A Reappraisal with Special Reference to South India, in *Hinduism Reconsidered*, ed. G. D. Sontheimer and H. Kulke, 29–49, New Delhi: Manohar.

Ganguli, K. M. (transl.). (1981–2) *The Mahabharata of Krishna – Dwaipayana Vyasa*, 12 –vols, Fourth Edition, New Delhi: Munishiram Manoharlal.

Ghadially, R. and P. Kumar. (1988) Bride-Burning: The Psycho-Social Dynamics of Dowry Deaths, in *Women in Indian Society: A Reader*, ed. R. Ghadially, 167–77, New Delhi: Sage Publications.

Grierson, Sir G. A. (1926) On the Adbhuta-Ramayana, *Bulletin of the School of Oriental Studies* vol. 4: 11–27.

Griffith, R. T. H. (transl.). (1963a) *The Hymns of the Ṛg Veda (Translated with a Popular Commentary)*, The Chowkhamba Sanskrit Studies vol. 35, 2 – vols, Fourth Edition, Varanasi: Chowkhamba Sanskrit Series Office.

—— (1963b) *The Ramayan of Valmiki*, Third Edition, Chowkhamba Sanskrit Studies vol. 29, Varanasi: Chowkhamba Sanskrit Series Office.

Gupta, L. (1991) Kali, the Savior, in *After Patriarchy: Feminist Transformations of the World Religions*, ed. P. M. Cooey, W. R. Eakin and J. B. McDaniel, Faith Meets Faith Series, ed. P. F. Knitter, 15–38, New York: Orbis Books.

Halhed, N. (transl.). (1777) *A Code of Gentoo Laws or Ordinations of the Pundits*, London: no publisher.

Hastings, W. (1772) Judicial Plan, quoted in B. K. Acharyya, *Codification in British India*, 153, Calcutta: Thacker, Spink 1914.

—— (n.d.) [Correspondence with the Board of Directors of the East India Company and Lord Mansfield], quoted in K. Feiling, *Warren Hastings*, 103, London: Macmillan 1954.

Heimsath, C. (1964) *Indian Nationalism and Hindu Social Reform*, Princeton: Princeton University Press.

Hiltebeitel, A. (1978) The Indus Valley 'Proto-Śiva', Reexamined through Reflections on the Goddess, the Buffalo and the Symbolism of vāhanas, *Anthropos* 73: 767–97.

Hindu Law Committee (HLC). (1947) *Report of the Hindu Law Committee*, Delhi: Government of India Press.

HLC, see under Hindu Law Committee.

Hobsbawm, E. (1984) Introduction: Inventing Traditions, in *The Invention of Tradition*, ed. E. Hobsbawm and T. Ranger, 1–14, Cambridge: Cambridge University Press.

Horner, I. B. (transl.). (1957) *The Collection of the Middle Length Sayings Majjhima-Nikāya*, vol. 2, *The Middle Fifty Discourses* (Majjhimapaṇṇāsa), Pali Text Translation Series no. 30, London: Pali Text Society.

Hume, R. E. (transl.). (1983) *The Thirteen Principal Upanishads (Translated from the Sanskrit with an Outline of the Philosophy of the Upanishads and an Annotated Bibliography)*, Reprint of Second Revised Edition, 1931, Delhi: Oxford University Press.

Jackson, R. (1996) The Construction of 'Hinduism' and its Impact on Religious Education in England and Wales, *Panorama* vol. 8 no. 2: 86–104.

Jesudasan, C. and H. (1961) *A History of Tamil Literature*, Heritage of India Series, Calcutta: YMCA Publishing House.

Kakar, S. (1988) *The Inner World: A Psycho-Analytic Study of Childhood and Society in India*, Second Edition, Delhi: Oxford University Press.

Kapur, R. and B. Cossman. (1995) Communalising Gender, Engendering Community: Women, Legal Discourse and the Saffron Agenda, in *Women and Right-Wing Movements: Indian Experiences*, ed. T. Sarkar and U. Butalia, 136–57, London: Zed Books.

Kinsley, D. (1987) *Hindu Goddesses: Visions of the Divine Feminine in the Hindu Religious Tradition*, Delhi: Motilal Banarsidass.

Kishwar, M. (1984) [Introduction to] *In Search of Answers: Indian Women's Voices from Manushi*, ed. M. Kishwar and R. Vanita, 1–47, London: Zed Books.

—— (1990a) In Defence of Our *Dharma*, *Manushi* no. 60: 2–15.

—— (1990b) Why I do not Call Myself a Feminist, *Manushi* no. 61: 2–8.

—— (1997) Yes to Sita, No to Ram! The Continuing Popularity of Sita in India, *Manushi* no. 98: 20–31.

Kishwar, M. and R. Vanita. (1987) The Burning of Roop Kanwar, *Manushi* no. 42–3: 15–25.

Krishnaswamy, S. (1988) Female Infanticide in Contemporary India: A Case-Study of Kallars of Tamilnadu, in *Women in Indian Society: A Reader*, ed. R. Ghadially, 186–95, New Delhi: Sage Publications.

Kumar, R. (1993) *The History of Doing: An Illustrated Account of Movements for Women's Rights and Feminism in India, 1800–1990*, London: Verso.

Larson, G. J. (1993) Discourse about 'Religion' in Colonial and Postcolonial India, in *Ethical and Political Dilemmas in Modern India*, ed. N. Smart and S. Thakur, 181–93, Basingstoke: Macmillan.

Levy, H. (1973) Indian Modernization by Legislation: the Hindu Code Bill, Ph.D. diss., University of Chicago.

Liddle, J. and R. Joshi. (1986) *Daughters of Independence: Gender, Caste and Class in India*, London: Zed Books.

Lipner, J. (1994) *Hindus: Their Religious Beliefs and Practices*, London: Routledge.

Lynton, H. R. (1995) *Born to Dance*, London: Sangam Books.

MacIntyre, A. (1988) *Whose Justice? Which Rationality?*, London: Duckworth.

Mahila Samta Sainik Dal (MSSD). (1976) Manifesto of the Mahila Samta

Sainik Dal, in *We Will Smash This Prison! Indian Women in Struggle*, G. Omvedt, 173–6, London: Zed Press 1980.

Malabari, B. M. (1888) Note 1 Infant Marriage in India [1884] 1–5, To the Shastris of Poona [1886] 190–2, in *The Life and Life-work of Behramji M. Malabari (Being a Biographical Sketch, with Selections from his Writings and Speeches on Infant Marriage, and also his 'Rambles of a Pilgrim Reformer')*, ed. D. Gidumal, Bombay: Education Society's Press.

Mandi, Rani of (Lalit Kumari Sahiba). (1929) All India Women's Conference, Presidential Address, *The Indian Social Reformer* vol. 39 no. 20: 310–3.

Mani, L. (1987) Contentious Traditions: The Debate on SATI in Colonial India, *Cultural Critique* (Fall): 119–56.

Mazumdar, V. (1983) Interviews with Vina Mazumdar and Chandralekha, interview by M. Dubey, *The Book Review* vol.7 pt 6: 267–74.

Mies, M. (1975) Indian Women and Leadership, *Bulletin of Concerned Asian Scholars*, vol. 7 pt 1: 56–? (Incomplete Photocopy Supplied).

—— (1980) *Indian Women and Patriarchy: Conflicts and Dilemmas of Students and Working Women*, First published in German 1973, New Delhi: Concept Publishing Company.

Miles, M. R. (1987) [Introduction to] *Immaculate and Powerful: The Female in Sacred Image and Social Reality*, ed. C. W. Atkinson, C. H. Buchanan and M. R. Miles, 1–14, London: Crucible.

Mill, J. (1972) *The History of British India*, vol. I, Reprint of Second Edition 1820, New Delhi: Associated Publishing House.

Mill, J. S. (1984) The Subjection of Women, in *Essays on Equality, Law, and Education* [1869], Collected Works of John Stuart Mill vol. XXI, 250–340, Toronto: University of Toronto Press.

MSSD, see under Mahila Samta Sainik Dal.

Mukherjee, P. (1983) The Image of Women in Hinduism, *Women's Studies International Forum* vol. 6 no. 4: 375–81.

Mukherjee, R, Swami Satswarupananda, K. N. Gopala Pillai and N. Lakshminarayan Rao. (1953) Great Indian Women of the Nineteenth Century, in *Great Women of India: The Holy Mother Birth Centenary Memorial*, ed. Swami Madhavananda and R. C. Majumdar, 395–413, Mayavati: Advaita Ashram.

Mukherji, S. C. (1934) Report of Last Year's Work [Report of Proceedings of All India Women's Annual Conference], *The Indian Annual Register* vol. II (July–December): 356–9.

Naidu, S. (1918a) Education of Indian Women [1906] 17–20, Ideals of Education [1908] 26–7, Mrs. Gandhi [1915] 29–32, Unlit Lamps of India [1915] 69–72, Women in National Life [1915] 96a–h, Address to Hindu Ladies [1916] 97–100, The Vision of Patriotism [1917] 107–20, Indentured Labour [1917] 121–9, Hindu–Muslim Unity [1917] 130–51, Ideals of Islam [1917] 164–76, Ideals of a Teacher's Life [1917] 177–98, The Hope of To-morrow [1917] 199–210, Self-government for India. 3. Speech at the Calcutta Congress [1917] 241–6, in *Speeches and Writings of Sarojini Naidu*, Madras: G. A. Nateson & Co.

—— (1918b). National Education of Indian Women [Speech at Bradlaugh Hall, Lahore, April] quoted in P. Sengupta, *Sarojini Naidu: A Biography*, 97, London: Asia Publishing House 1966.

—— (1925a) Advice to City Fathers of Karachi, *Forward* vol. 2 no. 239: 10.
—— (1925b) [The Speech Given by Mrs Sarojini Naidu as President of Indian National Congress] in Sm. Naidu's Presidential Address, *Forward* vol. 3 no. 52 Supplement (27 December).
—— (1934). [Presidential Address to the Women's Indian Association] Extract entitled How Sarojini Spoke: A Call to Women, *Roshni* vol. 9 pt 4:14 1957.
—— (1995). The Soul of India [1917] 148–52, Indian Women and the Franchise III: Memorandum, before Joint Committee of Lords and Commons [1919] 161–4, in *Sarojini Naidu: Selected Poetry and Prose*, ed. M. Paranjape, First Published 1993, New Delhi: Indus.
Natarajan, K et al. (1932) *Lady Tata : A Book of Remembrance*, Bombay: Commercial Printing Press.
Nehru, R. (1940) The All India Women's Conference Presidential Address, *The Indian Annual Register* vol. II (July–December): 334–6.
—— (1950) Women's Movement [1929] 10–12, Woman in the New Social Order [1940] 20–5, Reflections on the Women's Conference [1932] 27–31, The Hindu Code [1945] 39–41, in *Gandhi is my Star: Speeches and Writings of Shrimati Rameshwari Nehru*, ed. Prof. S. Dhar, Patna: Pustakbhandar.
Nethercot, A. H. (1963) *The Last Four Lives of Annie Besant*, Chicago: Chicago University Press.
Oldenburg, V. T. (1994) The Roop Kanwar Case: Feminist Responses, in *Sati, the Blessing and the Curse: The Burning of Wives in India*, ed. J. S. Hawley, 101–30, New York: Oxford University Press.
Omvedt, G. (1993) *Reinventing Revolution: New Social Movements and the Socialist Tradition in India*, Armonk: M.E. Sharpe.
—— (1995) *Dalit Visions: The Anti-Caste Movement and the Construction of an Indian Identity*, Tracts for the Times 8, London: Sangam Books.
Pandey, R. B. (1969) *Hindu Saṃskāras: Socio-Religious Study of the Hindu Sacraments*, Delhi: Motilal Banarsidass.
Patel, T. (1996) A Suitable Survey, *New Scientist* (26 October): 39–42.
Patel, V. (1989) Sex-Determination and Sex-Preselection Tests in India: Modern Techniques for Femicide, *Bulletin of Concerned Asian Scholars* vol. 21 no.1: 2–10
Petition against the Prohibition of Sati. (1829) in *The History of Doing: An Illustrated Account of Movements for Women's Rights and Feminism in India, 1800–1990*, R. Kumar, 12–13, London: Verso 1993.
Petition against the Legalisation of Widow Remarriage. (1856?) in *Ishvar Chandra Vidyasagar: A Story of his Life and Work*, S. C. Mitra, 310–17, Calcutta: Sarat Chandra Mitra, New Bengal Press 1902.
Piggott, S. (1974) *The Druids*, Harmondsworth: Penguin.
Pollock, S. (1993) Deep Orientalism? Notes on Sanskrit and Power Beyond the Raj, in *Orientalism and the Postcolonial Predicament: Perspectives on South Asia*, ed. C. A. Breckenridge and P. van der Veer, 76–133, Philadelphia: University of Pennsylvania Press.
Potter, K. H. (ed.). (1981) *Advaita Vedānta up to Śaṃkara and His Pupils*, Encyclopedia of Indian Philosophies, Princeton: Princeton University Press.
POW, see under Progressive Organisation of Women.

Progressive Organisation of Women (POW). (1974) Draft Manifesto of the Progressive Organisation of Women, in *We Will Smash This Prison! Indian Women in Struggle*, G. Omvedt, 169–73, London: Zed Press 1980.

Ranade, M. G. (1915) State Legislation in Social Matters [Introduction to] A collection by Mr. Vaidya containing the proceedings which led to the passing of Act XV of 1856 [1885], in *The Miscellaneous Writings of the Late Hon'ble Mr. Justice M. G. Ranade*, 70–86, Bombay: Manoranjan Press.

Ranade, R. (1938) *Himself: The Autobiography of a Hindu Lady*, transl. K. V. A. Gates, New York: Longmans, Green & Company.

Ratté, L. (1985) Goddesses, Mothers, and Heroines: Hindu Women and the Feminine in the Early Nationalist Movement, in *Women, Religion, and Social Change*, ed. Y. Y. Haddad and E. B. Findly, 351–76, New York: State University New York Press.

Ray, A. (1988) Native Response to the Movement for Abolition, in *Sati: Historical and Phenomenological Essays*, A. Sharma with A. Ray, A. Hejib and K. K. Young, 49–59, Delhi: Motilal Banarsidass.

Ray, R. (1952) The Background of the Hindu Code Bill, *Pacific Affairs* vol. 25 pt 3: 268–77.

Reddi, M. (1931) The All India Women's Conference Presidential Address, *The Indian Annual Register* vol. I (January–June): 367–73.

Regulation XVII of the Bengal Code. (1829) in *The History of Doing: An Illustrated Account of Movements for Women's Rights and Feminism in India, 1800–1990*, R. Kumar, 10–11, London: Verso 1993.

Roy, R. M. (1906) Abstract of the Arguments regarding the Burning of Widows Considered as a Religious Rite [1830], in *The English Works of Raja Rammohun Roy (With an English Translation of 'Tuhfatul Muwahhiddin')*, 365–72, Allahabad: Panini Office.

Ruskin, J. (1894) III, Ethics 107, Man and Woman (Excerpted from Sesame and Lilies [1865–9] II 67–8), in *Selections from the Writings of John Ruskin*, Second Series 1860–88, 263–5, London: George Allen.

Said, E. (1995) *Orientalism: Western Conceptions of the Orient*, Edition with new Afterword, Harmondsworth: Penguin Books.

Sakala, C. (1980) *Women of South Asia: A Guide to Resources*, Millwood: Kraus International Publications.

Sankaracharya (H.H. the Jagatguru Sri Sankaracharya Swamigal of Kamakoti Pitham). (1941) Answers to the Questionnaire Issued by the Hindu Law Committee: II by a Religious Head, *The Madras Law Journal* pt 1: 127–37.

Saraswati, D. (1970) *Light of Truth: An English Translation of Satyarth Prakash* [1875], Second Edition, New Delhi: Jan Gyan Prakashan.

Sarasvati, R. (1890) *The High-Caste Hindu Women*, First Published 1887, London: George Bell and Sons.

Schneir, M. (1972) [Introduction to] *Feminism: The Essential Historical Writings*, ed. M. Schneir, xi–xxi, New York: Vintage Books.

Sengupta, P. (1996) *Sarojini Naidu: A Biography*, Bombay: Asia Publishing House.

Shahnawaz, J. A. (1971) *Father and Daughter : A Political Autobiography*, Lahore: Nigarishat.

Sharma, A. (1988) *Sati: Historical and Phenomenological Essays*, Delhi: Motilal Banasidass.

Sharma, A. (1995) Interviews with Women, interview by S. Anitha, Manisha, Vasudha and Tavitha, in *Women and Right-Wing Movements: Indian Experiences*, ed. T. Sarkar and U. Butalia, 329–35, London: Zed Books.

Sharma, K. (1995) Interviews with Women, interview by S. Anitha, Manisha, Vasudha and Tavitha, in *Women and Right-Wing Movements: Indian Experiences*, ed. T. Sarkar and U. Butalia, 329–35, London: Zed Books

Shastri, H. P. (transl.). (1985) *The Ramayana of Valmiki*, 3 –vols, Reprint of Second Revised Edition, London: Shanti Sadan.

Shulman, D. D. (1980) *Tamil Temple Myths: Sacrifice and Divine Marriage in the South Indian Śaiva Tradition*, Princeton: Princeton University. Press.

Singer, M. (1989) Foreword. A Changing American Image of India: The Palimpsest of a Civilization, in *Contemporary Indian Tradition: Voices on Culture, Nature and the Challenge of Change*, ed. C. M. Borden, 1–17, Washington: Smithsonian Institution Press.

Singh, S. N. (1910) The English Woman's Battle for the Ballot, *The Modern Review* (September): 261–71.

Sircar, (1934) [Speech on the legal disabilities of women] quoted in Legal Disabilities of Women, *The Modern Review* (December): 752.

Sircar, D.C. (1953) Great Women in North India, in *Great Women of India: The Holy Mother Birth Centenary Memorial*, ed. Swami Madhavananda and R. C. Majumdar, 285–97, Mayavati: Advaita Ashrama.

Sorabji, S. (1929) Ramabai Ranade, in *Women in Modern India: Fifteen Papers by Indian Women*, ed. E. Gedge and M. Choksi, 25–37, Bombay: D.B. Taraporewala Sons & Co.

Stone, M. 1976. *The Paradise Papers: The Suppression of Women's Rites.* London: Virago.

Srinivasan, D. (1984) Unhinging Śiva from the Indus Civilization, *Royal Asiatic Society Journal*: 77–89.

Sullivan, H.P. (1964) A Re-Examination of the Religion of the Indus Civilization, *History of Religions* 4: 115–25.

Tahmankar, D. V. (1956) *Lokamanya Tilak: The Father of Indian Unrest and Maker of Modern India*, London: John Murray.

Tendulkar, D.G. (1960–3) *Mahatma: Life of Mohandas Karamchand Gandhi*, –vols 1–8, New Delhi: Publications Division, Ministry of Information and Broadcasting, Government of India.

Thakur, S.C. (1996) *Religion and Social Justice*, in Macmillan Library of Philosophy and Religion, ed. J. Hick, Basingstoke: Macmillan.

Thapar, R. (1987) Tradition versus Misconceptions, interview by M. Kishwar and R. Vanita, *Manushi* no. 42–3: 2–14.

—— (1988) In History, *Seminar* no.342: 14–19.

Thobani, S. (1989) Indian Woman, *Bulletin of Concerned Asian Scholars* vol. 21 no. 1: 10–11.

Tilak, B. G. (1881) *Mahratta* 1:22 1, quoted in S. Wolpert, *Tilak and Gokhale: Revolution and Reform in the Making of Modern India*, 47, Berkeley: University of California Press 1961.

—— (1891) The Express Texts of the Shastras Against the Age of Consent Bill, Poona: Arya-Bhushana Press.

van Buitenen, J. A. B. (transl.). (1973–8) *The Mahābhārata*, –vols 1–3, Chicago: Chicago University Press.

van Den Bosch, L. P. (1990) A Burning Question, *Numen* vol. 37 pt 2: 174–94.

Vasaria, S. (1984) No More Sitas, in *In Search of Answers: Indian Women's Voices from Manushi*, ed. M. Kishwar and R. Vanita, 298–9, London: Zed Books.

Vidyasagar, I. C. (1976) Marriage of Hindu Widows [1855] 1–17, Marriage of Hindu Widows: The Rejoinder [1855] 18–105, in *Marriage of Hindu Widows* [English Version of Two Pamphlets 1856], Introduction by A. Podder, Calcutta: K.P. Bagchi and Co.

Vivekananda, Swami (Narendranath Datta). (1972) Conversations and Dialogues 18 [1901], Conversations and Dialogues 1–35, in *The Complete Works of Swami Vivekananda*, vol. 7, Eighth Edition, 105–293, Calcutta: Advaita Ashrama.

—— (1973) On Indian Women – Their Present and Future [1898], in *The Complete Works of Swami Vivekananda*, vol. 5, Tenth Edition, 228–31, Calcutta: Advaita Ashrama.

von Stietencron, H. (1991) Hinduism: On the Proper Use of a Deceptive Term, in *Hinduism Reconsidered*, ed. G.D. Sontheimer and H. Kulke, 11–27, New Delhi: Manohar.

Warren, H.C. (1982) *Buddhism in Translations: Passages Selected from the Buddhist Sacred Books and Translated from Original Pali into English*, First Published 1896, New York: Atheneum.

Wilkinson, T. S. and M. M. Thomas (ed.). (1972) *Ambedkar and the Neo–Buddhist Movement*, Madras: Christian Literature Society.

Wolpert, S. A. (1961) *Tilak and Gokhale: Revolution and Reform in the Making of Modern India*, Berkeley: University of California Press.

Woodward, F. L. (transl.). (1960) *The Book of the Gradual Sayings (Anguttara-nikāya) or more numbered suttas*, vol. 1, (*Ones, Twos, Threes*), Pali Text Translation series no. 22, Reprint of First Edition 1932, London: Pali Text Society.

Zvelebil, K. V. (1974) *Tamil Literature*, A History of Indian Literature, ed. J. Gonda, vol. 10, Wiesbadan: Otto Harrassowitz.